Living a **Feminist** Life

SARA AHMED Living a
Feminist
Life

Duke University Press / Durham and London / 2017

Designed by Heather Hensley
Typeset in Arno Pro by Graphic Composition, Inc., Bogart, Georgia

Library of Congress Cataloging-in-Publication Data
Names: Ahmed, Sara, [date] author.
Title: Living a feminist life / Sara Ahmed.
Description: Durham : Duke University Press, 2017.
Includes bibliographical references and index.
Identifiers:
LCCN 2016032264 (print)
LCCN 2016033775 (ebook)
ISBN 9780822363040 (hardcover)
ISBN 9780822363194 (pbk.)
ISBN 9780822373377 (e-book)
Subjects: LCSH: Feminist theory. | Feminism.
Classification: LCC HQ1190.A36 2017 (print) | LCC HQ1190 (ebook) |
DDC 305.4201—dc23
LC record available at https:// lcn.loc.gov/ 2016032264

COVER ART: Carrie Moyer, *Chromafesto (Sister Resister 1.2)*, 2003, acrylic, glitter on canvas, 36 × 24 inches. © Carrie Moyer. Courtesy of DC Moore Gallery, New York.

To the many feminist killjoys
out there doing your thing:

THIS ONE IS FOR YOU.

CONTENTS

ACKNOWLEDGMENTS

This is the first time I have written a book alongside a blog. Thank you so much to those who encouraged me to start my blog, especially my feminist friends on Facebook. Thanks also to those with whom I have engaged on social media since. I have learned so much. Thanks to Mulka and Poppy for your furry brown companionship, then and now. Thanks to Leona Lewis for your voice and inspiration. My special thanks to my partner in feminist crime, Sarah Franklin. My appreciation to Duke University Press for working with me again, and to Ken Wissoker and Elizabeth Ault for sustaining your enthusiasm for this project throughout, as well as to Liz Smith for her patience at the late stages. To my feminist colleagues at Goldsmiths and beyond, I appreciate the care and connection, whether from near or afar, especially Rumana Begum, Sirma Bilge, Lisa Blackman, Ulrika Dahl, Natalie Fenton, Yasmin Gunaratnam, Heidi Mirza, Fiona Nicoll, Nirmal Puwar, Beverley Skeggs, Elaine Swan, and Isabel Waidner. To those who have participated in the Centre for Feminist Research and the Feminist Postgraduate Forum, thanks for working to make work a better and safer place, especially Tiffany Page and Leila Whitley. During the copyediting of this book, I made the difficult decision to resign from my post at Goldsmiths after three years of working with others to challenge how sexual harassment has become normalized in academic culture. I have been overwhelmed by the feminist solidarity and support I have received. Each message brought a message home to me, one I have been trying to write about in this book: living a feminist life is about how we connect with and draw upon each other in our shared project of dismantling worlds. We are chipping away, slowly, but we are chipping away!

INTRODUCTION *Bringing Feminist Theory Home*

What do you hear when you hear the word *feminism*? It is a word that fills me with hope, with energy. It brings to mind loud acts of refusal and rebellion as well as the quiet ways we might have of not holding on to things that diminish us. It brings to mind women who have stood up, spoken back, risked lives, homes, relationships in the struggle for more bearable worlds. It brings to mind books written, tattered and worn, books that gave words to something, a feeling, a sense of an injustice, books that, in giving us words, gave us the strength to go on. Feminism: how we pick each other up. So much history in a word; so much it too has picked up.

I write this book as a way of holding on to the promise of that word, to think what it means to live your life by claiming that word as your own: being a feminist, becoming a feminist, speaking as a feminist. Living a feminist life does not mean adopting a set of ideals or norms of conduct, although it might mean asking ethical questions about how to live better in an unjust and unequal world (in a not-feminist and antifeminist world); how to create relationships with others that are more equal; how to find ways to support those who are not supported or are less supported by social systems; how to keep coming up against histories that have become concrete, histories that have become as solid as walls.

It is worth noticing from the outset that the idea that feminism is about how to live, about a way of thinking how to live, has often been understood as part of feminist history, as dated, associated with the moralizing or even policing stance of what might be called or might have been called, usually dismissively, cultural feminism. I will return to the politics of this dismissal in chapter 9. I am not suggesting here that this version of feminism as moral police, the kind of feminism that might proceed by declaring this or that practice (and thus this or that person) as being unfeminist or not feminist, is simply a fabrication. I have heard that judgment; it has fallen on my own shoulders.[1]

But the figure of the policing feminist is promiscuous for a reason. Feminism can be more easily dismissed when feminism is heard as about dismissal; as being about making people feel bad for their desires and investments. The figure of the feminist policer is exercised because she is useful; hearing feminists as police is a way of not hearing feminism. Many feminist figures are antifeminist tools, although we can always retool these figures for our own purposes. A retooling might take this form: if naming sexism is understood as policing behavior, then we will be feminist police. Note that retooling antifeminist figures does not agree with the judgment (that to question sexism is to police) but rather disagrees with the premise by converting it into a promise (if you think questioning sexism is policing, we are feminist police).

In making feminism a life question, we will be judged as judgmental. In this book I refuse to relegate the question of how to live a feminist life to history. To live a feminist life is to make everything into something that is questionable. The question of how to live a feminist life is alive as a question as well as being a life question.

If we become feminists because of the inequality and injustice in the world, because of what the world is not, then what kind of world are we building? To build feminist dwellings, we need to dismantle what has already been assembled; we need to ask what it is we are against, what it is we are for, knowing full well that this *we* is not a foundation but what we are working toward. By working out what we are for, we are working out that *we*, that hopeful signifier of a feminist collectivity. Where there is hope, there is difficulty. Feminist histories are histories of the difficulty of that *we*, a history of those who have had to fight to be part of a feminist collective, or even had to fight against a feminist collective in order to take up a feminist cause. Hope is not at the expense of struggle but animates a struggle; hope gives us a sense that there is a point to working things out, working things through. Hope does not only or always point toward the future, but carries us through when the terrain is difficult, when the path we follow makes it harder to proceed.[2] Hope is behind us when we have to work for something to be possible.

A FEMINIST MOVEMENT

Feminism is a movement in many senses. We are moved to become feminists. Perhaps we are moved by something: a sense of injustice, that something is wrong, as I explore in chapter 1. A feminist movement is a collective political movement. Many feminisms means many movements. A collective is what does not stand still but creates and is created by movement. I think of feminist action as like ripples in water, a small wave, possibly created by agitation from weather; here, there, each movement making another possible, another ripple, outward, reaching. Feminism: the dynamism of making connections. And yet a movement has to be built. To be part of a movement requires we find places to gather, meeting places. A movement is also a shelter. We convene; we have a convention. A movement comes into existence to transform what is in existence. A movement needs to take place somewhere. A movement is not just or only a movement; there is something that needs to be kept still, given a place, if we are moved to transform what is.

We might say a movement is strong when we can witness a momentum: more people gathering on the streets, more people signing their names to protest against something, more people using a name to identify themselves. I think we have in recent years witnessed the buildup of a momentum around feminism, in global protests against violence against women; in the increasing number of popular books on feminism; in the high visibility of feminist activism on social media; in how the word *feminism* can set the stage on fire for women artists and celebrities such as Beyoncé. And as a teacher, I have witnessed this buildup firsthand: increasing numbers of students who want to identify themselves as feminists, who are demanding that we teach more courses on feminism; and the almost breathtaking popularity of events we organize on feminism, especially queer feminism and trans feminism. Feminism is bringing people into the room.

Not all feminist movement is so easily detected. A feminist movement is not always registered in public. A feminist movement might be happening the moment a woman snaps, that moment when she does not take it anymore (see chapter 8), the violence that saturates her world, a world. A feminist movement might happen in the growing connections between those who recognize something—power relations, gender violence, gender as violence—as being what they are up against, even if they have different words for what that what is. If we think of the second-wave feminist motto "the personal is political," we can think of feminism as happening in the very places that have historically been bracketed as not political: in domestic arrangements, at home, every room of the house can become a feminist room, in who does what where, as well as on the street, in parliament, at the university. Feminism is wherever feminism needs to be. Feminism needs to be everywhere.

Feminism needs to be everywhere because feminism is not everywhere. Where is feminism? It is a good question. We can ask ourselves: where did we find feminism, or where did feminism find us? I pose this question as a life question in the first part of this book. A story always starts before it can be told. When did *feminism* become a word that not only spoke to you, but spoke you, spoke of your existence, spoke you into existence? When did the sound of the word *feminism* become your sound? What did it mean, what does it do, to hold on to feminism, to fight under its name; to feel in its ups and downs, in its coming and goings, your ups and downs, your comings and goings?

When I think of my feminist life in this book, I ask "from where?" but also "from whom?" From whom did I find feminism? I will always remember a conversation I had as a young woman in the late 1980s. It was a conversation with my auntie Gulzar Bano. I think of her as one of my first feminist teachers. I had given her some of my poems. In one poem I had used *he*. "Why do you use *he*," she asked me gently, "when you could have used *she*?" The question, posed with such warmth and kindness, prompted much heartache, much sadness in the realization that the words as well as worlds I had thought of as open to me were not open at all. *He* does not include *she*. The lesson becomes an instruction. To make an impression, I had to dislodge that *he*. To become *she* is to become part of a feminist movement. A feminist becomes *she* even if she has already been assigned *she*, when she hears in that word a refusal of *he*, a refusal that *he* would promise her inclusion. She takes up that word *she* and makes it her own.

I began to realize what I already knew: that patriarchal reasoning goes all the way down, to the letter, to the bone. I had to find ways not to reproduce its grammar in what I said, in what I wrote; in what I did, in who I was. It is important that I learned this feminist lesson from my auntie in Lahore, Pakistan, a Muslim woman, a Muslim feminist, a brown feminist. It might be assumed that feminism travels from West to East. It might be assumed that feminism is what the West gives to the East. That assumption is a traveling assumption, one that tells a feminist story in a certain way, a story that is much repeated; a history of how feminism acquired utility as an imperial gift. That is not my story. We need to tell other feminist stories. Feminism traveled to me, growing up in the West, from the East. My Pakistani aunties taught me that my mind is my own (which is to say that my mind is not owned); they taught me to speak up for myself; to speak out against violence and injustice.

Where we find feminism matters; from whom we find feminism matters.

Feminism as a collective movement is made out of how we are moved to become feminists in dialogue with others. A movement requires us to be moved. I explore this requirement by revisiting the question of feminist consciousness in part I of this book. Let's think of why feminist movements are still necessary. I want to take here bell hooks's definition of feminism as "the movement to end sexism, sexual exploitation and sexual oppression" (2000, 33). From this definition, we learn so much. Feminism is necessary because of what has not ended: sexism, sexual exploitation, and sexual oppression. And for hooks, "sexism, sexual exploitation and sexual oppression" cannot be separated from racism, from how the present is shaped by colonial histories including slavery, as central to the exploitation of labor under capitalism. Intersectionality is a starting point, the point from which we must proceed if we are to offer an account of how power works. Feminism will be intersectional "or it will be bullshit," to borrow from the eloquence of Flavia Dzodan.[3] This is the kind of feminism I am referring to throughout this book (unless I indicate otherwise by referring specifically to white feminism).

A significant step for a feminist movement is to recognize what has not ended. And this step is a very hard step. It is a slow and painstaking step. We might think we have made that step only to realize we have to make it again. It might be you are up against a fantasy of equality: that women can now do it, even have it, or that they would have it if they just tried hard enough; that individual women can bring sexism and other barriers (we might describe these barriers as the glass ceiling or the brick wall) to an end through sheer effort or persistence or will. So much ends up being invested in our own bodies. We could call this a postfeminist fantasy: that an individual woman can bring what blocks her movement to an end; or that feminism has brought "sexism, sexual exploitation or sexual oppression" to an end as if feminism has been so successful that it has eliminated its own necessity (Gill 2007; McRobbie 2009); or that such phenomena are themselves a feminist fantasy, an attachment to something that was never or is no longer. We could also think of postrace as a fantasy through which racism operates: as if racism is behind us because we no longer believe in race, or as if racism would be behind us if we no longer believed in race. Those of us who come to embody diversity for organizations are assumed to bring whiteness to an end by virtue of our arrival (see chapter 6).

When you become a feminist, you find out very quickly: what you aim to bring to an end some do not recognize as existing. This book follows this finding. So much feminist and antiracist work is the work of trying to convince others that sexism and racism have not ended; that sexism and racism are fundamental to the injustices of late capitalism; that they matter. Just to talk about sexism and racism here and now is to refuse displacement; it is to refuse to wrap your speech around postfeminism or postrace, which would require you to use the past tense (back then) or an elsewhere (over there).[4]

Even to describe something as sexist and racist here and now can get you into trouble. You point to structures; they say it is in your head. What you describe as material is dismissed as mental. I think we learn about materiality from such dismissals, as I will try to show in part II, on diversity work. And think also of what is required: the political labor necessary of having to insist that what we are describing is not just what we are feeling or thinking. A feminist movement depends on our ability to keep insisting on something: the ongoing existence of the very things we wish to bring to an end. The labor of that insistence is what I describe in this book. We learn from being feminists.

A feminist movement thus requires that we acquire feminist tendencies, a willingness to keep going despite or even because of what we come up against. We could think of this process as practicing feminism. If we tend toward the world in a feminist way, if we repeat that tending, again and again, we acquire feminist tendencies. Feminist hope is the failure to eliminate the potential for acquisition. And yet once you have become a feminist, it can feel that you were always a feminist. Is it possible to have always been that way? Is it possible to have been a feminist right from the beginning? Perhaps you feel you were always that way inclined. Maybe you tended that way, a feminist way, because you already tended to be a rebellious or even willful girl (see chapter 3), who would not accept the place she had been given. Or maybe feminism is a way of beginning again: so your story did in a certain way begin with feminism.

A feminist movement is built from many moments of beginning again. And this is one of my central concerns: how the acquisition of a feminist tendency to become that sort of girl or woman, the wrong sort, or bad sort, the one who speaks her mind, who writes her name, who raises her arm in protest, is necessary for a feminist movement. Individual struggle does matter; a collective movement depends upon it. But of course being the wrong sort does not make us right. Much injustice can be and has been committed by those who think of themselves as the wrong sort—whether the wrong sort of women or the wrong sort of feminists. There is no guarantee that in struggling for justice we ourselves will be just. We have to hesitate, to temper the strength of our tendencies with doubt; to waver when we are sure, or even because we are sure. A feminist movement that proceeds with too much confidence has cost us too much already. I explore the necessity of wavering with our convictions in part III. If a feminist tendency is what we work for, that tendency does not give us a stable ground.

HOMEWORK

Feminism is homework. When I use the word *homework*, I think first of being at school; I think of being given an assignment by a teacher to take home. I think of sitting down at the kitchen table and doing that work, before I am allowed to play. Homework is quite simply work you are asked to do when you are at home, usually assigned by those with authority outside the home. When feminism is understood as homework, it is not an assignment you have been given by a teacher, even though you have feminist teachers. If feminism is an assignment, it is a self-assignment. We give ourselves this task. By homework, I am not suggesting we all feel at home in feminism in the sense of feeling safe or secure. Some of us might find a home here; some of us might not. Rather, I am suggesting feminism is homework because we have much to work out from not being at home in a world. In other words, homework is work on as well as at our homes. We do housework. Feminist housework does not simply clean and maintain a house. Feminist housework aims to transform the house, to rebuild the master's residence.

In this book I want to think of feminist theory too as homework, as a way of rethinking how feminist theory originates and where it ends up. What is this thing called feminist theory? We might at first assume that feminist theory is what feminists working within the academy generate. I want to suggest that feminist theory is something we do at home. In the first part of this book, I explore how in becoming feminists we are doing intellectual as well as emotional work; we begin to experience gender as a restriction of possibility, and we learn about worlds as we navigate these restrictions. The experiences of being a feminist, say at the family table, or at a meeting table, gave me life lessons, which were also philosophical lessons. To learn from being a feminist is to learn about the world.

Feminist theory can be what we do together in the classroom; in the conference; reading each other's work. But I think too often we bracket feminist theory as something that marks out a specific kind, or even a higher kind, of feminist work. We have to bring feminist theory home because feminist theory has been too quickly understood as something that we do when we are away from home (as if feminist theory is what you learn when you go to school). When we are away, we can and do learn new words, new concepts, new angles. We encounter new authors who spark moments of revelation. But feminist theory does not start there. Feminist theory might even be what gets you there.

Within the academy, the word *theory* has a lot of capital. I have always been interested in how the word *theory* itself is distributed; how some materials are understood as theory and not others. This interest can partly be explained by my own trajectory: I went from a PhD in critical theory to being a lecturer in women's studies. As a student of theory, I learned that theory is used to refer to a rather narrow body of work. Some work becomes theory because it refers to other work that is known as theory. A citational chain is created around theory: you become a theorist by citing other theorists that cite other theorists. Some of this work did interest me; but I kept finding that I wanted to challenge the selection of materials as well as how they were read.

I remember one theorist being taught as having two sides, a story of desire and a story of the phallus. We were told, basically, to bracket the second story in order to engage with and be engaged by the first. I began to wonder whether doing theory was about engaging with a body of work by putting questions like phallocentrism or sexism into brackets. In effect, we were being asked to bracket our concerns with the sexism at stake in what was read as theory as well as what we read in theory. I still remember submitting a critical reading of a theory text in which woman was a figure as one of my essays, a reading that was later to form part of the chapter "Woman" in my first book, *Differences That Matter* (Ahmed 1998). I was concerned with how statements made by the teacher, like "This is not about women," were used to bypass any questions about how the figure of woman is exercised within a male intellectual tradition. When the essay was returned to me, the grader had scrawled in very large letters, "This is not theory! This is politics!"

I thought then: if theory is not politics, I am glad I am not doing theory! And it was a relief to leave that space in which theory and politics were organized as different trajectories. When I arrived in women's studies, I noticed how I would sometimes be recruited by the term *feminist theory*, as a different kind of feminist than other kinds of feminists, those assumed, say, to be more empirical, which seemed to be conflated with less theoretical, or less philosophical. I have always experienced this recruitment as a form of violence. I hope always to experience this recruitment as a form of violence. Even though

I am relatively comfortable in critical theory, I do not deposit my hope there, nor do I think this is a particularly difficult place to be: if anything, I think it is easier to do more abstract and general theoretical work. I remember listening to a feminist philosopher who apologized every time she mentioned such-and-such male philosopher because he was so difficult. It made me feel very rebellious. I think that the more difficult questions, the harder questions, are posed by those feminists concerned with explaining violence, inequality, injustice. The empirical work, the world that exists, is for me where the difficulties and thus the challenges reside. Critical theory is like any language; you can learn it, and when you learn it, you begin to move around in it. Of course it can be difficult, when you do not have the orientation tools to navigate your way around a new landscape. But explaining phenomena like racism and sexism—how they are reproduced, how they keep being reproduced—is not something we can do simply by learning a new language. It is not a difficulty that can be resolved by familiarity or repetition; in fact, familiarity and repetition are the source of difficulty; they are what need to be explained. In the face of such phenomena, we are constantly brought home by the inadequacy of our understanding. It is here we encounter and reencounter the limits of thinking. It is here we might feel those limits. We come up against something that we cannot resolve. We can be brought home by the inadequacy of what we know. And we can bring what we know back home.

As I show in part II, my own experience of bringing up racism and sexism within the academy (of refusing to bracket these questions in a more loving digestion of the philosophical canon) replicated some of my earlier experiences of bringing up racism and sexism at the family table. This replication is another form of pedagogy: we learn from how the same things keep coming up. You are assumed to be interrupting a happy occasion with the sensation of your own negation. You are assumed to be doing identity politics as if you speak about racism because you are a person of color or as if you speak about sexism because you are a woman. Nirmal Puwar (2004) has shown how some become "space invaders" when they enter spaces that are not intended for them. We can be space invaders in the academy; we can be space invaders in theory too, just by referring to the wrong texts or by asking the wrong questions.

A question can be out of place: words too.

One response might be to aim to reside as well as we can in the spaces that are not intended for us. We might even identify with the universal of the university by agreeing to put our particulars to one side.[5] There is disruption, even invention, in that, of that I have no doubt. But think of this: those of us who arrive in an academy that was not shaped by or for us bring knowledges, as well as worlds, that otherwise would not be here. Think of this: how we learn about worlds when they do not accommodate us. Think of the kinds of experiences you have when you are not expected to be here. These experiences are a resource to generate knowledge. To bring feminist theory home is to make feminism work in the places we live, the places we work. When we think of feminist theory as homework, the university too becomes something we work on as well as at. We use our particulars to challenge the universal.

BUILDING FEMINIST WORLDS

I will come out with it: I enjoy and appreciate much of the work that is taught and read as critical theory. There were reasons I went there first, and I explain how this happened in chapter 1. But I still remember in the second year of my PhD reading texts by black feminists and feminists of color including Audre Lorde, bell hooks, and Gloria Anzaldúa. I had not read their work before. This work shook me up. Here was writing in which an embodied experience of power provides the basis of knowledge. Here was writing animated by the everyday: the detail of an encounter, an incident, a happening, flashing like insight. Reading black feminist and feminist of color scholarship was life changing; I began to appreciate that theory can do more the closer it gets to the skin.

I decided then: theoretical work that is in touch with a world is the kind of theoretical work I wanted to do. Even when I have written texts organized around the history of ideas, I have tried to write from my own experiences: the everyday as animation. In writing this book, I wanted to stay even closer to the everyday than I had before. This book is personal. The personal is theoretical. Theory itself is often assumed to be abstract: something is more theoretical the more abstract it is, the more it is abstracted from everyday life. To abstract is to drag away, detach, pull away, or divert. We might then have to drag theory back, to bring theory back to life.

Even though my earlier works did include examples from everyday life, they also involved substantial reference to intellectual traditions. I have no doubt I needed those traditions to make some of the steps in my arguments: in *The Promise of Happiness* (Ahmed 2010), I needed to place the figure of the feminist killjoy in relation to the history of happiness, to make sense of how she appears; in *Willful Subjects* (Ahmed 2014), I needed to place the figure of the willful subject in relation to the history of the will for her too to make sense. But once these figures came up, they gave me a different handle.

They acquired their own life. Or should I say: my writing was able to pick up these figures because of the life they had. These figures quickly became the source of new forms of connection. I began a new blog organized around them (feministkilljoys.com), which I have been writing as I have been working on this book. Since I began that blog, I have received communications from many students including not only undergraduates and postgraduates but also high school students about their own experience of being feminist killjoys and willful subjects. I have learned so much from these communications. In a genuine sense, the book comes out of them. I address this book to feminist students. It is intended for you.

To become a feminist is to stay a student. This is why: the figures of the feminist killjoy and willful subject are studious. It is not surprising that they allowed me to communicate with those who sensed in these figures an explanation of something (a difficulty, a situation, a task). I am still trying to make sense of something (a difficulty, a situation, a task), and this book is the product of that labor. One of my aims in *Living a Feminist Life* is to free these figures from the histories in which they are housed. I am trying to work out and work through what they are saying to us. In a way, then, I am retracing my own intellectual journey in this book. In going through the conditions of their arrival, how they come up for me, how they became preoccupying, I am going back over some old ground. An intellectual journey is like any journey. One step enables the next step. In this book I retake some of these steps.

I hope by retaking the steps to make some of my arguments in a more accessible manner: in staying closer to the everyday, feminist theory becomes more accessible. When I first began working on this book, I thought I was writing a more mainstream feminist text, or even a trade book. I realized the book I was writing was not that kind of book. I wanted to make a slow argument, to go over old ground, and to take my time. And I still wanted to make an intervention within academic feminism. I have been an academic for over twenty years, and I am relatively at home in the academic language of feminist theory. I am aware that not all feminists are at home in the academy, and that the academic language of feminist theory can be alienating. In this book, I do use academic language. I am working at home, so academic language is one of my tools. But I also aim to keep my words as close to the world as I can, by trying to show how feminist theory is what we do when we live our lives in a feminist way.

In retracing some of the steps of a journey, I am not making the same journey. I have found new things along the way because I have stayed closer to the everyday. I should add here that staying close to the everyday still involves attending to words, and thus concepts, like happiness, like will. I am still listening for resonance. I think of feminism as poetry; we hear histories in words; we reassemble histories by putting them into words. This book still follows words around just as I have done before, turning a word this way and that, like an object that catches a different light every time it is turned; attending to the same words across different contexts, allowing them to create ripples or new patterns like texture on a ground. I make arguments by listening for resonances; the book thus involves repeating words, sometimes over and over again; words like *shatter*, words like *snap*. The repetition is the scene of a feminist instruction.

A feminist instruction: if we start with our experiences of becoming feminists not only might we have another way of generating feminist ideas, but we might generate new ideas about feminism. Feminist ideas are what we come up with to make sense of what persists. We have to persist in or by coming up with feminist ideas. Already in this idea is a different idea about ideas. Ideas would not be something generating through distance, a way of abstracting something from something, but from our involvement in a world that often leaves us, frankly, bewildered. Ideas might be how we work with as well as on our hunches, those senses that something is amiss, not quite right, which are part of ordinary living and a starting point for so much critical work.

By trying to describe something that is difficult, that resists being fully comprehended in the present, we generate what I call "sweaty concepts." I first used this expression when I was trying to describe to students the kind of intellectual labor evident in Audre Lorde's work. I want to acknowledge my debt here. I cannot put into words how much I am indebted to Audre Lorde for the extraordinary archive she left for us. When I first read Audre Lorde's work, I felt like a lifeline was being thrown to me. The words, coming out of her description of her own experience, as a black woman, mother, lesbian, poet, warrior, found me where I was; a different place from her, yet her words found me. Her words gave me the courage to make my own experience into a resource, my experiences as a brown woman, lesbian, daughter; as a writer, to build theory from description of where I was in the world, to build theory from description of not being accommodated by a world. A lifeline: it can be a fragile rope, worn and tattered from the harshness of weather, but it is enough, just enough, to bear your weight, to pull you out, to help you survive a shattering experience.

A sweaty concept: another way of being pulled out from a shattering experience. By using sweaty concepts for descriptive work, I am trying to say at least two things. First, I was suggesting that too often conceptual work is understood as distinct from describing a situation: and I am thinking here of a situation as something that comes to demand a response. A situation can refer to a combination of circumstances of a given moment but also to a critical, problematic, or striking set of circumstances. Lauren Berlant describes a situation thus: "A state of things in which something that will perhaps matter is unfolding amidst the usual activity of life" (2008, 5). If a situation is how we are thrown by things, then how we make sense of things also unfolds from "the usual activity of life." Concepts tend to be identified as what scholars somehow come up with, often through contemplation and withdrawal, rather like an apple that hits you on the head, sparking revelation from a position of exteriority.

I became more aware of this academic tendency to identify concepts as what they bring to the world when doing an empirical project on diversity, which I discuss in part II. I had this tendency myself, so I could recognize it. In the project I interviewed those employed by the university as diversity officers. It brought home to me how, in working to transform institutions, we generate knowledge about them. Concepts are at work in how we work, whatever it is that we do. We need to work out, sometimes, what these concepts are (what we are thinking when we are doing, or what doing is thinking) because concepts can be murky as background assumptions. But that working out is precisely not bringing a concept in from the outside (or from above): concepts are in the worlds we are in.

By using the idea of sweaty concepts, I am also trying to show how descriptive work is conceptual work. A concept is worldly, but it is also a reorientation to a world, a way of turning things around, a different slant on the same thing. More specifically, a sweaty concept is one that comes out of a description of a body that is not at home in the world. By this I mean description as angle or point of view: a description of how it feels not to be at home in the world, or a description of the world from the point of view of not being at home in it. Sweat is bodily; we might sweat more during more strenuous and muscular activity. A sweaty concept might come out of a bodily experience that is trying. The task is to stay with the difficulty, to keep exploring and exposing this difficulty. We might need not to eliminate the effort or labor from the writing. Not eliminating the effort or labor becomes an academic aim because we have been taught to tidy our texts, not to reveal the struggle we have in getting somewhere. Sweaty concepts are also generated by the practical experience of coming up against a world, or the practical experience of trying to transform a world.[6]

Even as I have labored in this way, I have noticed (partly because readers have noticed) signs of not quite being able to admit a difficulty: for instance, when I discuss some of my own experiences of sexual violence and harassment, I keep using *you* and not *me*, allowing the second person pronoun to give me some distance. I tried putting in *me* after it was written, but that *me* felt too strained, and I let the *you* stay but with qualification. Feminism: it can be a strain. This strain is evident as tension in this text, sometimes revealed as a confusion of pronouns and persons; a tension between telling my own story of becoming feminist, being a diversity worker, handling what you come up against, and making more general reflections about worlds. I have tried not to eliminate that tension.

Feminism is at stake in how we generate knowledge; in how we write, in who we cite. I think of feminism as a building project: if our texts are worlds, they need to be made out of feminist materials. Feminist theory is world making. This is why we need to resist positioning feminist theory as simply or only a tool, in the sense of something that can be used in theory, only then to be put down or put away. It should not be possible to do feminist theory without being a feminist, which requires an active and ongoing commitment to live one's life in a feminist way. I encountered this problem of how feminist theory can be feminism in theory as a student in critical theory. I met academics who wrote essays on feminist theory but who did not seem to act in feminist ways; who seemed routinely to give more support to male students than female students, or who worked by dividing female students into more and less loyal students. To be a feminist at work is or should be about how we challenge ordinary and everyday sexism, including academic sexism. This is not optional: it is what makes feminism feminist. A feminist project is to find ways in which women can exist in relation to women; how women can be in relation to each other. It is a project because we are not there yet.

We should be asking ourselves the same sorts of questions when we write our texts, when we put things together, as we do in living our lives. How to dismantle the world that is built to accommodate only some bodies? Sexism is one such accommodating system. Feminism requires supporting women in a struggle to exist in this world. What do I mean by *women* here? I am referring to all those who travel under the sign *women*. No feminism worthy of its name would use the sexist idea "women born women" to create the edges of feminist community, to render trans women into "not women," or "not born women," or into men.[7] No one is born a woman; it as an assignment (not just a sign, but also a task or an imperative, as I discuss in part I) that can shape us; make us; and break us. Many women who were assigned female at birth, let us remind ourselves, are deemed not women in the right way, or not women at all, perhaps because of how they do or do not express themselves (they are too good at sports, not feminine enough because of their bodily shape, comportment, or conduct, not heterosexual, not mothers, and so on). Part of the difficulty of the category of women is what follows residing in that category, as well as what follows not residing in that category because of the body you acquire, the desires you have, the paths you follow or do not follow. There can be violence at stake in being recognizable as women; there can be violence at stake in not being recognizable as women.

In a world in which *human* is still defined as *man*, we have to fight for women and as women. And to do that we also need to challenge the instrumentalization of feminism. Even though feminism can be used as a tool that can help us make sense of the world by sharpening the edges of our critique, it is not something we can put down. Feminism goes wherever we go. If not, we are not.

We thus enact feminism in how we relate to the academy. When I was doing my PhD, I was told I had to give my love to this or that male theorist, to follow him, not necessarily as an explicit command but through an apparently gentle but increasingly insistent questioning: Are you a Derridean; no, so are you a Lacanian; no, oh, okay, are you a Deleuzian; no, then what? If not, then what? Maybe my answer should have been: if not, then not! I was never willing to agree to this restriction. But not to agree with this restriction required the help of other feminists who came before me. If we can create our paths by not following, we still need others before us. In this book, I adopt a strict citation policy: I do not cite any white men.[8] By *white men* I am referring to an institution, as I explain in chapter 6. Instead, I cite those who have contributed to the intellectual genealogy of feminism and antiracism, including work that has been too quickly (in my view) cast aside or left behind, work that lays out other paths, paths we can call desire lines, created by not following the official paths laid out by disciplines.[9] These paths might have become fainter from not being traveled upon; so we might work harder to find them; we might be willful just to keep them going by not going the way we have been directed.

My citation policy has given me more room to attend to those feminists who came before me. Citation is feminist memory. Citation is how we acknowledge our debt to those who came before; those who helped us find our way when the way was obscured because we deviated from the paths we were told to follow. In this book, I cite feminists of color who have contributed to the project of naming and dismantling the institutions of patriarchal whiteness. I consider this book primarily as a contribution to feminist of color scholarship and activism; this body of work is where I feel most at home, where I find energy as well as resources.

Citations can be feminist bricks: they are the materials through which, from which, we create our dwellings. My citation policy has affected the kind of house I have built. I realized this not simply through writing the book, through what I found about what came up, but also through giving presentations. As I have already noted, in previous work I have built a philosophical edifice by my engagement with the history of ideas. We cannot conflate the history of ideas with white men, though if doing one leads to the other then we are being taught where ideas are assumed to originate. Seminal: how ideas are assumed to originate from male bodies. I now think of that philosophical edifice as a timber frame around which a house is being built. In this book I have not built a house by using that frame. And I have felt much more exposed. Perhaps citations are feminist straw: lighter materials that, when put together, still create a shelter but a shelter that leaves you more vulnerable. That is how it felt writing this work as well as speaking from it: being in the wind; being blown about, more or less, depending on what I encountered. The words I sent out danced around me; I began to pick up on things I had not noticed before. I began to wonder how much I had in the past built an edifice to create a distance. Sometimes we need distance to follow a thought. Sometimes we need to give up distance to follow that thought.

In the chapters that follow, I refer to different kinds of feminist materials that have been my companions as a feminist and diversity worker, from feminist philosophy to feminist literature and film. A companion text could be thought of as a companion species, to borrow from Donna Haraway's (2003) suggestive formulation. A companion text is a text whose company enabled you to proceed on a path less trodden. Such texts might spark a moment of revelation in the midst of an overwhelming proximity; they might share a feeling or give you resources to make sense of something that had been beyond your grasp; companion texts can prompt you to hesitate or to question the direction in which you are going, or they might give you a sense that in going the way you are going, you are not alone. Some of the texts that appear with me in this book have been with me before: Virginia Woolf's *Mrs. Dalloway*, George Eliot's *Mill on the Floss*, Rita Mae Brown's *Rubyfruit Jungle*, and Toni

Morrison's *The Bluest Eye*. I could not have proceeded along the path I took without these texts. To live a feminist life is to live in very good company. I have placed these companion texts in my killjoy survival kit. I encourage you as a feminist reader to assemble your own kit. What would you include?

The materials we include in our kits could also be called feminist classics. By feminist classics, I mean feminist books that have been in circulation; that have become worn from being passed around. I do not mean classics in the sense of canonical texts. Of course, some texts become canonical, and we need to question how these histories happen, how selections are made; we need to ask who or what does not survive these selections. But the texts that reach us, that make a connection, are not necessarily the ones that are taught in the academy, or that make it to the official classics edition. Many of the texts that connect with me are the ones assumed to be dated, to belong to a time that we are in no longer.

The idea of feminist classics for me is a way of thinking about how books make communities. I was part of a feminist classics reading group held in women's studies at Lancaster University. This reading group was one of my favorite experiences of feminist intellectual life thus far. I loved the labor of going over materials that might now tend to be passed over, of finding in them some abundant resources, concepts, and words. To attend to feminist classics is to give time: to say that what is behind us is worth going over, worth putting in front of us. It is a way of pausing, not rushing ahead, not being seduced by the buzz of the new, a buzz that can end up being what you hear, blocking the possibility of opening our ears to what came before. What I also really enjoyed too in the reading group was the attention to the books themselves as material objects. Each of us had different copies, some of them tattered and well read, worn, and, as it were, lived in. You can, I think, live in books: some feminists might even begin their feminist lives living in books. Participating in the group with books made me aware of how feminist community is shaped by passing books around; the sociality of their lives is part of the sociality of ours. There are so many ways that feminist books change hands; in passing between us, they change each of us.

There are many ways of describing the materials I bring together in this book: companion texts and feminist classics are just two possible ways. The materials are books, yes, but they are also spaces of encounter; how we are touched by things; how we touch things. I think of feminism as a fragile archive, a body assembled from shattering, from splattering, an archive whose fragility gives us responsibility: to take care.

Living a Feminist Life is structured in three parts. In part I, "Becoming Feminist," I discuss the process of becoming a feminist, and how consciousness of gender is a world consciousness that allows you to revisit the places you have been, to become estranged from gender and heteronorms as to become estranged from the shape of your life. I start with experiences I had growing up, exploring how these individual experiences are ways of (affectively, willfully) being inserted into a collective feminist history. In part II, "Diversity Work," I focus on doing feminist work as a form of diversity work within universities, as the places where I have worked, as well as in everyday life. I show how questions of consciousness and subjectivity raised in the first part of this book, the work required to become conscious of that which tends to recede, can be understood in terms of materiality: walls are the material means by which worlds are not encountered, let alone registered. I explore experiences of being a stranger, of not feeling at home in a world that gives residence to others. In part III, "Living the Consequences," I explore the costs and potential of what we come up against, how we can be shattered by histories that are hard, but also how we become inventive, how we create other ways of being when we have to struggle to be. The history of creativity, of bonds made and forged, of what we move toward as well as away from, is a history that we need to keep in front of us; a feminist history.

It is the practical experience of coming up against a world that allows us to come up with new ideas, ideas that are not dependent on a mind that has withdrawn (because a world has enabled that withdrawal) but a body that has to wiggle about just to create room. And if we put ourselves in the same room, how much knowledge we would have! No wonder feminism causes fear; together, we are dangerous.

PART I Becoming Feminist

IN THIS FIRST PART OF THE BOOK, I explore the process of becoming feminist. Reflecting on this process can offer a way of doing feminist theory, a way of generating new insights into how gender works, as social system, or as machinery that tends to spit some bodies out. Insights into gender as well as race are worldly. Becoming a feminist involves coming up against the world.

What's my feminist story? Like you, I have many. As I will try to show, my own feminist biography is entangled with other aspects of my biography; how could it not be; how messy life is. I start this part of the book very simply, staying in chapter 1 as close to home as I can, beginning by recalling things that happened. I return to experiences that were painful and difficult, but that were animating, that gave me life because they were how I was directed along a feminist path. If we start close to home, we open ourselves out. I will try to show how, in making sense of things that happen, we also draw on histories of thought and activism that precede us. Throughout I thus reflect on how feminism itself can be understood as an affective inheritance; how our own struggles to make sense of realities that are difficult to grasp become part of a wider struggle, a struggle to be, to make sense of being.

In the process of describing how I became a feminist, this opening part of the book also offers a feminist approach to some keys areas of concern within feminist theory and beyond: the role of sensation in knowledge formation; the sociality of emotions; how power operates through directionality and orientation; and how to think about happiness, as well as the relationship between will and force. I show how becoming feminist is also about generating ideas about the worlds we encounter. Feminist theory, in other words, comes out of the sense-making process of becoming feminist and navigating a way through a world.

The figures of the feminist killjoy and willful subject are considered in this part of the book primarily in terms of how they relate to some of my early experiences of becoming and being a feminist. These figures will pop up all over the place. They are everywhere.

1 / FEMINISM IS SENSATIONAL

Feminism is sensational. Something is sensational when it provokes excitement and interest. Feminism is sensational in this sense; what is provocative about feminism is what makes feminism a set of arguments that is hard to deliver. We learn about the feminist cause by the bother feminism causes; by how feminism comes up in public culture as a site of disturbance.

When you speak as a feminist, you have to deal with strong reactions. To be committed to a feminist life might require being willing to elicit those reactions. When you speak as a feminist, you are often identified as being too reactive, as overreacting, as if all you are doing is sensationalizing the facts of the matter; as if in giving your account of something you are exaggerating, on purpose or even with malice. In this chapter I accept that feminism begins with sensation: with a sense of things. I want to explore how feminism is sensible because of the world we are in; feminism is a sensible reaction to the injustices of the world, which we might register at first through our own experiences. We might work over, mull over, these experiences; we might keep coming back to them because they do not make sense. In other words we have to make sense of what does not make sense. There is agency and life in this making. In this chapter, I share some of the experiences that led me to feminism, which I would describe as a bumpy rather than smooth process of coming to register something that is difficult; these experiences provided the raw materials of my feminist instruction.

SENSING WRONGS

A sensation is often understood by what it is not: a sensation is not an organized or intentional response to something. And that is why sensation matters: you are left with an impression that is not clear or distinct. A sensation is often felt by the skin. The word *sensational* relates both to the faculty of sensation and to the arousal of strong curiosity, interest, or excitement. If a sensation is how a body is in contact with a world, then something becomes sensational when contact becomes even more intense. Perhaps then to feel is to feel this even more.

Feminism often begins with intensity: you are aroused by what you come up against. You register something in the sharpness of an impression. Something can be sharp without it being clear what the point is. Over time, with experience, you sense that something is wrong or you have a feeling of being wronged. You sense an injustice. You might not have used that word for it; you might not have the words for it; you might not be able to put your finger on it. Feminism can begin with a body, a body in touch with a world, a body that is not at ease in a world; a body that fidgets and moves around. Things don't seem right.

Many of my early experiences of feeling wronged, as a girl, involved unwanted male attention. Things happened. They happened again. Already we sense some consequences: if becoming feminist cannot be separated from an experience of violence, of being wronged, then what brings us to feminism is what is potentially shattering. The histories that bring us to feminism are the histories that leave us fragile. Feminism might pick up (or more hopefully pick us up) from the experiences that leave us vulnerable and exposed. Feminism: how we survive the consequences of what we come up against by offering new ways of understanding what we come up against.

Feminist work is often memory work. We work to remember what sometimes we wish would or could just recede. While thinking about what it means to live a feminist life, I have been remembering; trying to put the pieces together. I have been putting a sponge to the past. When I think of my method, I think of a sponge: a material that can absorb things. We hold it out and wait to see what gets mopped up. It is not that memory work is necessarily about recalling what has been forgotten: rather, you allow a memory to become distinct, to acquire a certain crispness or even clarity; you can gather memories like things, so they become more than half glimpsed, so that we can see a fuller picture; so you can make sense of how different experiences connect.

There is one time I remember, very acutely, still. I was out jogging, just near my home. A man whirled passed on a bike and put his hand up the back of my shorts. He did not stop; he just carried on cycling as if nothing had happened, as if he had not done anything. I stopped, shaking. I felt so sick; invaded, confused, upset, angry. I was the only witness to this event; my body its memory.

My body its memory: to share a memory is to put a body into words. What do we do when these kinds of things happen? Who do we become? I kept on going. I began jogging again, but it was different: I was different. I was much more nervous. Every time someone came up behind me, I was ready, tense, waiting. I felt differently in my body, which was a different way of encountering the world.

Experiences like this: they seem to accumulate over time, gathering like things in a bag, but the bag is your body, so that you feel like you are carrying more and more weight. The past becomes heavy. We all have different biographies of violence, entangled as they are with so many aspects of ourselves: things that happen because of how we are seen; and how we are not seen. You find a way of giving an account of what happens, of living with what happens.

This you is me. You seem to receive the same message again and again: the flasher at school who keeps returning; the time you walk past a group of boys and girls on the way home when one of them shouts out to you to come back because you are "fuckable," and they all laugh; that time you come across a man masturbating under a tree in the city parklands who tells you to come and take a look and comes after you when you hurry away; the time when you are walking down a street with your sister and a man jumps out of the door exposing himself; the time you are waiting at a bus stop and a group of men in a car stop and ask you to get in, and you run away and they start jeering and shouting; the time when you fall asleep on a long flight under a blanket and you wake up with a man's fingers all over you.[1] I remember each of these occasions not only as an experience of being violated, but as a sensory event that was too overwhelming to process at the time. I can still hear the sound of the voices, the car as it slowed down, the bike that rushed past, the door that opened, the sound of the footsteps, the kind of day it was, the quiet hum of a plane as I woke up. Senses can be magnified, sometimes after the event.

At the time, each time, something happens. You are thrown. These experiences: What effects do they have? What do they do? You begin to feel a pressure, this relentless assault on the senses; a body in touch with a world can become a body that fears the touch of a world. The world is experienced as sensory intrusion. It is too much. Not to be assaulted: maybe you might try to close yourself off, to withdraw from proximity, from proximity to a potential. Or perhaps you try to deal with this violence by numbing your own sensations, by learning not to be affected or to be less affected. Perhaps you try to forget what happened. You might be ashamed. You might stay silent. You might not tell anyone, say anything, and burn with the sensation of a secret. It becomes another burden: that which is not revealed. Maybe you adopt for yourself a certain kind of fatalism: these things happen; what happens will happen; whatever will be, will be.

The violence does things. You begin to expect it. You learn to inhabit your body differently through this expectation. When you sense the world out there as a danger, it is your relation to your own body that changes: you become more cautious, timid; you might withdraw in anticipation that what happened before will happen again. It might be your own experiences that lead you here, to caution as withdrawal, but it might also be what you have learned from others. You are taught to be careful: to be full of care as to become anxious about the potential to be broken. You begin to learn that being careful, not having things like that happen to you, is a way of avoiding becoming damaged. It is for your own good. And you sense the consequence: if something happens, you have failed to prevent it. You feel bad in anticipation of your own failure. You are learning, too, to accept that potential for violence as imminent, and to manage yourself as a way of managing the consequences.

You are taught to care for yourself by being careful about others. I remember a policeman coming to our classroom one time, to teach us all about what they called "stranger danger." The lesson was given as it is usually given, as a simple instruction: don't talk to strangers. An image was conjured in my mind, derived not only from my own experience but from this instruction, of a stranger. An image, a body, a figure: it appears as if by magic. I began the first chapter of my book *Strange Encounters* by evoking this image: the stranger as a shadowy figure with a "grey mac shimmering at your feet" (Ahmed 2000, 19). The police, in evoking the stranger, also gave me a body in which to deposit my anxiety. If the stranger could be anyone, the stranger was someone I recognized; somebody I could look out for. Stranger danger is an effective as well as affective script: some bodies become dangerous, others endangered. As girls you learn to be cautious and careful in public spaces with that caution and care directed toward those who do not belong, whose presence or proximity is illegitimate. The stranger loiters. The stranger becomes a container of fear.

Violence becomes instruction when it is accompanied by a narrative, an explanation. When you have learned something, when you have received the message of this instruction, your feelings are given direction and shape. Your body reacts in the right way. Iris Marion Young (1990) in "Throwing like a Girl" asks how girls come to be "like girls" through how they come to inhabit their bodies. Girls come to take up less space by what they do, and by what they do not do. Girls come to restrict themselves through restricting how they use their bodies. Young calls this restriction an "inhibited intentionality," using the example of how girls learn to throw, by not getting their bodies behind an action.

Becoming a girl is here about how you experience your body in relation to space. Gendering operates in how bodies take up space: think of the intense sociality of the subway or train, how some men typically lounge around, with their legs wide, taking up not only the space in front of their own seat but the space in front of other seats. Women might end up not even having much space in front of their own seats; that space has been taken up. To become accommodating, we take up less space. The more accommodating we are the less space we have to take up. Gender: a loop, tightening.

A world can shrink when we shrink. Judith Butler (1993) taught us to think of "girling" as a social mechanism. A baby is born: we might say, "It's a girl!" or "It's a boy!" Even before birth: we might watch on the screen to see whether it's a girl or boy, where that is decided by virtue of the absence or presence of a penis. The attachment to gender rests from the very beginning on phallocentrism: on the penis as the decider of the future, two sexes as two paths: the sexual binary as fate, as fated, as fatalism. Even when we critique the sex-gender distinction, even when we learn from feminist critiques of this distinction (Gatens 1983; Butler 1990), we know that that distinction works as a form of sequencing: as if from sex, gender follows. We could call this sequencing "gender fatalism," as implied by the assumption that "boys will be boys." I remember that utterance "boys will be boys" as one often made by adults, often with a nod of the head and an intonation of forgiveness: an unruliness explained as boys being boys; aggression, violence, even. Gender fatalism rests on ideas about nature as well as time: what "will be" is decided by "what is." This is what boys are like; girls, too. But likeness becomes not only an explanation (he is being such boy; what a boy he is being) but an expectation. The "will be" in "boys will be boys" acquires the force of prediction. A prediction becomes a command. You will be boy. When you have fulfilled that command, you are agreeable; you have lived up to an expectation.

Sex is given as an assignment; homework. No wonder mere description (it's a girl; it's a boy!) provides the basis of a task (being boy! being girl!) as well as a command (You will be boy! You will be girl!). To receive an assignment is to be a given a sign: boy or girl. This *or* too is doing something, registering as opposition; one or the other. A sign: what means or denotes something. Right from the very beginning matter and meaning are deeply entangled; it is not matter (sex), then meaning (gender). You are in being assigned *x* or *y* also being assigned to a group; an assignment is what you receive from others that will determine how you are positioned in relation to others. We are more than these assignments right from the beginning.

We can feel at home in an assignment; or not; more or less. An assignment also means a task; like homework. To be assigned a sex in this binary system is a way of being directed toward a future, as I explore in more detail in chapter 2. Perhaps gender becomes more work for those who feel less at home in their original assignments. We might, early on, not be at home in a body by not being at home in a sign. And we might be perpetually reassigned; reminders of our assignment punctuate our lives like grammar. So of course girling moments do not stop happening, even after we are pronounced girls. As Judith Butler elaborates, "the girling of the girl does not end there" (1993, xvii). Rather, "that founding interpellation is reiterated by various authorities" (xvii). It is not simply that the sign denotes something. What matters is who addresses you through the sign; how you receive it.

Girling is enacted not only through being explicitly addressed as a girl, but in the style or mode of address: because you are a girl, we can do this to you. Violence too is a mode of address. Being girl is a way of being taught what it is to have a body: you are being told; you will receive my advances; you are object; thing, nothing. To become girl is to learn to expect such advances, to modify your behavior in accordance; to become girl as becoming wary of being in public space; becoming wary of being at all. Indeed, if you do not modify your behavior in accordance, if you are not careful and cautious, you can be made responsible for the violence directed toward you (look at what you were drinking, look at what you wearing, look at where you were, look look). You can be made responsible whether or not you have modified your behavior in accordance, because gender fatalism has already explained the violence directed against you as forgivable and inevitable. The violence of judgments that tend to follow violence against women and girls has been documented by feminists over generations. Documentation is a feminist project; a life project.

FEMINIST CONSCIOUSNESS

When did you begin to put the pieces together? Perhaps when you put the pieces back together you are putting yourself back together. We assemble something. Feminism is DIY: a form of self-assembly. No wonder feminist work is often about timing: sometimes we are too fragile to do this work; we cannot risk being shattered because we are not ready to put ourselves back together again. To get ready often means being prepared to be undone.

In time, with work, things begin to make more sense. You begin to recognize how violence is directed: that being recognized as a girl means being subjected to this pressure, this relentless assault on the senses; a body that comes to fear the touch of a world. Maybe you learn from that, from what that repetition does; you realize retrospectively how you came to take up less space. You might express feminist rage at how women are made responsible for the violence that is directed against them. Feminism helps you to make sense that something is wrong; to recognize a wrong is to realize that you are not in the wrong.

Becoming feminist: how we redescribe the world we are in. We begin to identify how what happens to me, happens to others. We begin to identify patterns and regularities. Begin to identify: this sounds too smooth. It is not an easy or straightforward process because we have to stay with the wrongs. And think about feeling: to direct your attention to the experience of being wronged can mean feeling wronged all over again.

We need to attend to the bumps; it is bumpy. You had already sensed something amiss. Maybe it was an uneasy feeling at first. As Alison Jaggar describes, "Only when we reflect on our initially puzzling irritability, revulsion, anger, or fear may we bring to consciousness our 'gut-level' awareness that we are in a situation of coercion, cruelty, injustice or danger" (1996, 181; see also Spelman 1989). A gut has its own intelligence. A feminist gut might sense something is amiss. You have to get closer to the feeling; but once you try to think about a feeling, how quickly it can recede. Maybe it begins as a background anxiety, like a humming noise that gradually gets louder over time so that it begins to fill your ear, canceling out other sounds. And then suddenly it seems (though perhaps it is not sudden) what you tried so hard not to notice is all you can hear. A sensation that begins at the back of your mind, an uneasy sense of something amiss, gradually comes forward, as things come up; then receding, as you try to get on with things; as you try to get on despite things. Maybe you do not even want to feel this way; feeling wrong is what brings a wrong home. Attending to the feeling might be too demanding: it might require you to give up on what otherwise seems to give you something; relationships, dreams; an idea of who it is that you are; an idea of who it is that you can be. You might even will yourself not to notice certain things because noticing them would change your relation to the world; it would change the world to which you exist in relation. We have to stay with the feelings that we might wish would go away; that become reminders of these things that happened that made you wary of being at all.

Perhaps there is just only so much you can take in. Perhaps you take in some things as a way of not taking in other things. As I have been putting a sponge to my own feminist past, I remembered another conversation. It was with a teacher of mine at university, Rosemary Moore, who taught the first feminist classes I took: Nineteenth-Century Women's Writing in 1988; Twentieth-Century Women's Writing in 1989. I hadn't thought about this conversation for a long time, though it is probably not true to say that I had forgotten it. I asked her whether my essay for the course had to refer to women or gender. Her answer was that it didn't but that it would be surprising if it didn't. Why did I ask her this question? I had come to university hoping to study philosophy. I was especially interested in what I called "scepticism," philosophies that proceeded by doubting what is as a way of questioning what's what. Sadly, philosophy at Adelaide University was pretty much straight analytical philosophy and scepticism was dismissed as self-refuting in the first lecture of Philosophy 101. To study the kind of work I was interested in, I ended up in the English literature department because there they taught what was referred to as "theory." And I chose the women's writing courses not because I was interested in feminist theory (even though I was passionate about feminism) but because I was interested in critical theory. I was interested in how we know things, in questions of truth, in perspective and perception, in experience and subjectivity. I wanted to ask how I know that what I see as green is what you see as green; those sorts of questions were my sort of questions.

Yes: I chose women's writing because I wanted to do critical theory. Our teacher was engaged with and by Lacanian psychoanalysis. If we began there, that wasn't what kept my attention; it was 1980s feminist literary theory and from there, feminist philosophy of science and feminist epistemology. I ended up writing my first feminist essay for that course.[2] So why did it happen this way around: from critical theory to feminist theory, given that I thought of myself as a feminist and had been such an outspoken feminist growing up?

I think there was only so much feminism I could take in. I had thought that to be philosophical or to ask questions about the nature of reality was not to do feminism: that feminism was about something particular not general, relative not universal, that feminism was about questioning and challenging sexual violence, inequality, and injustice and not the nature of reality as such. I did not understand that feminism was a way of challenging the universal. I did not appreciate how questioning sexism is one of the most profound ways of disrupting what we take to be given and thus learning about how the given is given. Feminist theory taught me that the universal is what needs to be exploded. Feminist theory taught me that reality is usually just someone else's tired explanation. So if in my introduction to this book I suggested that feminist theory is what gets you there, to the classroom, we might note how feminist theory can be what gets you out of there. By this I mean: I thought I wanted to be in the theory class; feminist theory taught me that that was not the class for me. Feminism is my theory class.

We learn also: how we recognize sexism or racism here can be a way of not recognizing it there. A location can be a reduction. Becoming feminist involves a process of recognizing that what you are up against cannot be located or reduced to an object or thing (which could then be discarded so we could start up again). The process of recognizing sexism was not smooth or automatic. I had multiple false starts because there was so much I resisted: I could take feminism in only bit by bit. Maybe there was only so much I could take in because it meant recognizing that I had been taken in. You can feel stupid for not having seen things more clearly before. You have to give up on a version of yourself as well as a version of events. And maybe we need to remember how hard it is to acknowledge that a world is not accommodating you because of the body you have. I didn't want feminism to be everywhere, as I didn't want to encounter these limits; I wanted there to be places to go where I could just leave my body behind.

If becoming feminist is not a smooth process, if we resist what we encounter because it is too much to take in, this is not to say when we do let go it is just difficult. When you begin to put the pieces together, it can feel magical: the wonder of the clicking moment, when things that had previously been obscured begin to make sense, when things fit into place. You blink and the world reappears: clarity can feel magical. For me reading feminist theory was a series of continuous clicks. And later, teaching women's studies was such a delight as you can participate in other people's clicking moments: what a sound it makes; how important it is that this sound is audible to others.

Finding feminism can be empowering as it is a way of reinhabiting the past. It is personal. There is no question: it is personal. The personal is structural. I learned that you can be hit by a structure; you can be bruised by a structure. An individual man who violates you is given permission: that is structure. His violence is justified as natural and inevitable: that is structure. A girl is made responsible for his violence: that is structure. A policeman who turns away because it is a domestic call: that is structure. A judge who talks about what she was wearing: that is structure. A structure is an arrangement, an order, a building; an assembly.

We need structure to give evidence of structure. To catalog instances of violence is to create a feminist catalog. I think one of the reasons I find the project *Everyday Sexism* so important and compelling is that it shows how the cataloging of instances of sexism is necessarily a collective project.[3] The project involves the creation of a virtual space in which we can insert our own individual experiences of sexism, sexual violence, or sexual harassment so that we show what we know: that this or that incident is not isolated but part of a series of events: a series as a structure. These recent feminist strategies have revived key aspects of second-wave feminism; we are in the time of revival because of what is not over. Consciousness-raising was also about this: reaching a feminist account, as an account for oneself with and through others, connecting my experience with the experience of others. We need a deposit system to show the scale of sexism. When there is a place to go with these experiences—and feminism is about giving women places to go—the accounts tend to come out: a "drip, drip" becomes a flood. It is like a tap has been loosened, allowing what has been held back to flow. Feminism: the releasing of a pressure valve.

Feminism can allow you to reinhabit not only your own past but also your own body. You might over time, in becoming aware of how you have lessened your own space, give yourself permission to take up more space; to expand your own reach. It is not necessarily the case that we take up this permission simply by giving ourselves permission. It does take time, to reinhabit the body, to become less wary, to acquire confidence. Feminism involves a process of finding another way to live in your body. We might learn to let ourselves bump into things; not to withdraw in anticipation of violence. Of course I am describing a difficulty; I am describing how ways of resolving problems can enact the problems we are trying to resolve. We know we are not responsible for resolving the problem of violence; changing how we relate to the world does not change the world. And yet in refusing to withdraw, in refusing to lessen how much space we take up, in insisting on taking up space, we are not receiving the message that has been sent out. In order to put the pieces together, you cannot but get the message wrong, the message that makes a wrong a right. No wonder then, as I explore later, to become a feminist is to be perceived as in the wrong.

As we begin this process of putting ourselves back together we find much more than ourselves. Feminism, in giving you somewhere to go, allows you to revisit where you have been. We can become even more conscious of the world in this process of becoming conscious of injustices because we had been taught to overlook so much. A world can flood once we have let it in, once we have unlocked the door of our own resistance. Feminism too can become a flooding experience: one book read that leads to another, a trail that leads you to find feminism, more and more feminism, new words, concepts, arguments, models: patriarchy, phallocentrism, rape culture, the sex-gender system. In finding feminism, you are finding out about the many ways that feminists have tried to make sense, already, of the experiences you had, before you had them; experiences that left you feeling all alone are the experiences that lead you to others. We still have sorting to do: some of these ways of making sense make more sense to you than others. But I will always remember that feeling; a sense that there are others like you out there, that you are not on your own, that you were not on your own. Your own difficult history is written out in words that are sent out. I often think of reading feminist books as like making friends, realizing that others have been here before.

Even if you still feel pain, frustration, and rage, even if you feel these feelings more as you have given them more attention, they are directed in a different way. Knowledge is this achievement of direction. Your feelings are directed neither at some anonymous stranger who happened upon you (or not only), nor toward yourself for allowing something to happen (or not just), but toward a world that reproduces that violence by explaining it away.

PROBLEMS WITH NAMES

Feminist consciousness can feel like a switch that is turned on. Turning off might be necessary to survive the world that we are in, which is not a feminist world. Feminist consciousness is when the on button is the default position. Unless you turn it off, you are on. Perhaps this is the reverse of the usual setting, where you have to be switched to be on. No wonder: it can be exhausting. Sometimes it might even seem that it is as or even more tiring to notice sexism and racism than to experience sexism and racism: after all, it is this noticing that makes things real. And at times, it can be tempting to think: it would be less difficult if I could just stop noticing sexism and racism. It would be easier to screen things out. Personally I don't think that is an easy option. And I don't think that it is always available as an option: because having let the world in, screening it out, would also require giving up on the subject you have become. I think this is a promise: once you become a person who notices sexism and racism, it is hard to unbecome that person.

If a world can be what we learn not to notice, noticing becomes a form of political labor. What do we learn not to notice? We learn not to notice some suffering, such that if the suffering of those deemed strangers appears, then it does so only dimly, at the edges of our consciousness. In fact this is another way we learn about the figure of the stranger: strangers are not simply those we do not recognize but those we recognize as strangers, not only those you do not know but those you should not know. As a child you might have been taught to turn away from homeless people on the street, to screen out not only their suffering but their very existence. They are not anything to do with you. Hurry on, move on. We are learning not only whose suffering should affect us, or how we should be affected by whose suffering; we are busy exercising the very distinction between friends and strangers, creating that distinction, between those who matter and those who do not. It is a distinction predicated on violence. It is a distinction enforced through violence. We are learning to screen out what gets in the way of our occupation of space. Once you have learned this something, you don't notice this someone.

If we have been taught to turn away, we have to learn to turn toward. Audre Lorde taught me how turning toward what is difficult, which can be a what with a who, is politically necessary, even if this turning can at times feel like we are making life more difficult for ourselves. She teaches us how some difficulties—when we come up against a world because of the body we have—resist being comprehended when they are experienced. In *Sister Outsider*, Audre Lorde describes the words *racism* and *sexism* as "grown up words" (1984a, 152). We encounter racism and sexism before we have the words that allow us to make sense of what we encounter. Words can then allow us to get closer to our experiences; words can allow us to comprehend what we experience after the event. We become retrospective witnesses of our becoming. Sexism and racism: if they are problems we have given names, the names tend to lag behind the problems.

Having names for problems can make a difference. Before, you could not quite put your finger on it. With these words as tools, we revisit our own histories; we hammer away at the past. It took a long time for me to get to the point where I could even describe how race and racism had structured my own world. Reading black feminist and feminist of color scholarship allowed me to revisit my own past, to occupy that past. I was brought up in Australia in a very white neighborhood. I went to a very white school (is there something very "very" about whiteness? One wonders.). There were just a few of us of color; we didn't quite know what to do with each other, though we knew we had something to do with each other. I had a white English mother and a brown Pakistani father who had kind of let go or almost let go of his own history in order to give us children a chance in a new world.[4] We had no Pakistani friends, but there was an occasional visit to Pakistan, and visits from Pakistani aunties. But they were occasional, fleeting moments, ones that did not leave me with a possibility I could grasp. I was brown, visibly different but with no real account of that difference; no real sense of where it or I was coming from. I kept feeling wrong, being treated as in the wrong, but I did not know what was wrong. Something was wrong. How to acquire the words for this something?

I had to leave home before I could find these words. I had to leave so I could come back again. I was writing a chapter of my PhD thesis on subjectivity. I needed an example. I remember looking around the room as if something lying around might provide me with inspiration. It is funny to recall this because later on I would turn to an object that was nearby: the table, an object that was to become another kind of writing companion (Ahmed 2006). As I was glancing around, it came back to me. A memory intruded into the present as if by its own will. I was ready for the intrusion. I recalled an experience I had when I was fourteen years old, walking close to home, along a street in Adelaide. Two policemen in a car pulled up next to me. The first asked, "Are you Aboriginal?" It turned out there had been burglaries in the area. Racism: how an association between Aboriginality and criminality is turned into a question. I will pick up this association in due course. The second policeman then quipped, "Or is it just a sun tan?" Although given as a quip it was a hostile address, and it was an unsettling experience at the time. It was an experience of being made into a stranger, the one who is recognized as out of place, as the one who does not belong, whose proximity is registered as crime or threat. Once I recalled this experience, so much else came back to me; a drip, drip became a flood.

The police at the school were friendly and taught me to fear strangers for my own protection. The police on the street were hostile and taught me that to become a stranger is to be stopped by how you are addressed. We learn from this difference: my first instruction was an instruction into whiteness and not just femininity. It is a white female body that is assumed to be vulnerable and in need of protection from others. In the second encounter, I was danger, not endangered; a brown body is not perceived as a fragile female body. My different experiences with the police show how the stranger is a racialized figure. What happened to me partly depended on how I would pass into or out of this figure. I return to this instance in chapter 5, to reflect on how I was able to start up again, and how being able to start up again was a form of class as well as racial privilege. But let's think about the stranger as a racialized figure. The racialization of the stranger is not immediately apparent; after all, we are taught the stranger could be anyone. My stranger memory taught me that the "could be anyone" points to some bodies more than others. You are stopped because they think you are Aboriginal; you are allowed to start up again when you pass as white.

Feminist and antiracist consciousness involves not just finding the words, but through the words, how they point, realizing how violence is directed: violence is directed toward some bodies more than others. To give a problem a name can change not only how we register an event but whether we register an event. Perhaps not having names is a way of turning away from a difficulty that persists whether or not we turn away. Not naming a problem in the hope that it will go away often means the problem just remains unnamed. At the same time, giving the problem a name does not make the problem go away. To give the problem a name can be experienced as magnifying the problem; allowing something to acquire a social and physical density by gathering up what otherwise would remain scattered experiences into a tangible thing. Making sexism and racism tangible is also a way of making them appear outside of oneself; something that can be spoken of and addressed by and with others. It can be a relief to have something to point to; otherwise you can feel alone or lost. We have different tactics for dealing with sexism and racism; and one difficulty is that these tactics can be in tension. When we give problems their names, we can become a problem for those who do not want to talk about a problem even though they know there is a problem. You can cause a problem by not letting things recede.

We need to acquire words to describe what we come up against. Becoming feminist; finding the words. *Sexism* is another such word. It often arrives after the event: we look back and we can explain things that happened as sexism. To name something as sexist does not make something there that was not there before; it is a sexist idea that to describe something as sexist is to make something sexist. But naming something as "sexism" does do something. It modifies a relation given that it does not create something from nothing. Connections can be what we have to struggle for, because there is so much silence about sexism: sexism makes it costly for women to speak about sexism. Because, after all, to name something as sexist is not only to name something that happens as part of a wider system (to refuse to give what happens the status of an exceptional event), but it is also to give an account of that something as being wrong and unjustifiable. To name something as sexist is not only to modify a relation by modifying our understanding of that relation; it is also to insist that further modification is required. When we say, "That's sexist," we are saying no to that, as well as no to the world that renders such a speech or behavior permissible; we are asking individuals to change such that these forms of speech and behavior are no longer acceptable or permissible.

Not just individuals: the point is that individuals are encouraged and rewarded for participating in sexist culture. It might be a reward given through affirmation from peers (the egging on that allows a group to solidify over how they address others as imposters). But institutions also enable and reward sexist behavior: institutional sexism. Sexual banter is so often institutionalized. You might participate in that banter because it is costly not to participate: you become the problem, the one who is disapproving or uptight. You are treated as policing the behavior of others simply by virtue of not participating in that behavior. Not participating can be judged as disapproval whether or not you make that judgment. You are judged as taking something the wrong way when you object to something. When we give an account of something as sexist or racist, we are often dismissed as having a faulty perception, as not receiving the intentions or actions of others fairly or properly. "I didn't mean anything by it," he might say. And indeed then by taking something said or done the wrong way, not only are you wrong, but you are understood as committing a wrong against someone else. When you talk about sexism and racism, you are heard as damaging the reputation of an individual or an organization. I return to this issue of damage in chapter 6 in my discussion of brick walls.

Sometimes it might be to our own advantage not to have a problem with how we are addressed. Another time, a rather long time ago when I was still in Australia, a woman told me how in a job interview a man asked her where she was from (some of us are always asked this question, as our being is in question, as I explore in chapter 5). She explains; she gives an account of herself.

She is mixed race. He then says to her that mixed-race women are beautiful. I was outraged when she told me this, but she shrugged it off: she said it was a compliment; she was offered the position. What a history I suspect is implied here: a history of how we shrug things off. To get on, you get along. I would use words like *racism* and *sexism* to describe how she becomes an exotic spectacle, but for her these words would probably have been experienced as impositions, as coming from the outside, as potentially requiring her to give up an opportunity that was available, to give up something, all over again.

These are complicated scenarios: you can receive some benefits by adapting yourself to a system that is, at another level, compromising your capacity to inhabit a world on more equal terms. I think for many women, becoming willing to participate in sexist culture is a compromise, even if it is not registered as such, because we have been taught (from past experience, from what we come up against) that being unwilling to participate can be dangerous. You risk becoming alienated from all of the existing structures that enable survival within an institution, let alone a progression. Here we can say: resistance to recognizing something might be a way of coping with or living with that thing. Resistance to recognition can be a form or manner of recognition; recognition as a form of resignation, even.

Sometimes: surviving the relentlessness of sexism as well as racism might require that you shrug it off, by not naming it, or even by learning not to experience those actions as violations of your own body; learning to expect that violence as just part of ordinary life; making that fatalism your fate. Sometimes: we have to teach ourselves not to shrug things off, knowing full well that by not doing something we will be perceived as doing too much. When we start using words like *sexism* and *racism*, words that make what we are asked not to notice all the more real, we sense there will be consequences. We sense the pain that might follow, as well as the punishment. Part III of this book reflects on living a feminist life as living with the consequences of being feminists who are willing to give problems their names. But I want to make a start here by turning to the figure of the killjoy. She has been waiting (rather impatiently) to speak to us.

BECOMING THE PROBLEM

As I have suggested, when you name something as sexist or as racist you are making that thing more tangible so that it can be more easily communicated to others. But for those who do not have a sense of the racism or sexism you are talking about, to bring them up is to bring them into existence.

When you expose a problem you pose a problem.

It might then be assumed that the problem would go away if you would just stop talking about it or if you went away. The charge of sensationalism falls rather quickly onto feminist shoulders: when she talks about sexism and racism, her story is heard as sensationalist, as if she is exaggerating for effect.[5] The feminist killjoy begins as a sensationalist figure. It is as if the point of making her point is to cause trouble, to get in the way of the happiness of others, because of her own unhappiness. I turn to the question of happiness and unhappiness in chapter 2. But note how the feminist killjoy begins her life as an antifeminist figure: we are retooling her for our own purpose.

Let me retell my story of becoming a feminist by turning to the figure of the feminist killjoy. I would begin this story with a table. Around the table, a family gathers.[6] Always we are seated in the same place: my father one end, myself the other, my two sisters to one side, my mother to the other. Always we are seated this way, as if we are trying to secure more than our place. We are having polite conversations, where only certain things can be brought up. Someone says something you consider problematic. At first you try not to say anything. But they keep saying something. So maybe you respond, carefully, perhaps. You say why you think what they have said is problematic. You might be speaking quietly, but you are beginning to feel wound up, recognizing with frustration that you are being wound up by someone who is winding you up. The feminist killjoy appears here: when she speaks, she seems wound up. I appear here. This is my history: wound up.

However she speaks, the one who speaks as a feminist is usually heard as the cause of the argument. She stops the smooth flow of communication. It becomes tense. She makes things tense. We can begin to witness what is being locked in this dynamic. The problem is not simply about the content of what she is saying. She is doing more than saying the wrong thing: she is getting in the way of something, the achievement or accomplishment of the family or of some *we* or another, which is created by what is not said. So much you are supposed not to say, to do, to be, in order to preserve that *we*. And yet, even if she is not supposed to react this way, her reaction is, at another level, willed. She is after all being wound up by someone who is winding her up. The family is performed by witnessing her being wound up, spinning around. Look, look at her spin! To make her the cause of a tension is another way of preserving the illusion that without her, the family would be civil. I think those of us who have been killjoys around family tables probably know this; how useful we are as containers of incivility and discord.[7]

Whenever we speak, eyes seem to roll, as if to say, well, you would say that. From these experiences we can condense a formula:

Rolling eyes = feminist pedagogy.

Eyes seem to roll wherever you go, whatever you say. In fact, you don't even have to say anything before eyes start rolling. It can seem as if eyes roll as an expression of collective exasperation because you are a feminist. Becoming a feminist is often about being lodged in a *because*. She says that because she is a feminist; or, even more strongly, she is only saying that because she is a feminist. In the introduction, I described how practicing feminism is about developing our feminist tendencies (becoming the kind of person who would be willing to speak out about sexism and racism). We can see now how feminism is refuted or dismissed as simply a personal tendency, as if she disagrees with something because she is being disagreeable; as if she opposes something because she is being oppositional. Feminists are then judged as being unable to help themselves, as if to be a feminist is to function on automatic pilot.[8] Feminism is treated as a removal from the world rather than engagement with the world. We are talking about how feminists are removed from the world because of the nature of their engagement; how feminist accounts are discounted as sensationalizing the facts of the matter.

We can appreciate, then, how the sensations that lead us to feminism are often the very same sensations that follow being a feminist. Through feminism you make sense of wrongs; you realize that you are not in the wrong. But when you speak of something as being wrong, you end up being in the wrong all over again. The sensation of being wronged can thus end up magnified: you feel wronged by being perceived as in the wrong just for pointing out something is wrong. It is frustrating! And then your frustration can be taken as evidence of your frustration, that you speak this way, about this or that, because you are frustrated. It is frustrating to be heard as frustrated; it can make you angry that you are heard as angry. Or if you are angry about something and you are heard as an angry person (an angry black feminist or an angry woman of color), then what you are angry about disappears, which can make you feel even angrier. If feminism allows us to redirect our emotions toward different objects, our emotions can become their objects. We are dismissed as emotional. It is enough to make you emotional.

And then of course the objects we are objecting to are reaffirmed as inappropriate objects for critique or complaint. I remember one time we were talking over the family table about the film *Kramer vs. Kramer*. I remember questioning how the mother is demonized. I make that point, that rather obvious feminist point, which is hard not to make once you have acquired a feminist tendency. And then: the noise, the noise! "Oh can't you just let us enjoy this lovely sweet film"; "Oh can't you see how special the relationship is between the father and son, how cruel she is"; "Oh you are always looking for problems," and so on. Feminists: looking for problems. It is as if these problems are not there until you point them out; it is as if pointing them out is what makes them there.

We become a problem when we describe a problem.

One time much later than my other killjoy moments over the family table, I was having dinner with my sister and her (then) partner. He began saying things about Aboriginal people and how they would complain about the army moving a rock because it was sacred. He was deeply offensive. I responded. Maybe I used the word *racism*. I can't remember if I used that word, but it was on my mind. Racism was on my mind because racism was in the room. Whatever I said, he became very angry, but an anger that took the form of silence and stares. He sat there, steely faced, for the rest of the dinner, not touching his food. Waiters hovered nervously. We spoke politely around him. When I woke the next morning, my mother called, and she had heard that I had put him off his food. When will you ever learn—I could hear those unuttered words.

Poor him

Mean

Memories of being a killjoy at the table flooded back to me, a burning sensation on skin; recalled as being the one who puts others off their food. You sense that an injustice follows pointing out an injustice. Another dinner ruined. So many dinners ruined. That flooding: it happens. It still happens. Feeling wrong, being wrong; being wronged. If sensation brings us to feminism, to become a feminist is to cause a sensation.

CONCLUSION: ALIENATION AS SENSATION

The feminist killjoy first came up for me in a painful and difficult situation. I have learned so much from returning to some of my early experiences of this assignment. In chapter 2 I complicate the scene of her arrival to show how the killjoy does not simply come up because of what she brings up. But it is important to start with my first sense of her as a figure, how she came up, for me; how she spoke to rather than simply of that feeling of alienation, of being alienated, from a world, a family, a set of arrangements. If you say something and eyes roll, you might end up in a state of wonder and disbelief: how can they not see it, what is right in front of us? You learn to doubt reality as such, because you doubt their reality, this reality. When you question sexism and racism it is hard not to question everything.

That is another promise.

To be a feminist can feel like being in a different world even when you are seated at the same table. If that is the case, then to be a feminist is to be in a different world. So much is reproduced by not being noticed: by receding into the background. What had receded into the background comes alive when you no longer participate in that recession. No wonder: the family becomes a more tangible thing the more you are alienated from it.

If the feminist killjoy comes up in a conversation over the table, she brings other things into view, including the family, as well as the table, as a series of arrangements. When feminists are dismissed as sensationalist, we experience the world as all the more sensational; what is ordinarily overlooked or looked over appears striking. The world registers yet again as sensory intrusion; the events you might have tried to forget come more and more into focus as you make feminism your stance. The past is magnified when it is no longer shrunk. We make things bigger just by refusing to make things smaller. You experience the world on a different scale.

The experience of being feminist is often an experience of being out of tune with others. The note heard as out of tune is not only the note that is heard most sharply but the note that ruins the whole tune. Of course it sounds negative: to ruin something. We are heard as negative: ruining something; dinners, as well as photographs, as I explore in chapter 2. We need to ruin what ruins. We could think of ruining not only as an activity that leads to something collapsing or falling down but as how we learn about things when we dismantle things, or by dismantling things.

I think of Toni Morrison's *The Bluest Eye*. This is a text that begins by dismantling the happy family, by literally sentencing it to death: the nuclear family, the white family of the picture book, becomes garbled when the punctuation of the story is removed. I would describe the narrator of this novel, Claudia, as a black feminist critic. She is studious not only about whiteness but also about gender. She teaches us about intersectionality in how she pokes things; how she pokes around in things. In one scene Claudia reflects on how it began:

> It had begun with Christmas and the gift of dolls. The big, the special, the loving gift was always a big, blue-eyed Baby Doll. From the clucking sounds of adults I knew that the doll represented what they thought was my fondest wish. . . . [What was] supposed to bring me great pleasure, succeeded in doing quite the opposite. . . . [I] traced the turned-up nose, poked the glassy-blue eyes, twisted the yellow hair. I could not love it. But I could examine it to see what it was that all the world said was lovable. . . . I destroyed white baby dolls. (1979, 13–14)

Claudia encounters the doll she is supposed to wish for, that she is supposed to love, as an unlovable thing. Attunement is here a technique of power: by clucking, adults are trying to tell her the appropriate ways of handling the white baby doll. Attunement matches an affect with an object. Claudia knows by their clucking that she is supposed to love the white baby doll. Claudia's misattunement is expressed in how she handles the thing (she pokes and twists the doll rather than clucking), a handling that will, no doubt, be registered by others as violence and aggression; as disaffection, disloyalty, ingratitude. If misattunement is expressed as a mishandling of things, then misattunement is worldly. Objects bring worlds with them. In Claudia's case, she is alienated not only from dolls as things but from patriarchal whiteness that elevates such things as lovable things. To be misattuned is to be out of sync with a world. Not only that: it is to experience what is in tune as violence. Claudia could also be described as a black feminist killjoy: she dismembers rather than clucks at what she has been given to love, the white baby doll; she uses the gift to generate counterknowledge.

If alienation is sensation, it is not then just or only the sensation of negation: of experiencing the impress of a world as violence, although it includes those feelings. Alienation is studious; you learn more about wishes when they are not what you wish for. We can think of alienation then as wonder: we wonder about things; we marvel at their assembly. The dolls we do not want are not simply discarded or left behind, lifeless limp rags left on the table. When dolls are dismembered, they are the object of our attention; we learn not only what they are like (the turned-up nose, the glassy-blue eyes, the yellow hair) but from them what we are supposed to like or even be like; from them we learn about the very stuff of human aspiration. It is when we are not attuned, when we do not love what we are supposed to love, that things become available to us as things to ponder with, to wonder about. It might be that we do destroy things to work them out. Or it might be that working them out is perceived as destroying things.

When we sense a wrong, we withdraw from a wish. Having a sense of things as palpable things is thus not unrelated to having a sense of injustice. A feminist life is how we get in touch with things. How astonishing.

2 / ON BEING DIRECTED

In chapter 1, I explored how becoming feminist puts us in touch with a world through alienation from a world. I want to build from this discussion of the sensational nature of feminism by developing an account of what I had begun to notice through feminism: how power works as a mode of directionality, a way of orientating bodies in particular ways, so they are facing a certain way, heading toward a future that is given a face. As you become aware of how the social world is organized, norms appear as palpable things. I think of those times, say, when you walk into a toy shop and it is striking. You might pick up the vacuum cleaner, a toy vacuum cleaner, and feel like you are holding the future for girls in a tangible thing. You can pick up a toy gun, and also feel this: the future for boys held as a tangible thing.

Norms become striking: holdable as palpable things.[1] Once we are stricken, there is still much work left to do. The hardest work can be recognizing how one's own life is shaped by norms in ways that we did not realize, in ways that cannot simply be transcended. A norm is also a way of living, a way of connecting with others over or around something. We cannot "not" live in relation to norms. In this chapter, I thus explore how feminism can be experienced as life alienation, how we can become estranged from the lives we are living in the very process of recognizing how our lives have been shaped or have taken shape. This analysis of power as directionality will enable me to introduce the feminist killjoy in another way.

TRAFFIC SYSTEMS

I want to begin with another of my companion texts, Virginia Woolf's ([1925] 1996) extraordinary novel *Mrs. Dalloway*. She will keep coming up in this chapter because I think we need to be curious about this novel and why it holds such a place in feminist imagination. It is a novel set in one day. It is about an immersion in a day, one day, in the ordinary; one day as another day; every day as another day. Mrs. Dalloway is busy. She is throwing a party. She walks out into London, down the street, to get some flowers for her party; what an ordinary thing. There she is: out and about. She looks up to the sky and sees a plane making letters. Like those nearby, she strains to try to make out the letters. What are they going to be; what is it going to say? Woolf captures something here, how sociality can be achieved temporarily—you happen upon those who happen to be walking down the same street at the same time; you are passing by others who are passing you by, but just for a moment, just a moment, you look up at the same thing. She captures something: the oddness of a connection, the queerness of a gathering.

Mrs. Dalloway, she is busy; she is occupied. But she too can be distracted by what she encounters, looking up, not forward; distraction is how she is thrown into a common world, thrown off her track, her purpose. Suddenly in the middle of her day, when she is immersed in what she is doing, she has another sense of herself. She becomes aware of her own body as what she is wearing: "But often now this body she wore (she stopped to look at a Dutch picture), this body, with all its capacities, seemed nothing—nothing at all. She had the oddest sense of being herself invisible; unseen; unknown; there being no more marrying, no more having children now, but only this astonishing and rather solemn progress with the rest of them, up Bond street, this being Mrs. Dalloway; not even Clarissa anymore; this being Mrs. Richard Dalloway" ([1925] 1996, 14). This being Mrs. Richard Dalloway: in becoming wife, she loses herself. When it is no more, she is no more: no more marrying, no more having children now; becoming woman, being no more. Becoming Mrs. Dalloway is a form of disappearance: to follow the paths of life is to feel that what is before you is a kind of "astonishing and rather solemn progress." You are just going the same way others are going.

She is walking with others when she catches sight of her own disappearance. We learn with Mrs. Dalloway how life itself can be understood as a path or a trajectory. There are points you should reach, points that become like punctuation: how we stop and start, how we measure our progression.[2] We proceed in a direction through reaching certain points. A path gives life a certain shape, a direction, a sequence (birth, childhood, adolescence, marriage, reproduction, death). How we begin, how we end, what happens along the way.

When we share a direction, the traffic flows. Up Bond Street: Mrs. Dalloway, or should we call her Clarissa now; she is part of the traffic. Let's think of that traffic; human traffic, cars, bikes; roads as well as pavements. Traffic is organized. There are rules that enable us to travel more safely, rules that help us to avoid bumping into each other; rules intended to ease our progression. Some of these rules are formal or written down; other rules are more informal; they are habits, ways of acting and being in relation to others that have become second nature over time. When you are a stranger—maybe you are a tourist, or just newly arrived, and you don't know these unwritten rules (How can you? There is nothing to consult)—you can become quite an imposition, a burden, a thing. You feel awkward, as locals frown at you as they bump into you because you are not going the right way, or because you pause or hesitate when they are busy, or because you stop to ask directions; they are hurrying, going the way they are going, getting somewhere. It is when Mrs. Dalloway herself is hurrying—she has to get the flowers for the party—that she is distracted. Something can be revealed in these moments of distraction.

Once a flow is directed, it acquires a momentum. A crowd is often directed by the machinery of man-made geography, as well as timetables, by the political economies that render life and work more separated for more; transportation becomes necessary for work. There is congestion because there is a pattern. A pattern is the generalization of tendency. Once a momentum is acquired, it is directive. You can be carried along by the force of a direction. You are getting off a busy commuter train and you are making your way to the exit. So many others are making the same way. A "with" can be simultaneously mobile and thick. When there are so many, you have a crowd, a thickening, a density. You are carried by that flow: it might even save you energy. But if you drop something, if you have to stop for some reason, the crowd thickens; a crowd can frown. You become an obstacle; an inconvenience. And you would then experience that flow as a tangible thing: what stops you from stopping; what slows you down.

A crowd is directed. Once a crowd is directed, a crowd becomes directive. We are directed by what is in front of us; what is in front of us depends on the direction we have already taken. In my book *Queer Phenomenology* (Ahmed 2006), I suggested paths are good to think with. Take the phrase "a path well-trodden." A path can be made by the repetition of "being trodden" upon. We can see the path as a trace of past journeys. When people stop treading, the path might disappear. On the one foot: we walk on the path as it is before us. On the other foot: it is before us as an effect of being walked upon. A paradox of the footprint emerges. A path is created by being followed and is followed by being created. We can use a path insofar as we do use a path. *Can* is here a consequence of doing. If we can because we do, then we *do can* rather than *can do*.

To sustain a direction is to support a direction. The more people travel upon a path, the clearer the path becomes. Note here how collectivity can become a direction: a clearing of the way as the way of many. Perhaps there is encouragement just in this: you are encouraged to go in that direction when the progression is eased. When it is harder to proceed, when a path is harder to follow, you might be discouraged; you might try to find an easier route.

Remember Mrs. Dalloway: becoming Mrs. Dalloway as like the steady and solemn progress of bodies going in the same direction along a street. Our lives might be directed in some ways, rather than others, because of this easing of progression. Leaving a well-trodden path can be so difficult: it can mean leaving a support system. I am tempted to redescribe what Adrienne Rich (1993) called "compulsory heterosexuality" in these terms: compulsory heterosexuality is a traffic system as well as a support system. The route is kept clear through collective labor: the attempt to stop too many obstacles from getting in the way. You are given support by others when you follow the route: as long as your choices are different sex (and sometimes more: a suitable match is often same class, same race), your loves can be celebrated collectively; your losses are mourned collectively. Stopping and starting: at the same points. What some scholars call "homonormativity" (Duggan 2003; Halberstam 2005) is the politics of trying to make being gay about reaching the same destination: stopping and starting at the same points. Gay marriage: (can be) another way of reaching the same destination.

And yet it is important to remember that life is not always linear, or that the lines we follow do not always lead us to the same place. It is not incidental that the drama of life, moments of crisis that require a decision, is represented by the following scene: you face a fork in the road, and you have to decide which path to take. This way or that one, you must decide. And then you go one way. Maybe you go that way without being sure that's the right way to go. Maybe you go that way because the path seems clearer. The longer you proceed on this path, the harder it is to turn back. You keep going in hope that you are getting somewhere. Hope is an investment that the paths we follow will get us somewhere. Turning back risks the wasting of time, as a time that has already been expended or given up.

Sometimes what happens is not simply a matter of a conscious decision. Something unexpected happens that throws you. You feel thrown when you are thrown off course. You might be redirected by an unexpected encounter; a little sideways movement can open up new worlds. Sometimes encounters might come as the gift of a lifeline; other times they might not; they might be experienced purely as loss. What happens when we are knocked off course depends on the psychic and social resources we have behind us. Such moments of being thrown off course can be experienced as a gift, as opening up a possibility; or they can be traumatic, registered as the loss of a desired future, one that you are grasping for, leaning toward.

We might sense how a life has a shape when it loses shape. Think of how Mrs. Dalloway comes to apprehend her own life as if it is a stranger's life. She becomes aware of becoming Mrs. Dalloway as an inevitable and solemn progress toward a point she has already reached. In chapter 1, I considered how feminist consciousness is achieved. Perhaps feminist consciousness also means becoming aware of one's life as a marvel or even marvelous. Being estranged from one's own life can be how a world reappears, becoming odd. You might become conscious of a possibility once it has receded. In Mrs. Dalloway's consciousness, other people, other possibilities, flicker as memory. To become conscious of possibility can involve mourning for its loss. You can feel the sadness of what could have been, but was not to be. Maybe we realize: it would have been possible to live one's life in another way. We can mourn because we didn't even realize that we gave something up. The shape of a life can feel like a past tense; something we sense only after it has been acquired.

But we might also know this: we can leave a life. It is not too late to leave a life. Many feminist books that are what I called feminist classics in my introduction are stories of women who leave a life. Some of these texts are lesbian classics: stories of women who realize, perhaps later on in life, that being a lesbian is not something you had to give up. Not giving up: feminism can be experienced or narrated as giving life, or as taking one's own life back, a life that you might have experienced as what you have given to others or even what has been taken by other people's expectations. Maybe the world comes to appear differently when you recognize that your life is not working. Think about how you can prepare to leave a situation before you leave. When you begin to leave, your body is no longer attuned to a set of requirements.

I think one of the reasons that I became interested in the very question of direction was because in the middle of my life, middle as muddle, I made a dramatic redirection. I left a certain kind of life and embraced a new one. I became a lesbian. I had tried heterosexuality. Rather like Mrs. Dalloway's description of her relation to her own body, heterosexuality was something I was wearing. When you have to try hard to convince yourself of something, it usually means you are not convinced. Heterosexuality did not fit. When I was wearing it, I found it wearing. In pursuing a path partway, in turning back, I learned about that path. To leave a path can be to leave a life even though when you leave heterosexuality you still live in a heterosexual world. But this is what leaving heterosexuality felt like: leaving a life, leaving a life that is supported; leaving a world where your being is supported. You have to create your own support systems, as I explore in more detail in part III. Queer and feminist worlds are built through the effort to support those who are not supported because of who they are, what they want, what they do.

THE PATH OF HAPPINESS

It is a loop: we are directed by what is in front of us; what is in front of us depends on how we are directed. And it is here we can think of how happiness is itself understood as a path. A path, remember, can be what you follow in order to reach somewhere. How do you know which way to go? What are you hoping for in going for? As I explored in my book *The Promise of Happiness* (Ahmed 2010), happiness is often assumed to be an end point: as what we want to reach, as the point of life, the aim of life. The path we should follow is the path that would lead us to happiness.

Some things, more than others, are assumed to lead to happiness. A path might be cleared by the very expectation that happiness is what you should reach. Maybe these are the very points that Mrs. Dalloway experiences as having reached: marrying, having children, now. For example, the child might be asked to imagine happiness by imagining certain events in the future, such as the wedding day. The wedding day is imagined as the "happiest day of your life," before it happens. Maybe this before is also how and why: how the day happens; why it happens.

How quickly we learn: for the child, especially the girl child, her happiest day *will be* the moment of marrying. What I have called gender fatalism is tied to happiness: Girls *will be* girls; girls *will be* happiest when they get married. Maybe that "will be" can also be heard not only as prediction but as a moral instruction: not only will she do this, but she will do this happily. The happiness path becomes a straight path: what leads you in the right way, to the right destination. So we might think today that heterosexuality is no longer the only option. But a cursory glance at images and narratives of happiness in popular culture teaches us that old investments can be sustained through minor alterations and variations in form. The happy stories for girls remain based on fairy-tale formulas: life, marriage, and reproduction, or death (of one kind or another) and misery. Maybe there are compromises; maybe there is a diversification of styles of feminine accomplishment; maybe heterosexuality can now be done in more ways than one; but the investments remain rather precise.

We encounter this precision everywhere. Even small children are talked about as having heterosexual futures, often through reading their conduct in heterosexual terms ("He is one for the girls"; "He will be one for the girls").[3] The future is solidified as something that can be grasped or refused. When you refuse to grasp something, it is often understood as because you failed to get it. What we could call presumed heterosexuality means that not to be presumed as heterosexual, you have to unbecome one. Such an unbecoming is narrated as the loss of the possibility of becoming happy. And then: it is assumed you are trying very hard not to be sad. Sad: it is a consequence we are supposed to avoid. It is a judgment as well as a feeling. How sad; she is sad.

Happiness: what we end up doing to avoid the consequence of being sad. Happiness is a way of being directed toward those things that would or should make you happy. Happiness can thus also be a form of pressure. Pressure does not always feel harsh. A pressure can begin with a light touch. A gentle encouragement: Go this way, go that way. Be happy, don't be happy. Are you having children? When are you having children? A concerned look. Questions, questions: insistence on a when: when will this happen, this will happen when. Questions can be wrapped up with warmth, even kindness: she will be so much happier when, so when?

Not to be heading in the right direction can mean being put under pressure, or under more pressure, whether or not that pressure is intended. Maybe we can feel this *more*, this gradual increase in pressure as time goes on. We need to describe what this feels like: the opposition that you encounter to your own opposition (where this opposition is not something you want, but something you are judged as being because of what you want). As I noted earlier, you can come up against a momentum when you are not going the right way. This is why we can talk of oppression as something that can be felt or experienced; oppression as a tangible thing. Marilyn Frye takes us back to the root of the word *oppression*, which is from *press*: "The press of the crowd; pressed into military service; to press a pair of pants; printing press; press the button. Presses are used to mold things or flatten them or reduce them in bulk, sometimes to reduce them by squeezing out the gases or liquids in them. Something pressed is something caught between or among forces and barriers which are so related to each other that jointly they restrain, restrict or prevent the thing's motion or mobility. Mold. Immobilize. Reduce" (1983, 54). Oppression: how we feel pressed into things, by things, because of who we are recognized as being.

To be is to be pressed. It might be the words of a parent or a friend, or the way an image of a good life is screened in front of you; you can experience images as weights, as heavy. Expectations, eyes raised, when. A pressure is the ratio of force to an area over which it is distributed. You feel forced, when you experience a requirement as being imposed upon you. Maybe fewer people are more forced because more people are less forced.

Maybe then, maybe then, if you start going in the right direction you experience a relief of pressure. You feel a lessening, a reduction or removal of pressure, as when a hand that was holding you down is gradually withdrawn. You might go faster as your passage is eased. Eventually you are going that way of your own accord. When you no longer have to be pushed, in order to proceed in that direction, you do not experience yourself as having been pushed. As I explore in chapter 3, this is how being willing can be a consequence of force; you become willing to avoid being forced. In willingly proceeding in the right direction, you experience a relief from pressure. How often do we proceed one way in order to be relieved of a pressure to go that way? One wonders. But sometimes we won't change direction; we accept the pressure; maybe we even become used to that press. Maybe a pressure becomes part of us at the moment we have been relieved of pressure.

We need a feminist account of such techniques of redirection. Happiness is one technique for redirection. One very feminine boy I knew was encouraged to play sports. His mother was worried he would be teased by his peers for being "sissy." She imagined his future as a future of unhappiness; a future of being teased, left out, hurt. She wanted him to man up to avoid this consequence. Eventually, the little boy did start playing sports; he began to love sports, to enjoy them. The little boy now plays sports with other little boys. He has pretty much discarded his soft cuddly toys, leaving them behind as a way of leaving one version of himself behind. Maybe he is even happier; who knows? When it is hard to know; who knows?

What does it mean to redirect children out of fear that they would be unhappy? Of course we can understand these desires for redirection; we can understand the anxiety about a child going in a direction that might be harder or more difficult. We want him to be happy; perhaps we cannot bear his sad face; I mean, who could? But what do we want when we want a child's happiness? What does it mean, what does it do, to say, "I just want you to be happy?" The intonation can vary: sometimes these words are said in frustration. I want you to be happy, so don't do that! Don't be that! But in a way, the desire for the child's happiness seems to offer a certain kind of freedom, as if to say, "I don't want you to be this, or to do that; I just want you to be or to do whatever makes you happy." The desire for the child's happiness seems to be predicated on a kind of indifference. A *whatever* seems open; like giving someone an empty box that can be filled with the content of her own desire.

But remember how the fear of unhappiness gave content to a future: not being boy enough meant being hurt, damaged by other boys who were boy enough. To want happiness is to want to avoid a certain kind of future for the child. Avoidance too can be directive. Wanting happiness can mean wanting the child to be in line to avoid the costs of not being in line. You want a boy to be a boy because not being a boy might be difficult for a boy. Boying here is about inclusion, friendship, participation, approval. Boying here is about avoiding the cost of not being included. To want happiness for a child can be to want to straighten the child out. Maybe sometimes, too, a boy might "self-boy," realizing that he might have more friends, enjoy himself more, if he does the same things that other boys do. I will return to the idea of self-boying and self-girling in due course.

Not to want your children to be unhappy can mean in translation: not to want them to deviate from the well-trodden paths. No wonder then that in some parental responses to a child coming out, this unhappiness is expressed not so much as being unhappy about the child being queer, but as being unhappy about the child being unhappy. Queer fiction is full of such speech acts in which the parents express their fear that the queer child is destined to have an unhappy life. One example is from Julie Ann Peters's novel *Keeping You a Secret*. Here a mother laments after her daughter comes out: "I want her to be happy. That's all Tom and I ever wanted for our kids. We want so much for our kids to grow up and have things we never had. We have high hopes for you. Expectations, dreams. Then, something like this" (Peters 2003, 190). Note how first the mother says that happiness is all she ever wanted for her child. The happiness wanted then becomes: wanting the child to have the things that she did not have. Wanting happiness becomes a high hope: a hope for a certain kind of life for the child. Becoming lesbian, "something like this," is imagined to compromise not only the happiness of the child, but the happiness of the parents, who gave up a certain kind of life in the hope the child would have that life. To disappoint an expectation is to become a disappointment.

We can pick up on this implied relation between happiness and debt: if the parents gave up happiness for you, then you must give them their happiness back. This is how: if some people come first, their happiness comes first. Parents might want for the children what they think would cause their happiness when it is really their own happiness they are referring to. No wonder then that the social struggle within families involves a struggle over the causes of unhappiness. Perhaps the parents are unhappy as they think their daughter will be unhappy if she is queer. They are unhappy with her being unhappy. The daughter is unhappy because they are unhappy with her being queer. Perhaps the parents would then witness the daughter's unhappiness as a confirmation of their fear: that she will be unhappy because she is queer. Even happy queers would become unhappy at this point.

Perhaps these debts of happiness become even more powerful or heavy for immigrant families like my own. You are constantly being reminded of what your parents gave up for you: their home, their country, their status, their family. You need to pay them back by living the life they gave up for you. And if you do not: how selfish; how could you; don't you know what we have done for you? If you happily deviate from an expectation, your joy becomes a theft of theirs. But it is more complicated, inevitably. Certainly if you are a queer child of a migrant family, a brown one at that, a Muslim one or mixed Muslim one at that: it is more complicated than this. As I argued in *The Promise of Happiness* (Ahmed 2010), the unconventional child of the migrant family provides a conventional form of social hope.[4] The queer child might be described as an unconventional child, who has to struggle against her family to come out. In the case of a brown migrant family, the family is imagined as a dead weight: there is an expectation that her family will be more oppressive, less tolerant; less supportive of her freedom. To be directed toward happiness is to be directed away from your family, who come up in the national imaginary as what or who are holding you back or holding you down. And then custom and culture become things that this brown queer child has to leave behind; happiness is assumed to require getting out. Translation: happiness becomes proximity to whiteness. Camel Gupta (2014) notes how it is sometimes assumed that brown queers and trans folk are rescued from unhappy brown families by happy white queer and trans communities. We are not a rescue mission. But when you deviate, they celebrate. Even happy brown queers would become unhappy at this point.

MISDIRECTION AND DISAFFECTION

If we do not change direction to avoid causing unhappiness, we cause unhappiness. The killjoy comes up again here. You might receive this assignment just because you do not want what others want you to want. And it can seem that by not wanting what other people want (which is also what they want you to want), you are somehow rejecting and devaluing their wants.

We can return to the family table. The family gathering around the table; these are supposed to be happy occasions. We work hard to keep the occasion happy, to keep the surface of the table polished so that it can reflect back a good image of the family. This labor eliminates the signs of itself: to polish is to remove traces of polish. You can get in the way of family happiness just by not polishing the surface. Not wanting the right things becomes tarnishing that surface.

No wonder: I was already a killjoy before I began speaking up. When I was growing up, I found the requirement to be a girl oppressive. I found dresses, and girly styles, irritating. In my mid to late teens I was regularly called a tomboy, although, looking back, I was just a girl not that interested in being girly, in dresses, or makeup, or talking about boys (I am sliding heterosexuality in here because heterosexuality often slides in here). That a not-girly girl is called a tomboy teaches us how restricted *girl* can be as a category of emergent personhood. If you experience being a girl as a restriction, you do not have to say anything. An affective disposition can speak for you, on your behalf, a grumpy face, or other nonverbal signs of resignation when you are asked to wear a dress for a special occasion. I remember many battles over dresses.

Party.

Dress, sigh.

Down, downer.

The feminist killjoy comes up without you having to say anything. You can kill joy just by not being made happy by the right things. Or maybe whether you are happy or not is not the question: you have to appear happy at the right moments. How many times have you been told you ruined the photograph because of your grumpy face? So many dinners ruined; so many photographs; holidays too. You can kill joy by not looking happy enough. If you are already known as a feminist, then not looking happy enough will be referred back to the fact of feminism, as if not smiling in the photograph is a political protest (whether or not it is). Feminism can be gender trouble (Butler 1990): you can be seen as not a girl—or a not-good girl or a not-happy girl—by virtue of how you act. Marilyn Frye argues that oppression involves the requirement that you show signs of being happy with the situation in which you find yourself. For Frye, "anything but the sunniest countenance exposes us to being perceived as mean, bitter, angry or dangerous" (1983, 2). Perceptions can be sticky. Not smiling enough: being mean.

Not smiling at the party was for me something to do with who I was required to be at the party: wearing a dress, looking pretty, even singing on command. Sometimes I felt like a clown, other times a machine, sometimes a show pony. I suspect my resignation about gender, my sense of this requirement as a burden, my identification of parties with downers (what a party pooper!), was also a resignation about human beings. One of the reasons I love horses so much—there are many queer stories to tell about girls and horses, as Elspeth Probyn (1996) has shown—was because they represented an escape from humans, and thus from the requirement to be a girl. I will introduce you to my horse Mulka in my survival kit. He had quite a role to play in freeing me from a sense of requirement. I was profoundly shy growing up, and my sense of human sociality was of something from which I was barred: almost like a room with a locked door for which I did not have the key. Perhaps that was it: gender seemed like a key to a lock, which I did not have, or which I did not fit. Looking back, I think I decided to self-girl when I went to university, as I was exhausted by not fitting or not fitting in. I have no doubt that my own exhaustion was as much to do with being surrounded by whiteness as it was from being alienated by gender; an exhaustion with difference. I remember the very first time I went to a boutique hairdresser after I left school at the age of eighteen. It was a quite deliberate decision. I looked in the mirror sadly and waited for a different version of myself to appear. I knew enough to know: inclusion might require becoming more willing to occupy femininity and to make it my own. I knew enough to know: this option was not available to everyone. Sometimes, then, we might redirect ourselves to relieve ourselves from pressure, from the sadness of not participating in something, or of feeling alone or cast out. We might worry that it is our own future we are cutting off.

This is difficult: I am not saying that to align yourself with something makes you wrong or your desires less authentic. I am certainly not saying being girly as a girl is only or just about fitting in even if, for me, it began that way. You might even feel an obligation to "de-girl" when being girly is not deemed right or appropriate. As Ulrika Dahl (2015) explores, in some feminist spaces, being girly as a girl can make you not fit in; to use the terms I work with in chapter 3, you might have to become willful to be willingly feminine in feminist spaces. I think now I can enjoy being girly (though I still do not wear dresses; I just don't like how they feel) because it is not something that is required, nor is it assumed by myself (or others) as a way of directing attention to boys. A queer girl stretches the meaning of *girl*.

So I am not suggesting self-girling is inauthentic. I am reflecting upon how we resolve those moments when we become conscious of being in or out of line with others. Feminism heightens consciousness of there being lines at all and thus requires us to make decisions when before decisions might have been made before us, or even without us. Sometimes we are tired or we experience an anticipatory exhaustion: we line ourselves up to avoid the consequences of being out of line because we have been there before and we can't face it anymore. And then when that line unfolds, other things happen along the way. Other times we might realize: we are willing to pay the costs of not being in line because getting in line would compromise too much. And we might find, too, other things can happen along the way.

We know about alignment as a mechanism because of an experience of being out of line. I turn to alignment in relation to institutional politics in part II. I want to stay here with the question of gender. Once you haven't got something right, there are lots of ways to get things wrong, and not all of them are intentional. I often got gender wrong or just got things wrong, whether or not I meant to. One time, when I was in my early twenties, I sent a congratulations card to my sister after the birth of her child. We spoke on the phone, and she said rather crossly, "Why do you always have to make a feminist point!" I had gotten her a blue card. She had had a girl. The thing was: I didn't do this intentionally. I hadn't meant to make a feminist point; I hadn't even noticed the color of the card. But that presumes, perhaps, a having become feminist, having already reached a feminist point: that you do not recognize immediately that the color system is a gender system. When the gender system does not become a habit, you have failed to be habituated. And that is how feminism can be lived: as the failure to be habituated to a gender system.

A gender system is not at work simply in how you do or do not express gender: it is also about how you perform within a wider system that matches meaning and value to persons and things. Once you have properly accommodated to this system, you can be unthinking; you can pick up the right card automatically. If you are not fully accommodated, you have to think what would be the right thing to get the thing right. If you don't think about what is right, you probably won't get gender right: you get it wrong. This is how you can end up making feminist points without even intending them. Getting gender wrong becomes getting things wrong.[5] And note then: you can killjoy not as a deliberate or intentional act; you might even be trying to participate in the joy of others. You can killjoy because you are not properly attuned to the requirements of a social system.

Another instance: when I was younger, someone said to me that in not shaving my legs I was "making a feminist statement." Not to go along with an expectation, you are making a statement. I think we learn from this. Whether or not we make feminist points, whether or not we speak, not complying with codes of appearance is heard as speech, almost as if your legs are a mouth and they are shouting: look at me! I had not thought I was making a feminist point, though perhaps in not assuming my legs had to be shaved legs, I was living out a feminist assumption. But in a way, the ordinariness of girls having unshaven legs is what is rendered impossible. Any acts that are not in compliance with the order of things become an imposition of a feminist agenda on the order of things.

Getting things wrong can mean: to be affected wrongly by things. We are misdirected by how we are affected or not affected. Arlie Russell Hochschild explores in her classic book *The Managed Heart* how if the bride is not happy on the wedding day and even feels "depressed and upset," then she is experiencing an "inappropriate affect" ([1983] 2003, 59) or is being affected inappropriately.[6] She has to save the day by feeling right: "Sensing a gap between the ideal feeling and the actual feeling she tolerated, the bride prompts herself to be happy" (61). The capacity to save the day depends on the bride being able to persuade herself or others that she is happy. To correct her feelings is to become disaffected from a former affectation: the bride makes herself happy by stopping herself from being miserable. Of course we learn from this example that it is possible not to inhabit fully one's own happiness, or even to be alienated from one's happiness, if the former affection remains lively, or if one is made uneasy by the labor of trying to make oneself feel a certain way. Uneasiness might persist in the very feeling of being happy, as a feeling of unease with the happiness you are in.

We cannot always make ourselves feel happy when we are supposed to be happy. A *cannot* does not always feel like a restriction; a *cannot* can be an opening. Maybe you are disappointed, with yourself or with a world, because you are not as happy as you expected to be. Disappointment can also involve an anxious narrative of self-doubt (Why am I not made happy by this? What is wrong with me?), or a narrative of rage against a world that promises happiness by elevating some things as good. We might become strangers in such moments. When you are alienated by virtue of how you are affected, you are an affect alien. A feminist killjoy is an affect alien. We are not made happy by the right things.

AN UNHAPPY ARCHIVE

It is time to return to Mrs. Dalloway. You will recall how Mrs. Dalloway becomes aware of the trajectory of her own life; how she witnesses her own disappearance as she walks up Bond Street. Getting married, having children become not only things she has done, things she has accomplished, but how she loses herself along the way; how she ceases to be Clarissa, with so many possibilities in front of her. Marrying, having children now: these are not only punctuation points, they are also moments of ceremony; what women do in order to be happy. Mrs. Dalloway does not feel happy. She might not know how she feels; she might not reveal her feelings to herself or to others; but she does not feel happy. She becomes alienated from her own life, conscious of possibilities only after they have been given up, possibilities that shimmer like the old friends she remembers in the passage of her day.

Feminism is full of stories like this: of women who are not made happy by what is supposed to make them happy. This is not to say unhappiness is everywhere, but rather that the expectation of happiness, the expectation that women should smile and the world will smile with them, is what puts so much on hold; a life on hold. The expectation of happiness does not necessarily create unhappiness but it might make unhappiness harder to bear. In the late twentieth century, feminist sociologists such as Ann Oakley wrote at length about how the expectation that in becoming mothers women will become happy worked to pathologize unhappiness. She describes "post-natal depression" as "a pseudo-scientific tag for the description and ideological transformation of maternal discontent" (1980, 277). The romantic myths of childbirth as maternal bliss make maternal blues a social as well as biological problem.

This early feminist work emphasized the importance of women telling their own stories that dislodged the happiness myth, stories that are not simply about unhappiness but about the complex, ambivalent, and messy feelings that women have. There are stories of women workers too, for example, in

Arlie Hochschild's ([1983] 2003) *The Managed Heart*, women who have to smile as their job, who are as alienated from their smiles as factory workers would be from their arms, when those arms are given in service to the industrial machine. I return to the question of labor (and arms) in chapter 3. Here I want to explore how happiness is what you can be required to perform in private as well as public spaces. I am sure many girls and women have heard comments like "Smile, love, it could be worse" when they walk out and about without cheerfulness planted on their faces. Smiling becomes a feminine achievement. But smiling can also be what you have to do to compensate when you are perceived as not feminine enough. You might have to soften your appearance because (or when) you are perceived as too hard. A black woman or woman of color might have to smile all the more because she is perceived as angry or too assertive: smiling then becomes what you have to do in order to dislodge an expectation. Expectations can be confirmed by the very effort to dislodge them. Even a smile can be too assertive if you are already judged as being assertive.

Happiness as a form of emotional labor can be condensed in the formula: making others happy by appearing happy. The labor is most successful when you become as happy as you appear; the more you strain, the more your smile would seem strained. Feminism might be what we need to resist this formula. By this I do not mean that to become feminists is to aim to make others unhappy. Rather you are no longer willing to appear happy, or to become as happy as you appear, in order to make others happy. Feminism might matter at the other end of the formula. By this I mean: you are not made happy by the appearance of happiness. We acquire, as feminist feeling, sympathy for women who are not happy when they are meant to be happy. Feminist sympathy involves a different direction to unhappiness. We would understand unhappiness not as the failure to be happy and thus as causing yet more unhappiness, but a refusal, a claim, a protest, or even just some ordinary thing, a texture of a life being lived. To be sympathetic to unhappiness is often to be perceived as unsympathetic. I think of the film *Waitress* (dir. Adrienne Shelly, 2007). Jenna, an unhappily married woman, arrives at a doctor's office and says she is pregnant. The doctor responds sympathetically by offering her his congratulations. His sympathy is not in response to how she does feel (miserable) but rather to how she should feel (happy). She is alienated by his sympathy, even though that sympathy is in accordance with an everyday judgment (that pregnancy for married women is a happy event). The waitress is alienated by virtue of her response to being pregnant, such that to be in sympathy with her response of alienation (to offer your condolence) would be to share her alienation: "Poor you, stuck with him." A feminist sympathy is sympathetic to an alienation from happiness.

Affect aliens sympathize with alien affects. We can be alienated by sympathy when sympathy is given in accordance with an expectation of how we should feel rather than how we do feel. I think that is why there has been such an outpouring of feminist sympathy for Mrs. Dalloway's predicament. Feminism might involve the cultivation of sympathy for women who are unhappy with the situation they find themselves in. It is interesting that in Clarissa's case it is not clear what she is unhappy about. For Clarissa the rather uncanny sensation of becoming Mrs. Dalloway as a loss of possibility, as an unbecoming, or becoming nothing at all, does not enter her consciousness in the form of sadness about something. The sadness of this book—and for me it is a sad book—is not presented as a point of view. Mrs. Dalloway does not explain the causes of her grief. She is too busy getting ready for her party. So much sadness revealed in the need to be busy. So much grief expressed in the need not to be overwhelmed by grief.

And it is at the party that Mrs. Dalloway is put in touch with grief. It is not her grief but the grief of a stranger, somebody she does not know, that takes her away from the party. Lady Bradshaw says to Mrs. Dalloway, "'Just as we were starting, my husband was called up on the telephone, a very sad case. A young man (that is what Sir William is telling Mr Dalloway) had killed himself. He had been in the army.' Oh! Thought Clarissa, in the middle of my party, here's death, she thought" (Woolf [1925] 1996, 279). In the middle of the party, words accumulate as a narrative, telling the story of a death, of a suicide, of a man whose suffering was too much to bear. The reader has already been witness to his death as well as his suffering. Clarissa has not witnessed his death, but she imagines it, almost as something happening to herself: "always her body went through it first, when she was told, suddenly, of an accident; her dress flamed, her body burnt" (280). When she is given the details of his death, his death becomes flesh: "Up had flashed the ground; through him, blundering, bruising, went the rusty spikes. There he lay with the thud, thud, thud in his brain, and then a suffocation of blackness" (281). The violence of an encounter becomes a violence she encounters. It is not simply that Clarissa is being empathetic, but that at this moment, a death becomes real or material because it has been allowed in. A death spreads as words into worlds. What is striking about *Mrs. Dalloway* is how suffering enters her consciousness from the edges, through the arrival of another, who is a stranger, an intruder, who has not been invited into the room. Suffering enters not simply or only as self-consciousness—as a consciousness of one's own suffering—but as a heightening of consciousness, a world-consciousness in which the suffering of those who do not belong disturbs the atmosphere.

It is at this point, the point when consciousness becomes worldly, that we open up what it means to consider feminism as an unhappy archive. We would not simply be thinking of unhappiness as a feeling that goes from the inside out; the unhappiness lodged in a figure such as the housewife; nor even as a feeling shared through empathetic witnessing. Rather we would be exploring how we can become more attuned to what is already in the world; to the violence of a world that can be obscured by life's chatter. The arrival of suffering from the edges teaches us about the difficulty of becoming conscious of suffering. It is hard labor to recognize sadness and disappointment when you are living a life that is meant to be happy but is not happy, which is meant to be full but feels empty. It is difficult to give up an idea of one's life when one has lived one's life according to that idea. We learn not only that consciousness of unhappiness is achieved but also how such consciousness puts us in touch with the world; allowing a world to pierce a seal, what I call the happiness seal. So much inequality is preserved through the appeal of happiness, the appeal to happiness. It is as if the response to power and violence is or should be simply to adjust or modify how we feel; for instance, by transforming a social relation of exploitation into a personal feeling of empowerment.

Feminism: how we break through a happiness seal. Even when unhappiness is a familiar feeling, it can arrive like a stranger, to pierce the stillness with the "thud, thud, thud" of violence. In the case of Mrs. Dalloway, it is a stranger who disturbs the familiar. But she still has something to do with it. Maybe, just maybe that is why this day matters so much: she was getting ready, to allow her past to flicker with life; she was getting ready to be undone. A seal is broken through a combination of forces. And so, in the middle of her party, something other than happiness happens. If a stranger disturbs the familiar, being a stranger can become familiar. I will return to experiences of being a stranger in chapter 5. Just note that when you recognize yourself as the stranger, you become estranged not only from happiness but from yourself. You might be the one whose arrival causes a disturbance. What then is disturbed? Audre Lorde, who offered us one of the most powerful feminist critiques of happiness (I will turn directly to her critique in my killjoy survival kit), shows how the past can be what is disturbed:

> Tensions on the street were high, as they always are in racially mixed zones of transition. As a very little girl, I remember shrinking from a particular sound, a hoarsely sharp, guttural rasp, because it often meant a nasty glob of grey spittle upon my coat or shoe an instant later. My mother wiped it off with the little pieces of newspaper she always carried in her purse. Sometimes she fussed about low-class people who had no better sense nor manners than to spit into the wind no matter where they went, impressing upon me that this humiliation was totally random. It never occurred to me to doubt her. It was not until years later once in conversation I said to her: "Have you noticed people don't spit into the wind so much the way they used to?" And the look on my mother's face told me that I had blundered into one of those secret places of pain that must never be spoken of again. But it was so typical of my mother when I was young that if she couldn't stop white people spitting on her children because they were Black, she would insist it was something else. (1984b, 17–18)

To remember violence is to bring the sound of violence into the present, that "hoarsely, sharp, guttural rasp." But a memory can obscure the violence brought up. For Audre Lorde's mother cannot bear to speak of racism, and creates an impression that the violence directed toward her black child is random. When the child reminds her mother about what happened, or what she thought used to happen because that was what she was told used to happen, when she brings it up in conversation, she has ventured into "one of those secret places of pain." When violence is no longer dismissible as random, violence is witnessed as directed: toward a black body, for Audre Lorde, toward her own black body, shrinking from its sound. Some forms of taking cover from pain are meant to protect those we love from being hurt. That cover still fails. When the cover fails, racism is revealed. Another way of saying this: the past can be what is sealed. When the seal has been broken; pain floods in.

To reflect on how we take cover from pain is to return with a different handle to the question of consciousness explored in chapter 1. We are learning *how* we learn not to be conscious of what happens right in front of us. Even when something happens to us, an event that is traumatic, we are not witnessing what is happening because of the handle we are given to make sense of it. We could use the term "false consciousness" to describe this process of taking cover. False consciousness here would not refer to something an individual suffers from: as if she herself screens out what gets in the way of her own happiness. Rather we would use this term to show how there is something false about our consciousness of the world. We can thus inherit false consciousness. Feminist consciousness can be thought of as consciousness of the violence and power concealed under the languages of civility, happiness, and love, rather than simply or only consciousness of gender as a site of restriction of possibility. You can venture into the secret places of pain by recalling something. You can cause unhappiness by noticing something. And if you can cause unhappiness by noticing something, you realize that the world you are in is not the world you thought you were in.

CONCLUSION: A FEMINIST INHERITANCE

The sadness of a feminist book: it is pedagogy. *Mrs. Dalloway*: she touches a nerve. Feminism: living in proximity to a nerve. When I think of how *Mrs. Dalloway* is evoked and recalled, I think of how sadness can be an inheritance, a feminist inheritance. I think of all the books that caught my attention not just because of the sadness they expressed, but because of the rebellion they enacted in this expression. It can be rebellious not to be made happy by what should make you happy. This sadness is not always or only about a personal revelation; even when eyes well with tears, those tears do not always form words. It is a sadness that can be too difficult to reveal to ourselves, let alone to others, because it is sadness with the world and thus sadness in the world. So often this sadness is distributed in things that surround a body; her body, allowing a space to be registered as confinement, as restriction. So when I spoke of feminism as sensory intrusion in chapter 1, here we might think of how becoming feminist puts us in touch with all that sadness, all those emotions that represent a collective failure to be accommodated to a system as the condition of possibility for living another way.

When we are being accommodating, when we are busy, we might not notice certain things. Perhaps this is why feminist readers can pick up so much from Mrs. Dalloway: we are not quite in the lives we are supposed to be in. Take the film *The Hours* (dir. Stephen Daldry, 2002). In one scene, Laura Brown, an unhappy housewife in the 1950s, is reading *Mrs. Dalloway*. A book becomes a feminist companion; it is a trace of a history that is not gone, of a past that lingers. Laura's sense of companionship with Mrs. Dalloway derives from a desire not to be in her life, to be suspended from its time and rhythms: she wants to spend time with the book to avoid spending time with her husband and child. It is a day, one day. It is another day. It is her husband's birthday; but Laura wants to be with Mrs. Dalloway, to take her to bed. Later, when her husband has gone, her friend Kitty arrives and asks her about the book. Laura says of Mrs. Dalloway, "Because she is confident everyone thinks she is fine. But she isn't." Laura identifies with Mrs. Dalloway by sharing her grief, as a grief that is not revealed to others. It is as if she says: like you, my life is about maintaining the appearance of being fine, an appearance which is also a disappearance.

Like you

I am not fine

Like you

What happens when domestic bliss does not create bliss? Laura tries to bake a cake. She cracks an egg. The cracking of the egg becomes a common gesture throughout the film, connecting the domestic labor of women over time. To bake a cake ought to be a happy activity, a labor of love. Instead, the film reveals a sense of oppression that lingers in the very act of breaking the eggs. Not only do such objects not make you happy; they embody a feeling of disappointment. The bowl in which you crack the eggs waits for you. You can feel the pressure of its wait. The empty bowl feels like an accusation. Feminist archives are full of scenes of domesticity, in which domestic objects become strange, almost menacing.

An empty bowl that feels like an accusation can be the beginning of a feminist life. In other words, to begin a feminist life is to hear an accusation; it is to hear that others understand you as failing to carry out your duties in the right way. But despite that accusation, you persist in living your feminist life. You keep going. And perhaps this is also why you pick up that book, or see that film, and find solace in an empty bowl. It is how you know you are not alone. When the happiness seal is broken, when violence has intruded into scenes of bliss, we begin to hear the ghosts of feminists past. The feminist ghosts clamor around; they surround; we listen.

To break the seal is to allow the past into the present. A feminist past becomes proximate; it is brought closer to you. Feminism: how we inherit from the refusal of others to live their lives in a happy way. But our feminist ghosts are not only miserable. They might even giggle at the wrong moments. They might even laugh hysterically in a totally inappropriate manner. After all, it can be rebellious to be happy when you are not supposed to be happy, to follow the paths happily that are presumed to lead to unhappiness: not marrying, not having children, now. She is called by some childless; she calls herself child-free. She multiplies the objects upon which she bestows her affections. An affect alien is made happy by the wrong things. So often her happiness is discredited: seen as selfish, silly, or inauthentic, as a substitute for the real thing. But she persists with it. It might take willfulness to persist with it. And it is to willfulness that I now turn.

3 / WILLFULNESS AND FEMINIST SUBJECTIVITY

A feminist history is affective: we pick up those feelings that are not supposed to be felt because they get in the way of an expectation of who we are and what life should be. No wonder feminism acquires such a negative charge: being against happiness, being against life. It is not simply that we first become feminists and later become killjoys. Rather, to become feminist is to kill other people's joy; to get in the way of other people's investments. In living a feminist life, we learn about judgments. We learn from how they fall. Words surround us, thick with meaning and intensity. We hear these words. We learn from what we are called. It is a feminist calling.

Words surround us, thick with meaning and intensity. In this chapter, I reflect on willfulness as one such word that surrounds us, a pointed or sharp word. Feminists are often called willful; judged as being willful, as suffering from too much will. Why willful? Let me share with you a typical definition of willfulness: "asserting or disposed to assert one's own will against persuasion, instruction, or command; governed by will without regard to reason; determined to take one's own way; obstinately self-willed or perverse." To be called obstinate or perverse because you are not persuaded by the reasoning of others? Is this familiar to you? Have you heard this before?

It is familiar to me. I have heard it before. Just the word *feminism* is heard as an assertion of will "against persuasion, instruction, or command." If feminists are often called willful, then feminism is understood as a problem of will: a way of going one's own way, a way of going the wrong way. The word *willfulness* exists in close relation to other words, such as stubborn, obstinate, and contrary, as words that imply a problem of character. If feminists speak of wrongs, this speech is understood not only as unreasonable, but as a product of having an obstinate and unyielding nature. I will be building on my discussion in chapter 1 of how speaking of a wrong is heard as being in the wrong. When I refer to "feminist subjectivity," then, I am considering how feminism is diagnosed as a symptom of failed subjectivity, assumed as a consequence of an immature will, a will that has yet to be disciplined or straightened out.

Willfulness: a way of addressing whose subjectivity becomes a problem. This perception of feminist subjects as having too much will, or too much subjectivity, or just as being too much, has profound effects on how we experience ourselves as well as the worlds we come up against. If to be a killjoy is to be the one who gets in the way of happiness, then living a feminist life requires being willing to get in the way. When we are willing to get in the way, we are willful. In this chapter, I first explore the figure of the willful girl before reflecting on how willfulness has been, and can be, taken up by feminists in doing our collective work. I explore how willfulness is not only what we are judged as being but how we convert a judgment into a project.

WILLFUL GIRLS

To become feminist can often mean looking for company, looking for other girls, other women, who share in that becoming. This search for feminist companionship began for me through books; I withdrew into my room with books. It was willful girls who caught my attention. Some of my most loved characters turn up in this chapter. In writing my book *Willful Subjects* (Ahmed 2014), I formalized my pursuit of willful girls into a research trajectory. Once I began to follow the figure of a willful girl, I found she turned up all over the place. It was by following this figure that I came to encounter new texts, ones that had a ghostly familiarity, even if I had not read them before. One of these texts was titled "The Willful Child." It is a grim story, and a Grimm story. Let me share this story, for those of you who have not read it before:

> Once upon a time there was a child who was willful, and would not do as her mother wished. For this reason God had no pleasure in her, and let her become ill, and no doctor could do her any good, and in a short time she lay on her death-bed. When she had been lowered into her grave, and the

earth was spread over her, all at once her arm came out again, and stretched upwards, and when they had put it in and spread fresh earth over it, it was all to no purpose, for the arm always came out again. Then the mother herself was obliged to go to the grave, and strike the arm with a rod, and when she had done that, it was drawn in, and then at last the child had rest beneath the ground.[1]

What a story. The willful child: she has a story to tell. This story can be treated as a teaching tool, as well as a way of teaching us about tools (the rods, the machinery of power). We learn how willfulness is used as an explanation of disobedience: a child disobeys because she is willful, when she is not willing to do what her mother wills her to do. We do not know in the story what it was that the child was not willing to do. Disobedience is not given content because disobedience as such becomes a fault: the child must do whatever her mother wishes. She is not willing, whatever.

What is striking about this story is how willfulness persists even after death: displaced onto an arm, from a body onto a body part. The arm inherits the willfulness of the child insofar as it will not be kept down, insofar as it keeps coming up, acquiring a life of its own, even after the death of the body of which it is a part. Note that the rod, as that which embodies the will of the parent, of the sovereign, is not deemed willful. The rod becomes the means to eliminate willfulness from the child. One form of will judges the other wills as willful wills. One form of will assumes the right to eliminate the others.

We might note here how the very judgment of willfulness is a crucial part of the disciplinary apparatus. It is this judgment that allows violence (even murder) to be understood as care as well as discipline. The rod becomes a technique for straightening out the willful child with her wayward arm. I return to this wayward arm in due course. She too has a feminist history. She too is a feminist history.

This Grimm story forms part of a tradition of educational writing that Alice Miller (1987) in *For Your Own Good* calls "poisonous pedagogy," a tradition that assumes the child as stained by original sin, and which insists on violence as moral correction, as being for the child. This history is condensed by the brutish maxim "spare the rod, spoil the child." Just consider that in this story the only time that the child is at rest is when she is beneath the ground. By implication, when the child gives up or gives up her will, when she stops struggling against those she must obey (her mother, God), when she is willing to obey, she will be at ease.

Becoming willing to obey would avoid the costs of not being willing. A willing girl, who does not appear in this story, is willing to obey, which is to say, she is willing not to have a will of her own. The willing girl does not appear, but she is the one to whom the story is addressed: the story is a warning of the consequences of not being willing to obey. In the original Grimm story the child is not given a gender; and sometimes in English the story is translated using "he," although the child is usually "she." I would make an argument out of this usually: willfulness is assigned to girls because girls are not supposed to have a will of their own. Of course boys act in ways that might be judged willful. It is useful to note that the meaning of *willfulness* in "the positive sense of strong willed" is described by the *Oxford English Dictionary* as both obsolete and rare. The negative senses of *willfulness* are deeply entrenched. Willfulness thus has more of a feminist than a masculinist sense.

Perhaps boys are more likely to be described as strong willed and girls as willful because boys are encouraged to acquire a will of their own. Another willful girl who might help us to make sense of the gendered nature of the assignment is Maggie Tulliver. Maggie appears in George Eliot's ([1860] 1965) *The Mill on the Floss* and has been one of my co-travelers in my journeys into the histories of unhappiness as well as willfulness. As I noted in my introduction to *Willful Subjects* (Ahmed 2014), I first embarked on my research into willfulness because I was so struck by how Maggie's will was used to explain what was behind her troubles. We might put this in another way: Maggie seems willingly to get into trouble, which is not the same thing as saying she has any choice in the matter.

When girls exercise their own will, they are judged willful. The novel contrasts Maggie and her brother Tom, not by suggesting Maggie is willful and Tom is not, but by showing how although they both act in ways that might ordinarily be designated as willful, Tom escapes the consequences of being judged in these terms: "Tom never did the same sort of foolish things as Maggie, having a wonderful distinctive discernment of what would turn to his advantage or disadvantage; and so it happened, that although he was much more willful and inflexible than Maggie, his mother hardly ever called him naughty" (Eliot [1860] 1965, 59). The narrator here describes Tom as even more willful or inflexible than Maggie but as not suffering the judgment. Tom is allowed to get away with it; Maggie not. Gender becomes a matter of consequence. The same actions have different consequences for boys and girls.

We learn from this: to suffer the cost of a judgment can be about who you are rather than what you do. Maggie is already designated a problem child (a girl who is not willing to obey) such that if there is a problem, she is assumed to be the one behind it: "It was Mrs. Tulliver's way, if she blamed Tom, to refer his misdemeanour, somehow or other, to Maggie" (114). This is how the judgment of willfulness falls: figuring who is behind the problem creates a figure, the one who is behind a problem; you might catch someone lurking just because you expect to find her there. Willfulness falls on the fallen.

If Maggie is led astray by her will, it is the will that provides Maggie with a solution. A key moment in the text is when Maggie reads a Christian book about the renunciation of will and has an epiphany. The answer to her troubles is to give up her will, which means for Maggie to stop making herself the center of things: "It flashed through her like the suddenly apprehended solution of a problem, that all the miseries of her young life had come from fixing her heart on her own pleasure as if that were the central necessity of the universe" (306). Maggie decides that her misery is tied to her own inclination; her own willful will is a will that is wanting. She willingly gives up her will as a way of giving up what she wants.

From the point of view of the parents, their daughter has become good because she has submitted to their will: "Her mother felt the change in her with a sort of puzzled wonder that Maggie should be 'growing up so good'; it was amazing that this once 'contrary' child was becoming so submissive, so backward to assert her own will" (309). Note how becoming good is about not being contrary; it means straightening one's wayward ways, no longer opposing one's own will to the will of others. The mother can love this daughter, who can support the family by staying in the background: "The mother was getting fond of her tall, brown girl, the only bit of furniture now in which she could bestow her anxiety and pride" (309). When you treat someone like furniture, you put them into the background. To recede into the background requires giving up a will other than the will of others, or learning to will what is willed by others. Renunciation can be thought of as will work: you have to work to recede, or work to become part of the background. To be willing to obey is to be willing to recede. Perhaps femininity as such becomes a willing resolution. If femininity becomes a problem of will, then femininity is to be resolved by will. Girls must be willing to give up their will.

Maggie of course fails to solve her problem; even becoming willing to obey is judged as a symptom of willfulness (she is too willing to be willing), and she hurtles toward her unhappy fate. For girls, what follows being willful is unhappiness or death. There is another story about Jane, a willful girl, which teaches us how willfulness is used to describe some kinds of girls and not others. Willfulness thus becomes a warning to girls: not to become that kind of girl. We begin with Jane herself: "Jane was a willful girl. She did not submit cheerfully to those whom it was her duty to obey, but was always contriving to how she could have her own way, as much and as often as possible" (Trowbridge 1855, 16). Note here how obedience is associated with good cheer: to be willing is to be happy to obey. She is happily willing or willing happily. The girl who does not cheerfully submit is the girl who insists on getting her own way.

This story of the willful girl borrows from old lexicons. What happens? The girls from the school are told by the teacher not to go to the orchard. The teacher makes this command because the apples in the orchard are ripe and she knows the girls will be tempted to eat them. Jane disobeys: she eats the apples. She wants them; she has them. Eating the forbidden fruit, the story of Jane, becomes a thread in the weave of the stories of willful women: returning us to Genesis, to the story of a beginning, to Eve's willful wantonness as behind the fall from Grace. The willfulness of women relates here not only to disobedience but to desire: the strength of her desire becoming a weakness of her will. In the history of willfulness, women are found wanting.

From this story we get another sense of the kinds of girls who are diagnosed as willful. When Jane is "determined" to go to the orchard and eat the apples, she declares her intent by exercising the language of injustice: "She declared that it was very unjust in their teacher not to permit them to play there" (17). The declaration of injustice, we might note, becomes, in the story, yet another piece of evidence of the child's willfulness. Maggie, too, when she speaks of injustice is heard as being willful. She speaks out about the injustice of her extended family's lack of compassion in response to her father's loss of the mill; she is described as bold and thankless (Eliot [1860] 1965, 229). Speaking out against injustice becomes yet another symptom of willfulness; and being heard as such is dismissed as such.

In the end, Jane's friend Lucy tries to dissuade Jane from her course of action, but her "obstinate will" carries her in this direction, as if her will has acquired its own will. She is carried by her will to the wrong place. Willfulness becomes here a will weakness: an inability to stop yourself from doing the wrong thing. So what happens to Jane? The teacher, when realizing Jane has disobeyed, does not address her as the guilty party but a class of children as if they are all guilty parties. She gives them a lesson on the right of some to govern: "Whose will should govern in this classroom?" And then, "I see from the looks on your faces that you do not wish to be governed by the will of any one of the pupils who attend it" (Trowbridge 1855, 19). Only then does the teacher speak of the willful disobedience of one child. The children identify with the teacher by making Jane's willfulness into an obstacle to their general will. Willfulness becomes how an individual in going astray gets in the way of the happiness of others. And the moral lesson is assumed by Jane as a willingness to become willing: "She also resolved that she will try never to be willful again" (20). Jane assumes in the firmness of a resolution a will to eliminate willfulness from her own character.

I can hear something in Jane's forgotten but familiar story. I can hear how willfulness is used to judge a girl who is becoming feminist. Her will becomes a willful will insofar as it is defined against a collective or general will. Her own will is deemed to get in the way of what the collective wills. A willful will becomes identified as the will to govern the others. Her willfulness, in other words, is interpreted as a will to power, as if protesting against something masks a desire for that very thing. And then when she speaks the language of injustice, that speech is heard as just another way she imposes her own will on others. The language of injustice is treated as a screen behind which a will lurks: a will that is wanting.

WILLFUL FEMINISTS

The word *willfulness* surrounds us when we become feminists. Already by taking up the unhappy fate of three willful girls from folklore and literature, we have acquired a handle on why this is the case. To be willful is to have a will that is wanting. By implication, feminists are judged as willful women as a way of dismissing feminism as a screen behind which a will lurks: a will that is wanting.

The word *willfulness* implies the problem with being feminist is feminist being. To be filled with will is to be emptied of thought: as if speaking about injustice, about power, about inequality, is just another way of getting your way. Those who get in the way are often judged as getting their own way. It is a way of diagnosing critique and opposition as self-interest (having too much subjectivity, being too much). No wonder that this figure of the willful girl, the one who is becoming feminist, who speaks the language of injustice to mask her own desire or will for power, creates such a strong impression.

She certainly made an impression upon me. I lived with that impression. I picked up the figure of the willful girl and put her into words because I had been her. I too had been called a willful child. It is not just concepts that sweat; figures too; they become containers for what is difficult, even excruciating.

A figure is evoked by just a word because that word carries a history with it. I remember what it felt like, that word. I remember how it falls, harshly as an accusation. I know how that word is used because it was used against me. Words can be tools. Words can be weapons.

My father would often call me willful when he was being violent. I was one of three sisters but the only one that my father was physically violent toward; I experienced that violence as being singled out. I find it hard now to disentangle this violence from my memories of becoming feminist. There was one experience when I was beaten with my own ruler. The ruler had holes in it: intended as different shapes you could trace onto paper; squares, circles, triangles. Those shapes became shapes left on my own skin; squares, circles, triangles. I remember that feeling of being marked by violence in the very shapes of my childhood. This history enacted on our bodies is one that we carry with us.

I think of this embodied history as my own history of willfulness. And that too is a challenge to the discourse of stranger danger, which assumes that violence originates outside of home. Stranger danger could be used to retell this story as the story of the violence of the Muslim father. Here the story becomes complicated: it is a feminist of color kind of complication. When we speak of violence directed against us, we know how quickly that violence can be racialized; how racism will explain that violence as an expression of culture, which is how racism and religion become entangled. Violence would then again be assumed to originate with outsiders. Some forms of violence become cultural, and other forms of violence remain individual and idiosyncratic: the *some* of this distinction is racism. I return to the racism at stake in this potential reframing of my own story in chapter 7. We must still tell these stories of violence because of how quickly that violence is concealed and reproduced. We must always tell them with care. But it is risky: when they are taken out of hands, they can become another form of beating.

Willfulness comes up in part as a mechanism for justifying violence by those who are violent. And why I mention this here, this very ordinary experience of violence directed against girls and women by fathers or husbands within the supposed safety of home (that this is ordinary is why we must mention it) is that my own father's blows were always accompanied by words. He would ask insistently punishing questions: Why do you want so much? Why are you never satisfied? Why do you not do better at school? In other words, being judged as willful was a technique for justifying violence in the midst of violence. You are being punished for your subjectivity, for being the being you are. You can be beaten by a judgment.

And then: you become the cause of the violence directed against you. I did work out what to do, and found my own ways of stopping it. I began to scream really loudly when he went for me. He would stop very quickly after I screamed. Why did this work?[2] So often people do not recognize their actions as violent; we know this. Hitting a willful girl, after all, has been justified as discipline and moral instruction: for her own good. By screaming, I announced my father's violence. I made it audible. And I learned from this too: becoming a feminist was about becoming audible, feminism as screaming in order to be heard; screaming as making violence visible; feminism as acquiring a voice.

Willfulness: the acquisition of a voice as a refusal to be beaten. My memories of being called willful relate to experiences at school as well as at home. In one instance, I recall contradicting the teacher (on a point about grammar). I learned that the teacher has a right to be right and the first right meant that even if the second right was wrong, the teacher was right. I learned the wrong of this right. I was sent to the headmistress's office for my disrespectful attitude to the teacher's authority. I often ended up in that office: the fate of many willful children, one suspects. I find it curious that the sore point was grammar. These experiences were perhaps a lesson in the grammar of the will.

There was another time as well during a PE class (How I hated PE classes!) when some of us got in trouble for being disruptive. I can't quite remember how or why we were being disruptive, though I do know I used to want to wiggle out of sports whenever I could. But rather than punishing some of us, the teacher punished all of us (I was reminded of this experience by Jane's story). We were all sent to the library to write an essay about sports. I much preferred the library to the playing field and happily wrote an essay on horseback riding. I took care and pride in this essay. But in the middle of the essay, I wrote a paragraph about why I thought it was wrong to punish all for some. My teacher found that paragraph. She could not understand why I would complete the task while protesting against the task. Again: back to the headmistress's office. These experiences are wearing: you come to understand how you are judged as being wrong for pointing out a wrong. You become a spoilsport. It is not only that we ruin their sport. To be called willful is an explanation of why we ruin things. We are assumed to cause our own ruin, as well as to ruin things for others. This assumption is expressed in the story of being spoiled; as if we get our own way because we have been allowed to have our own way.

Indeed it is the perception of having had our own way that leads us not to be spared; that leads in fact to the rod, to the law, to punishment.

A history of willfulness is a history of violence. An experience of violence might lead us to a sense of things being wrong, and when we sense things being wrong we are punished by violence. A feminist history is thus also a history of disobedience, of how we risk violence because we sense something being wrong. This history seems to condense in a set of figures: from Eve to Antigone. These figures are not the whole history, but they have a history, a feminist history as a history of women who pulse with life before law.

If feminists are willful women, then feminism is judged as a product of those who have too much will or too much of a will of their own. This judgment is a judgment of feminism as being wrong, but also an explanation of feminism in terms of motivation: the act of saying something is wrong is understood as being self-motivated, a way of getting what you want or will. Virginia Woolf (1920) wrote of a room of one's own, a room we have to fight for. We can think of feminism as having to fight to acquire a will of one's own.

Of course now when we hear the expression "a will of one's own," we might assume this claim as an assertion of the primacy of an individual. But *own* can be rebellious in a world that assumes some beings are property for others (being for others): to claim to be one's own or to have a will of one's own can be a refusal to be willing to labor or to provide services for others. Perhaps willing women means being willing to be for. When you are assumed to be for others, then not being for others is judged as being for yourself. Perhaps willfulness could be summarized thus: not being willing to be owned. When you are not willing to be owned, you are judged as willing on your own. This is why willfulness as a judgment falls on some and not others. It is only for some that ownness is rebellion; only some owns become wrongs. Remember Maggie and Tom: when boys are inflexible they are becoming themselves, becoming own as being supported rather than having to support. For some, ownness is a command not only to own oneself but to own oneself through others.

We sense why willfulness is such a useful charge. Through this charge, feminists become the cause of the problem we cause; almost as if to say, to become feminist is to cause a problem for oneself by making oneself one's own cause. Subjectivity (as a fantasy of self-causality) becomes something we have to give up. A solution thus becomes: not to cause oneself problems by making oneself the cause of oneself or by making oneself one's own cause. A solution thus also becomes: to make one's own cause the cause of others, to make one's own cause the happiness of others. The killjoy is one who does not make the happiness of others her cause. When she is not willing to make their happiness her cause, she causes unhappiness. My killjoy manifesto rests on these principles.

There are two senses of causality at stake here. Something is a cause when it brings about certain effects and something is a cause when it is being pursued. I suspect that when willfulness becomes a feminist character diagnosis, both senses of *cause* are in operation. A feminist is caused by her own will (such a will is a willful will, an error of motivation in how we begin or proceed), and she takes her own will as her cause (such a will is a willful will, an error of consequence in the end that is being aimed for). When a feminist will is described as a willful will, then a feminist is diagnosed as beginning or ending with herself. Her willfulness or obstinacy means that she makes the world about herself.

This is how to become feminist is to be assigned as being willful: you are not willing to recede. The costs of willfulness as a diagnosis are high; I think we know this. And from our own experience of these costs, we also learn how power works: how power works through will, not simply against will. You might become willing to avoid the costs of being willful. In chapter 2, I explored how bodies are directed toward certain ends. We can certainly rethink these processes in terms of will. Someone says, "Are you going to let me or do I have to make you?" We can hear in this statement a will directive: if you are not willing, you will be forced. Being forced to do something would be worse than doing something willingly, even if you are not willing to do something. When willing is a way of avoiding the consequence of being forced, willing is a consequence of force. Once you are willing to do what you have been compelled to do, less pressure needs to be exerted. To become willing offers a relief from pressure. To refuse to become willing requires accepting more and more pressure (the effort to make you do what you are not willing to do). Willfulness might be required to refuse to become willing.

The will as such becomes a moral technology. We can return to the Grimm story. The story warns girls of the danger of having a will of their own. Indeed, we might note the diagnosis of the story is medical as well as moral: to be willing would be to avoid becoming ill. Willfulness becomes that which compromises the health or well-being of the child. If feminism encourages girls to have a will of their own, then feminism becomes bad for health as well as happiness. Feminism becomes a diagnosis: what stops or prevents girls from giving up their will, or what in giving girls permission to desire leads to girls becoming agitated by their desires. Becoming willing is here: accepting one's fate, willing as fatality. Feminism as a form of activity becomes the cause of illness. We can be made ill by a diagnosis of being ill. So many feminist women lived their lives at the border of sanity. Feminists have paid a high price for the failure to give up their will and their desire. A feminist history is thus hard to disentangle from a diagnostic history, a mad history, or a history of madness.[3] Not only have feminists been agitators, many have, in agitating, crossed the border between sane and mad, a crossing that has led to confinement and death. Many feminists became what Shayda Kafai (2013) calls astutely "mad border bodies," bodies that expose the instability of the distinction between sanity and madness in how they travel through time and space.

I want to turn here to another one of my companion texts: Charlotte Perkins Gilman's "The Yellow Wallpaper" ([1892] 1997). "The Yellow Wallpaper" could be read as a feminist rewriting of the Grimm story. Gilman was herself diagnosed with neurasthenia, a nervous order, and has since been understood as suffering from postnatal depression. The treatment for neurasthenia is rest; it is a reduction of stimulus. The treatment of a mental condition is close to the requirements of femininity for middle-class and upper-class women: activities become disturbances, thoughts become agitations, life an endless series of distractions from the task of getting well or being well. "The Yellow Wallpaper" is a story of an unnamed woman, who suffers this very diagnosis; whose husband is a physician; a woman whose cure is rest. Right from the beginning she exercises the faculties she is supposed to rest: she is "absolutely forbidden to 'work.'" She counters, "Personally, I disagree with their ideas. Personally, I believe that congenial work, with excitement and change, would do me good" (1). Indeed, this repetition of *personally* is cutting; making explicit that to speak personally is to rebel against the impersonality of a medical diagnosis.

This story is a story of how female and feminist rebellion is a rebellion against restriction, a rebellion that requires the walls that house femininity to come alive. She is a writer; she writes the story for us; a feminist life is written into existence. Even writing itself is rebellion, what she has to do on the sly or "else meet with heavy opposition" (2). When activity is opposed, activity becomes even more laborious. Feminist writing: to write with opposition.

One can immediately see how feminism itself becomes a nervous condition. Feminism is too stimulating. The story is also a story of wallpaper, of willful wallpaper. At first, when she meets the wallpaper, it disgusts her. It is revolting. It is "too much" to take in; it overwhelms her senses. She can smell the yellow. Objects acquire qualities that confound our ways of dividing senses: colors that smell; smells that have colors. It is menacing, this refusal of things to respect the precision of our human divisions. The wallpaper stares back at her: "This paper looks to me as if it knew what a vicious influence it had" (5). The wallpaper has life; it is animated. Of course, for the physician this way of sensing the paper makes no sense; it is fanciful. A feminist consciousness of the liveliness of things might be diagnosed by others as fanciful. When she feels a restriction, she is too much; she registers too much; she leaks from her container.

She is too much.

She is too much, too.

She is too, too.

She's in the paper, a woman struggling to get out, another woman: "The front pattern *does* move and no wonder! The woman behind it shakes it" (12). The pattern moves because the woman behind it shakes it. She becomes the woman behind it. And so: her own life, her own freedom from the restriction of rest, becomes bound up with the life of the wallpaper. She gets out by pulling the wallpaper off the wall, by changing the pattern: "'I've got out at last,' said I, 'in spite of you and Jane. And I've pulled off most of the paper, so you can't put me back!'" (15).

What is narrated as death in the Grimm story becomes, in this feminist rewriting, liberation; under the ground, behind the wall. She escapes by taking on the very assignment she has been given, by making herself ill, by stimulating her own will and desire with activity. Feminist willfulness: when we change the pattern, we become aware of other women too, whose willfulness might be behind how the world shakes. If, as I discuss in chapter 2, we can become attuned to the ghosts of past suffering, we can also be energized by the words that have been put down; by the collective refusal to put down our pens. The feminist writer can be embraced as part of a feminist history of willfulness. In the next section, I explore how willfulness can be reclaimed as a collective source of energy, a way of being sparked into life by others, and how this reclaiming requires opening up the drama of willfulness beyond the domestic sphere.

RECLAIMING WILLFULNESS

Willfulness is used to explain how subjects become the cause of their own unhappiness. Perhaps then feminism involves being willing to be willful. To claim to be willful or to describe oneself or one's stance as willful is to claim the very word that has historically been used as a technique for dismissal. Not surprisingly, feminist histories are full of self-declared willful women. Take the

Heterodoxy Club that operated in Greenwich Village in the early twentieth century, a club for unorthodox women. They described themselves as "this little band of willful women" (Schwarz 1986, 103). Heterodoxy refers to what is "not in agreement with accepted beliefs." To be willful is, here, to be willing to announce your disagreement, and to put yourself behind it. Feminist, queer, and antiracist histories can be thought of as histories of those who in being willing to be willful are turning a diagnosis into an act of self-description.

Willfulness: an act of self-description. Alice Walker describes a "womanist" in the following way: "A black feminist or feminist of color . . . usually referring to outrageous, audacious, courageous or *willful* behavior. Wanting to know more and in greater depth than is considered 'good' for one . . . responsible. In charge. *Serious*" (2005, xi, emphasis in original). Alice Walker suggests here that the word *willful* conveys what being a black feminist or feminist of color is all about. Black feminists and feminists of color might acquire certain qualities because of what they fight against. The very behaviors that are dismissed as weakness or immaturity become not only strengths but signs of not being willing to be subordinate. She is serious, she knows things; she is responsible.

A womanist is a willful woman. To claim willfulness as womanist provides an alternative commentary on the grim history of will. As James Saunders notes, "The emphasis is on 'willfull' because for so long, so many black women have not been considered to be in possession of their own free wills" (1988, n.p.). Any will is a willful will if you are not supposed to have a will of your own. A willful will is what you will need when it is presumed you do not have a will of your own. And: willfulness becomes a judgment when some refuse to be owned.

Alice Walker explicitly identifies black feminists or feminists of color in evoking what womanism is about. I am pondering her words as a nonblack feminist of color and the generosity of the implication that feminists of color are part of this tradition.[4] I need to be responsible in receiving that implication; I need to recognize that there are important differences in our histories. For Walker also makes clear that womanism derives specifically from black culture, language, and history. *Womanist* is from "the black folk expression of mothers to female children, 'You acting womanish, i.e., like a woman'" (Walker 2005, xi). To be woman is not to be girl or girlish, "i.e., frivolous, irresponsible, not serious" (xi). Black folk expression might offer an alternative to the Grimm story. In the Grimm story, the daughter is deemed willful because she disobeys the mother. The daughter is likely to be understood as irresponsible and silly. In black folk expression, the daughter's willfulness is womanist:

responsible and serious. Womanism gives expression not to the disobedience of the female child, but to how she is becoming woman.

Willful womanism thus offers us another handle on the story of the willful girl. In the Grimm story, the girl who is deemed willful (from the point of view offered by the fable) is going out on her own limb; she separates herself from her family, an act of separation that is sustained by the transfer of willfulness to her arm, which appears as a limb on its own. The mother appears on the side of the rod/God: she takes up the rod to stop her daughter's arm from coming up. In a willful womanist rewriting of the story, the mother would be on the daughter's side. Willfulness becomes a *connecting tissue* between mothers and daughters; it is a style of being or a behavior that mothers recognize in their daughters, "outrageous, audacious, courageous or *willful* behavior" (Walker 2005, xi). That connection might even be the source of disobedience. After all, as Christina Sharpe reminds us, "in North American slavery black women were regularly separated from their children, who were sold away or sent to other women in the plantation to be taken care of" (2010, 18). When histories demand a separation (mothers from daughters, people from people), willfulness might be required to refuse or resist that separation. Read through this history, reclaiming willfulness would involve not only a protest against violence but a demand for a return: a return of the child who had been wrenched from her family; a return of the severed arm.

When separation becomes a command, willfulness is what returns; willfulness not as severance but as perseverance. When the arm perseveres, when it keeps coming up, it sustains a connection; willful womanism could be understood as a manifestation of that connection. After all, Alice Walker insists that a womanist is not a separatist (2005, xi). She is referring of course to the accusation that a womanist, as a black feminist, separates herself from black men. Walker insists throughout the body of her work that it is not separatism to point out violence committed against black women by black men within their homes and communities; even if that point can be heard as separatism, even if it remains risky and complicated to point out that violence given the ongoing existence of racism directed against black men as well as black women. It is because a willful womanist is responsible and in charge that she exposes sexual as well as racial violence, wherever and whenever it happens; she exposes the violence because she is concerned with the survival of people. If she comes up because she is necessary for collective survival, then she is a record of that survival.

In the Grimm story the drama of willfulness might appear to be restricted to the drama of the family. But other sources of authority are evoked: the doctor, God. The police are not in the story because the police are the rods.[5] It is these other sources that open up what it means to reclaim willfulness. If we think of willful womanism as a rewriting of the Grimm story of the willful girl, we are showing how poisonous pedagogy has its roots in the ruling of people as well as the domination of children.[6] We know after all that the enslaved and the colonized were positioned as children, as those for whom discipline was moral instruction, who were not supposed to have a will of their own; who must be willing to obey.

The Grimm story is there.

She is there; she is right there.

There she is.

Education was of course one of the crucial technologies of colonial rule.[7] The Grimm story of the willful child could also then be understood as circulating throughout the empire. The willful child is also the story of the subaltern: she is addressed as a member of the subordinate class. She is insubordinate when she refuses to be a member of that class. The demand to be willing is here articulated as the demand to obey the colonizer (who takes the place of the parent): the rod comes to embody his sovereign will. The willful child would function as an early warning system for subalterns at large: she is warned of the consequences of insubordination; her fate is a warning. In persisting, she converts that warning into a promise: she is not willing to be subordinate. As Gayatri Spivak (1988) famously argued, the subaltern does not speak. We might add: she does not speak to us directly through the archives provided by folklore and fables. Perhaps her arm speaks. Even then the arm cannot be understood as testimony. If we hear arms, we do so only through other limbs. The arm: a ghost, a menace, a trace.

If she persists, she is willful. And her arm comes up. When a history is not over, the arm comes up. The arm testifies to the survival of willfulness after the death of the body of which it is a part. This is why willfulness acquires different valences when understood as a black feminist and feminist of color inheritance. The violence that we have to survive is not only gender-based violence, or violence that might take place at home; although it includes these forms of violence. It is the violence of enslavement, of colonization, of empire. It is the requirement to give up kin, culture, memory, language, land. We reclaim willfulness in refusing to give up; and in refusing to forget the severances that have been performed and narrated as the spread of light to the dark corners of earth; to persevere embodies that refusal.

We have to embody that refusal. Histories are still. In the United Kingdom today, brown and black children of the (formerly) colonized are still managed by exercising the figure of the willful child. That figure functions to justify violence: the administration of sovereign will as the elimination of willfulness. For example, when the so-called riots happened in the summer of 2011—that is, the protests that began in response to the police murder of an unarmed black man, Mark Duggan, a killing later justified by law as lawful—the willful child quickly came up. I return to the significance of being unarmed in chapter 6. Just note: the protests were explained away by politicians and mainstream media as being a result of the failure to discipline the children, as a result of the failure to use the rod.[8] The brutish maxim, "spare the rod, spoil the child," becomes "spare the rod, spoil the nation." The rod reappears as a melancholic object, a lost object: as that which must be exercised because it has been too quickly given up, as that which would give coherence to the national body by straightening out the wayward child.

We must learn from where and when the willful child comes up. As soon as she appears, the rod comes quickly after. She tells us what might happen if we refuse to give up. She tells us what we become when we keep coming up, when we protest against the violence of the rod, when we challenge how some are beaten as if beating is a right: black bodies, brown bodies. Some have to become willful to survive a history. We cannot "not" start there, which is to say, here. We have to become willful to say this history is still; that it has not gone; that it goes on. I turn to how willfulness is required to insist on what is not over in chapter 6. We can just say, here, hear: the wayward arm in this grim story is speaking to us. She is trying to speak to us. She has something to say to us. Listen.

One history of will is a history of the attempt to eliminate willfulness from people; those deemed a different class, a different race. Given this, willfulness might be required to recover from the attempt at its elimination. Willfulness is not only a judgment that leads to punishment; it is a punishment. Willfulness can also be a protest against punishment; protest and punishment share the same terms. The term *willfulness* is a charge not only in the sense of a burden and an accusation but also as a load and a responsibility: it is how we carry something forward. When we are charged with willfulness, we can accept and mobilize this charge. Willfulness then becomes a charge in Alice Walker's sense: being in charge. To accept a charge is not simply to agree with it. Acceptance can mean being willing to receive.

A charge can be energy you receive. In chapter 2, I have referred to the momentum of a crowd. Let's think more about the experience of going the wrong way in a crowd. Everyone seems to be going the opposite way than the way you are going. No one person has to push or shove for you to feel the collective momentum of the crowd as pushing and shoving. For you to keep going, you have to push harder than any of those who are going the right way. The body going the wrong way is in the way of the will acquired as momentum. For some bodies, mere persistence, "to continue steadfastly," requires great effort, an effort that might appear to others as stubbornness or obstinacy, as an insistence on going against the flow. You have to become insistent to go against the flow. You are judged to be going against the flow because you are insistent.

Willfulness: a life paradox. You might have to become what you are judged as being. You might have to become what you are judged as being to survive what you are judged as being. The consequence of the judgment requires that we fulfill that judgment. It can take energy and effort not to go with the flow. We can thus distinguish between willfulness as a character diagnosis (as what is behind an action) and willfulness as the effect of a diagnosis (as what is required to complete an action). Sometimes you can stand up only by standing firm. Sometimes you can hold on only by becoming stubborn.

Willfulness becomes a style of politics when we are not willing to go with the flow; when we are willing to cause its obstruction. However, this is not a story of a lonely person fighting against the tide of social traffic. No: this is not that story. Loneliness might be what we are threatened with if we persist in being or doing what we are being or doing. We must not be intimidated by threats of what or who we lose. To reclaim willfulness is how a *we* can be brought forth by the willingness to go the wrong way. Alice Walker (2005, xi) stresses how womanism is also about connections between women, loving connections, between those who recognize in each other that willful stance. Loving connections are live connections, electric connections. A charge can be what you receive from proximity to others who have themselves received that charge. Proximity can be what you struggle for; separation what you fight against. In other words, the charge itself can be a connection: a way of relating to others similarly charged. The language can be our lead: if willfulness is an electric current, it can pass through each of us, switching us on. Willfulness can be a spark. We can be lit up by it.

We can be lit up by it. And so: we demonstrate; we strike. Demonstrations and strikes only work when there are enough bodies. You aim to stop things: the flow of an economy, people getting to work, the flow of traffic. Bodies, in becoming barriers, are stopping something from moving that would otherwise be moving. A barrier is only possible if enough gather; you can only counter a momentum by achieving a countermomentum.

We might also be willing to stop the flow of a conversation. This is why feminist killjoys are willful subjects: when we speak, a flow is stopped. A feminist flow can be what we stop. And this is why reclaiming willfulness as a feminist inheritance requires centering on the experiences of black women and women of color. Because, so often we are heard as stopping the flow of a feminist conversation. As Audre Lorde describes so well, "When women of Color speak out of the anger that laces so many of our contacts with white women, we are often told that we are 'creating a mood of helplessness,' 'preventing white women from getting past guilt,' or 'standing in the way of trusting communication and action'" (1984a, 131). To speak out of anger about racism is to be heard as the one who is standing in the way, who is blocking the flow of communication, who is preventing the forward progression sometimes described as reconciliation. We have to be willful to bring racism up within feminism, as I discuss in more detail in chapter 7.

We might have to become willful to keep going, to keep coming up. Willfulness is thus required in ordinary places: where we live; where we work. Willfulness too is homework. Throughout this book I share examples of the willfulness required just to be something or to do something (see especially chapters 5 and 9). Sometimes: to be something or do something, you are fighting against something. It is important, however, that we not reduce willfulness to againstness. There is a family of words around willfulness (*stubborn, obstinate, defiant, rude, reckless*), which creates a structure of resemblance (we feel we know what she is like). This familialism also explains how easily willfulness is confused with, and reduced to, individualism. We need to resist this reduction. The reduction is how willful subjects are dismissed.

And yet a dismissal can be an opportunity. It is because willfulness is assumed to stand out, to be so striking, that it becomes possible to act willfully by not standing out at all. She might be plotting. She might know how she tends to appear (whatever she says, whatever she does). She might resist a tendency that is not her own. She might not go on a smile strike, or she might smile in order to strike. She might pass as willing in order to be willful. I return to the question of willful passing in chapter 4.

Indeed, we should note here that even if to be willful is to have too much will we are often called willful when we are not willing. If feminist will is will that is wanting, feminist will is also will that is unwilling. When we are not willing to participate in sexist culture, we are willful. When we are not willing to participate in racist culture, we are willful. When we are not willing to adjust, we are maladjusted. Perhaps willfulness turns the diagnosis into a call: do not adjust to an unjust world! As with other political acts of reclaiming negative terms, reclaiming willfulness is not necessarily premised on an affective conversion, that is, on converting a negative into a positive term. On the contrary, to claim willfulness might involve not only hearing the negativity of the charge but insisting on that negativity: the charge, after all, is what keeps us proximate to scenes of violence. In willingly receiving the charge of willfulness, we stay close to those scenes of violence; as we must.

CONCLUSION: A FEMINIST ARMY

The arm: it came up in a story of violence. The striking arm of the Grimm story: the arm comes alive after death. The arm is life after death. Before the grim ending, the arm is held up in a moment of suspension. The arm becomes, despite the morbid nature of this story, a signifier of hope; the arm in suspension is still rising. Even after the willful child has been brought down, something, some spark, some kind of energy, persists. The arm gives flesh to this persistence. The arm has to disturb the ground, to reach up, to reach out of the grave, that tomb, that burial. Willfulness is persistence in the face of having been brought down. We have to reach the arm to carry that spark, to feel the pulse of its fragile life. We catch the arm in that moment of suspension.

Mere persistence can be an act of disobedience. And then: you have to persist in being disobedient. And then: to exist is disobedient.

And it is not that the child is willful because she disobeys but that the child must become willful in order to disobey. In order to persist with her disobedience, the child becomes her arm. Perhaps it is not that the arm inherits willfulness from the child. Perhaps the child inherits willfulness from her arm. Her arm: a willful becoming. She claims her arm as her own. No wonder the arm in the Grimm story appears all alone. This is how the story operates most powerfully as ideology: the implication that disobedience is lonely and unsupported. We can willfully hear the story as a plea: to join arms, to show the arms as joined. We assemble a feminist army in response to this plea. A feminist army of arms would pulse with shared life and vitality. Feminist arms do not lend their hand to support the familial or the social order. We support those who do not support the reproduction of that order. The arm that keeps coming up might not be willing to do the housework, to maintain his house, to free his time for thought. When women refuse to be helping hands, when we refuse to clean for him, up after him, when we refuse to be his secretary, the keeper of his secrets, his right hand, we become willful subjects.

We can understand why, of all her limbs, the arm matters. An arm is what allows you to reach, to carry, to hold, to complete certain kinds of tasks. Arms are identified throughout history as the limbs of labor or even the limbs of the laborer. Arms are supposed to be willing to labor. But not all arms. Arlie Hochschild describes how "the factory boy's arm functioned like a piece of machinery used to produce wallpaper. His employer regarded that arm as an instrument, claimed control over its speed and motions. In this situation, what was the relation between the boy's arm and his mind? Was his arm in any meaningful sense his *own*?" ([1983] 2003, 7, emphasis in original). When the laborers' arms become tools in the creation of wealth, the laborers lose their arms. To become his arm is to lose your arm. The factory owner does not only acquire the laborers' arms; he has his own arms freed. We can hear another sense in which arms are striking. To go on strike is to clench your fist, to refuse to be handy. When workers refuse to allow their arms to be the master's tool, they strike. The clenched fist remains a revolutionary sign for labor movements, internationally. The arm in the grim story belongs to this history, too: the arm is a revolutionary limb; a promise of what is to come, of how history is still but not yet done.

A feminist does not lend her hand; she too curls her fist. The clenched fist contained within the sign for woman is a key image for the women's liberation movement. The clenched fist is a protest against the sign *woman* (by being in the sign *woman*) as well as resignifying the hands of feminism as protesting hands. Feminist hands are not helping hands in the sense that they do not help women help. When a hand curls up as a feminist fist, it has a hand in a movement.

Arms remind us too that labor, who works for whom, is a feminist issue. Labor includes reproductive labor: the labor of reproducing life; the labor of reproducing the conditions that enable others to live. Black women and women of color; working-class women; migrant women; women who have worked in the factories, in the fields, at home; women who care for their own children as well as other children; such women have become the arms for other women whose time and energy has been freed. Any feminism that lives up to the promise of that name will not free some women from being arms by employing other women to take their place. Feminism needs to refuse this division of labor, this freeing up of time and energy for some by the employment of the limbs of others. If the freeing up of time and energy depends on

other people's labor, we are simply passing our exhaustion on to others. We can recall bell hooks's critique of Betty Friedan's solution to the unhappiness of the housewife, to the "problem that has no name." hooks notes, "She did not discuss who would be called in to take care of the children and maintain the home if more women like herself were freed from their house labor and given equal access with white men to the professions" (2000, 1–2).

When being freed from labor requires others to labor, others are paying the price of your freedom. That is not freedom. A feminist army that gives life and vitality to some women's arms by taking life and vitality from other women's arms is reproducing inequality and injustice. That is not freedom. For feminism to become a call to arms, we have to refuse to allow the arms to become dead labor. We have to refuse to support the system that sucks the blood, vitality, and life from the limbs of workers. We need to hear the arms in the call to arms. A call is also a lament, a passionate expression of grief and sorrow. I suggested earlier that willfulness might be not only a protest against violence but a demand for return: a return of the child, a return of her arm. We can begin to understand what is being demanded: a demand for return is also a demand for recognition of the theft of life and vitality from bodies; from arms. It is a demand for reparation.

A call of arms is thus a recall. We can recall Sojourner Truth speaking to the suffragettes, having to insist on being a woman as a black woman and former slave: "Ain't I a woman," she says. "Look at me," she says. "Look at my arm." It is said that Sojourner Truth, during her insistent speech, "bared her right arm to the shoulder, showing her tremendous muscular power" (cited in Zackodnick 2011, 99). In *Women, Race and Class*, Angela Davis notes how Truth in pointing to her arm is challenging the "weaker sex" arguments that were being used by those who opposed the suffragette cause. These were arguments that rested on flimsy evidence of flimsy bodies: "that it was ridiculous for women to desire the vote, since they could not even walk over a puddle or get into a carriage without the help of men" (Davis 1983, 61). Sojourner Truth in her speech as it has been recorded by others evokes her own laboring history: "I have ploughed and planted and gathered into barns and no man could head me. . . . I have borne thirteen children and seen them most all sold off to slavery" (99). The muscularity of her arm is an inheritance of history; the history of slavery shown in the strength of the arm, the arm required to plow, to plant, to bear the children who end up belonging to the master.

The arms of the slave belonged to the master, as did the slaves, as the ones who were not supposed to have a will of their own. Remember: any will is a willful will if you are not supposed to have a will of your own.[9] Of course we cannot simply treat the arm evoked here as Truth's arm. The arm does not provide its own testimony. It was Frances Dana Barker Gage, a leading white feminist, reformer, and abolitionist, who gave us this well-known account of Truth's speech as well as her "army testimony." This account is itself a citation: our access to Sojourner Truth's address is possible only through the testimony of others; to be more specific, through the testimony of white women.[10] We learn from this to be cautious about our capacity to bear witness to the labor and speech of arms in history: we might be able to hear the call of arms only through the mediation of other limbs. This mediation does not mean we cannot hear truth. Patricia Hill Collins notes this lack of access as a "limitation" in her account of Truth's speech: "Despite this limitation, in that speech Truth reportedly provides an incisive analysis of the definition of the term *woman* forwarded in the mid-1800s" (2000, 12). Collins thus treats Truth's speech as an example of an intellectual at work: Truth deconstructs the category woman by exposing the gap between her own embodied experiences as an African American woman and the very category "woman" (12–13).

In different hands, arms can become deconstructive limbs, or intersectional points. Arms can embody how we fail to inhabit a category. Arms can be how we insist on inhabiting a category we are assumed to fail. Arms can throw a category into crisis. The arms go on strike when they refuse to work; when they refuse to participate in their own subordination. No wonder we must *look to the arm*, if we are to understand the history of those who rise up against oppression. Arms: they will keep coming up.[11] Willfulness: how some rise up by exercising the very limbs that have been shaped by their subordination. And: it is those women who have to insist on being women, those who have to insist willfully on being part of the feminist movement, sometimes with a show of their arms, who offer the best hope for a feminist revolution.

The arms that built the house are the arms that will bring it down.

PART II Diversity Work

IN THE FIRST PART OF THIS BOOK, I explored some of my own experiences of becoming a feminist. I have been considering how we generate feminist theory by living a feminist life. Life can be our work. We work in our life. To live a feminist life is also to be a feminist at work. In this part of the book, I thus turn to the question of feminist work. My own working life has been based in universities: I was a student for around ten years and I have been an academic for over twenty years. What I know is shaped by where I have been located. So the university provides the setting for many (but not all) of the examples in this part. I hope, however, my discussion of being a feminist at work will be relevant to other working environments. Most of us with feminist commitments end up working for organizations that do not have these commitments. We often acquire commitments to do something because of what is not being done. To work as a feminist often means trying to transform the organizations that employ us. This rather obvious fact has some telling consequences. I have learned about how power works by the difficulties I have experienced in trying to challenge power.

In this part I thus explore some of my own involvement in trying to transform universities. Universities often describe their missions by drawing on the languages of diversity as well as equality. But using the language does not translate into creating diverse or equal environments. This "not translation" is something we experience: it is a gap between a symbolic commitment and a lived reality. Commitments might even be made because they do not bring something about. Indeed, equality and diversity can be used as masks to create the appearance of being transformed.

We need to challenge this appearance. In making this challenge, I draw on my experiences as a woman of color academic. My inspirations include Chandra Talpade Mohanty (2003), M. Jacqui Alexander (2005), and Heidi Mirza (2015), who offer powerful critiques of uses of diversity within the academy as a way of building feminist of color and black feminist counterinstitutional knowledge. I am also inspired by the monumental collection *Presumed Incompetent: The Intersections of Race and Class for Women in Academia* (Gutiérrez y Muhs et al. 2012), which by offering reflections by women of color students and faculty on their experiences within the academy gives us important new insights into how the academy works. We need to share our stories of arrival and progression; how we enter, exit, move forward, get stuck.

All of the chapters in this part draw on data I collected on diversity work in higher education from 2003 to 2006. I first presented these data in *On Being Included: Racism and Diversity in Institutional Life* (Ahmed 2012). In the project, I interviewed practitioners employed by universities to write and disseminate race equality and diversity policies. I also participated in what we could call simply the diversity world, attending meetings and conferences that were aimed or intended for diversity practitioners working across the public sector. This was my first experience of doing qualitative research, having previously worked with texts (not only literary and film texts but also policy documents).[1] When I looked back on this project (as well as the book), I had thought of it as a distinct phase of my career as well as a research trajectory, or even as a departure or deviation from the work I usually do. While writing *Living a Feminist Life*, I realized that this way of thinking was not quite right. Although the project was the first time I officially conducted interviews, although the book was the first in which examples were quotes from data I had gathered myself, I realized that I have been collecting stories of diversity and equality within universities since my arrival. And I would claim that women of color are already ethnographers of universities; we are participating, yes, but we are also observing, often because we are assumed not to belong or reside in the places we end up. So much of our collective humor comes from sharing observations about "the natives" within universities—the rather peculiar habits of white heteropatriarchy.

We are doing what I call diversity work, whether or not we think of ourselves as doing this work. I use *diversity work* in two related senses: first, diversity work is the work we do when we are attempting to transform an institution; and second, diversity work is the work we do when we do not quite inhabit the norms of an institution.[2] I structure this part of the book by taking the two senses of diversity work in turn, which will allow me to show how efforts to transform organizations such as universities relate to everyday existence. Sometimes the effort is to transform an existence (chapter 4). Sometimes existence itself becomes the effort (chapter 5). In chapter 6, I then consider what we learn about worlds from our efforts to transform an existence, or from our efforts to exist. I show how diversity workers come up against brick walls and ask what these walls teach us about the materiality of power. I describe brick walls as "the hardenings of history," the building materials of power.

My aim throughout this part is to show how diversity work is feminist theory: we learn about the techniques of power in the effort to transform institutional norms or in the effort to be in a world that does not accommodate our being.

4 / TRYING TO TRANSFORM

In this chapter, I explore diversity work in the first sense: the work we do when we are trying to transform an institution; or, to be more specific, the work we do when we are trying to open up institutions to those who have historically been excluded from them. I draw on interviews as well as informal conversations I have had with those appointed by universities as diversity officers, as well as some of my own experiences as a member of diversity and race equality committees. One of my central commitments in this chapter is to praxis: it is through the effort to transform institutions that we generate knowledge about them.

It might seem that as an academic as well as a diversity practitioner I have drawn upon ideas I came up with from being the former to help me do the latter, that is, that the academy gave me theories, which I then implemented as a practitioner. This is not the case. If anything, the reverse would be more the case: my theoretical understanding of how institutions work has been shaped by my work as a practitioner as well as by listening to other practitioners talk about their work. When we are trying to intervene in the reproduction of power, we have to think differently; we have to think on our feet. I suspect an academic illusion (and perhaps even an academic conceit) is that theory is what we do, because we can afford to withdraw from the requirement to act quickly; time for contemplation is assumed as time away from action. There is an academic tendency to think of strategy as what you do when you stop thinking. I have learned from diversity practitioners that strategy can be not only thought in action but thought sharpened by action.

When we have to think strategically, we also have to accept our complicity: we forgo any illusions of purity; we give up the safety of exteriority. If we are not exterior to the problem under investigation, we too are the problem under investigation. Diversity work is messy, even dirty, work. Diversity work too generates sweaty concepts, concepts that come out of the effort to transform institutions that are often not as behind that transformation as they appear to be.

WORKING THE SYSTEM

To be appointed as a diversity practitioner, or to be given diversity and equality as one of your duties, is to be put into an oblique relation to the institution. You are appointed by an institution to transform the institution. To this extent, an appointment can signify that an institution is willing to be transformed. However, as I learned from my own experiences as well as from my conversations with practitioners, being appointed to transform an institution does not necessarily mean the institution is willing to be transformed.

I began my qualitative study of diversity and higher education just after a change in equality legislation, the Amendment to the Race Relations Act (2000), which required all public organizations in the United Kingdom to have and to disseminate race equality policies. The amendment to the legislation led to many new appointments of diversity practitioners within the higher education sector. Appointments were made not only in order that organizations could comply with law (and doing something in order to comply with the law often falls short of willing something) but so that somebody within the organization would become responsible for meeting compliance. Diversity work becomes embodied in the diversity worker: institutions do this work insofar as they employ somebody to do this work. This is how: an institution being willing to appoint someone (to transform the institution) is not the same thing as an institution being willing to be transformed (by someone who is appointed). An appointment can even be about an appearance: being given a diversity mandate might be how an institution appears willing to be transformed.

We learn from the conditions of our appointment. Most of my interviews began with practitioners sharing the story of their appointment. This is one practitioner's story: "I came to [the university] three and a half years ago and the reason that they appointed someone, I think, was because of the compliance with the Race Relations Amendment Act. . . . You come into a position like this and people just don't know what kind of direction it's going to go in. You're not, sort of, there's nobody helping to support you. This job does not have support mechanisms and you know maybe you're just there, because if you're not there then the university can't say that it's dealing with legislation." An appointment can be how you are not given institutional support, as if being "just there" is enough.

Many practitioners describe their task as integrating or embedding diversity into the ordinary work or the daily routines of the organization. In other words, they want to generalize what they do so the whole organization does it. Another practitioner explains, "My role is about embedding equity and diversity practice in the daily practice of this university. I mean, ideally I would do myself out of a job, but I suspect that's not going to happen in the short term, so I didn't want to do that and I haven't got the staff or money to do it anyway." The diversity worker has a job precisely because diversity and equality are not daily practice. When your task is to remove the necessity of your existence, your existence is necessary for the task.

To embed diversity within an institution involves working with the institution as a physical entity: getting diversity into the organizational flow of things. Doing diversity requires expanding one's means of circulating information; for practitioners, diversity work is often about developing diverse communication strategies. We might even say that diversity workers are communication workers. Of course, all institutional work involves the gradual refinement of systems for getting information through to those employed by the institution. But when your task is to get information out that is less valued by an organization, the techniques for moving information become even more important. Diversity work becomes about diversifying the pathways for information so it is more likely to get to the right destination. One practitioner describes her communication strategy as follows: "I have a general circulation that goes to diverse groups of people, and if it doesn't get through one way it will get through another. By using about two or three different strategies of the circulation pool, in the end it must get there." The more paths that are blocked, the more paths you need. We can begin to see a connection between diversity work and my discussion of being directed in chapter 2. A path is cleared not only for bodies but for information. The information that challenges which paths are maintained or kept clear might be the very information that is blocked.

To do diversity work is to do work that is less supported. Another practitioner describes how persistence is required: "You need persistence and I think that's what you need to do because not everyone has an interest in equity and diversity issues, so I think it needs to be up there in people's— well, not right in their face, but certainly up there with equal billing with other considerations, so that it's always present, so that they eventually think of it automatically and that it becomes part of their considerations." The aim is to make thought about equality and diversity automatic. Diversity workers must be persistent because this kind of thought is not automatic. We have to persist because there is an institutional resistance. The requirement to persist becomes a job requirement.

Even when you have been appointed to bring about certain kinds of change, you encounter resistance to what you are trying to bring about. An expression that came up in a number of my interviews was of the institution as a "brick wall." One practitioner describes very powerfully: "So much of the time it is a banging your head on the brick wall job." A job description becomes a wall description. The feeling of doing diversity work is the feeling of coming up against something that does not move; something solid and tangible. Although the practitioner has been appointed by an institution to transform that institution, she experiences that institution as a wall, as the very thing that blocks her efforts. Perhaps her efforts are blocked, not despite being given an appointment, but through being given an appointment. Note then: the institution becomes that which you come up against. The official desire to institutionalize diversity does not mean that institution is opened up; indeed, the wall might become all the more apparent, all the more a sign of immobility, the more the institution presents itself as being opened up.

When things are not working, when what you aim for is not brought about, you have to work out what that's about. You have to work the system by working out the mechanisms whereby the system is not transformed. You have to work out where things get stuck. Diversity workers could be described as institutional plumbers: they develop an expertise in how things get stuck, as well as where they get stuck. Diversity workers come to have a different set of knowledges about institutions: they acquire practical knowledge of the mechanisms that allow some things to happen and not others. As one practitioner describes, "There are informal influences that act as blocking agents that stop conversations from even taking place." The mechanical aspect

A job description

of diversity work is revealed most explicitly when the system is working. In other words, a system is working when an attempt to transform that system is blocked.

STRATEGIC WORK

Diversity work can be frustrating as it takes the form of repeated encounters with what does not and will not move. Diversity work is thus often about trying; that is, it not only involves effort, it often becomes about the effort required to bring about certain kinds of change. Diversity workers can often find people within the organization who can participate in this effort, who can build a momentum or even a countermomentum, that is, a momentum to counter what one practitioner described as "institutional inertia."

When we say *trying*, we might be referring simply to an attempt to do something; to strive for something or to carry something out. But something can also be called trying when it is annoying or difficult, or when it strains one's patience or goodwill. I turn to the question of patience in chapter 8. We sometimes say "trying" to separate an effort from an outcome or to value efforts even though they do not lead to outcomes ("at least she tried"). I think all of these senses capture the sense of diversity work as trying. It is the effort to bring something about that means you encounter certain difficulties: diversity work is often the experiences of these difficulties. You have to keep trying because it is not working.

Diversity workers become conscious of the resistance to their work. A strategy is what is developed in the effort to overcome this resistance. So diversity workers might "try on" different styles or methods of argumentation (the business case for diversity, the social justice case, and so on) as well as different words, or even different styles of dress because of this resistance. Many practitioners have a critical awareness that much of what counts as diversity work for organizations is not about structural transformation: diversity is often a technique for rearranging things so organizations can appear in a better or happier way. One practitioner notes, "So now we'll talk about diversity and that means everybody's different but equal and it's all nice and cuddly and we can feel good about it and feel like we've solved it, when actually we're nowhere near solving it." Diversity is a way of rearranging a series that does not disrupt that series. This is why it is possible to talk about an image of diversity and everyone knows what you are referring to.

For diversity workers, words become tools; things you can do things with. This means that some strategies might aim not to cause too much disruption. Decisions about words are decisions about usefulness: you use the words that are useful, the words that travel furthest, or that enable you to get a message through. Many practitioners spoke to me about how certain words become tired from being overused. You use words more the more things are not working. But the more you use the words, the less they seem to do. As one practitioner notes:

> I think it [equity] became a tired term because it was thrown around a lot,[1] and I think . . . well I don't know . . . because our title is equity and social justice, somebody the other day was saying to me, "Oh there's equity fatigue. People are sick of the word *equity*." . . . Oh well, okay, we've gone through equal opportunity, affirmative action—they are sick of equity— now what do we call ourselves?! They are sick of it because we have to keep saying it because they are not doing it [laughs].

The tiredness or even sickness with the old terms is here a symptom of a certain institutional reluctance: you have to repeat the terms because they are not doing it, and because they are not doing it you have to repeat the terms. The implication of the arguments about equity fatigue is that in using less tired words, practitioners might themselves be energized or be perceived as more energetic: "Those terms had got tired and I think that there's a bit of 'If one thing gets tired, looks like you've got tired as well.'" Here a strategy is about rebooting, about creating more energy or avoiding becoming depleted. The hope: in rebooting the diversity worker, you reboot the system.

You can block the effort to transform institutions by not hearing those who are appointed to make the effort. They do not hear you because they expect you to speak in a certain way. The diversity worker could be described as an institutional killjoy. As this practitioner describes, "You know, you go through that in these sorts of jobs where you go to say something and you can just see people going, 'Oh here she goes.'" We both laughed, recognizing that each other recognized that scene. That scene, so familiar: I could even see the eyes rolling. In chapter 1, I introduced the following equation:

Rolling eyes = feminist pedagogy.

It is worth sharing here that I began putting this equation into words when I listened to diversity practitioners and mulled over their words. It is interesting to me, on reflection, that it can be others who put into words something you have experienced. A killjoy: so often she borrows her words from others. So yes, we both recognized that each other recognized that scene. The familiarity was partly from my own experience in women's studies, of being the feminist at the table, but it also came from my own experience of being a feminist killjoy at the family table that I described in chapter 1. As I noted then, however she speaks, the one who speaks as a feminist is usually heard as causing the argument. *Another dinner ruined.* Institutions also have tables around which bodies gather. Some more than others are at home in these gatherings. The diversity practitioner can be heard as the obstacle to the conversational space before she even says anything: she too poses a problem because she keeps exposing a problem. *Another meeting ruined.*

How you are perceived (as a problem, as causing a problem) can be what stops you from being able to get a message through. You become, if you like, identified as the blockage point such that it can even feel to you that you are the one stopping yourself from getting through. If so, what to do? A strategy for a diversity worker can be the effort to change how she appears to others within the organization. Diversity work becomes a form of image management: the diversity worker has to manage how she appears to others. Listen to the words of this practitioner: "This office two and a half years ago, which was when I started here, was the office of gender equity. They had done some good work and I certainly don't mean in any way to minimize or denigrate my predecessor, but I think, to be totally frank, that it had become a bit dated and it had actually begun to alienate and become marginalized from the business of the university."

The language of *dated* is not unsurprisingly related to *alienation*; equity work becomes alienated from the core business of the university. The word *diversity* might be more appealing as it might be more in tune with the languages employed to redescribe what universities are themselves doing. Diversity could even be described as a form of attunement. The old office was out of time as well as out of tune; the task of the practitioner is to reverse the marginalization. This practitioner thus claims a home (or can be more at home) within the university by disassociating herself from the historic work of the equality office: "I've had people say to me, you know, they thought they were the feminazis in the equity office and so there was a significant amount of resistance and people just weren't included. They weren't seen to be anything other than peripheral. Generally the office was not engaged with the university community in a really good way." I was struck during this interview by the willingness to repeat rather violent stereotypes of feminist and equality work in order to create room for another kind of work ("feminazis"). There is no doubt an agreement in the repetition: an agreement with the judgment that certain kinds of feminist and equality work didn't work because they were too extreme. Rather than challenging the perception, the strategy becomes to generate a different kind of image. If that is what they are thought to be, then you have to modify the thought by creating a new image. Those who are trying to transform a world are required to modify themselves in order to proceed within that world.

The diversity officer can take up the place at the table by not being the one who speaks in a problematic language or a language of problems. Some practitioners thus aim quite explicitly to avoid the problems I described in part I: they try to avoid becoming the problem by not naming the problem. Rather, they seek to redefine the relationship between diversity work and institutional work in less problematic or more positive terms. As this practitioner describes, "If I start off by saying, 'I'm here to change your values,' I suspect that that's not a terribly helpful way to develop a collaborative working relationship." The shift from the language of equality to the language of diversity becomes linked to a shift from a confrontational to a collaborative working model. Using the language of diversity can be a way of avoiding confrontation. But what else do we avoid if we avoid confrontation?

It is important for me to note, however, that the identification with the institution and its core values might only be an impression. An impression can be strategic. This practitioner also describes herself as a "counterhegemonic worker." Her redefining of the relationship between the equity office and the institution was thus about creating an illusion of working with or being in line with in order to enable her to work against institutional norms and values more effectively. Indeed, her aim was to create an impression of identification: and to create such an impression can be a form of disidentification. The alignment of diversity with the institution is maintained only at the level of appearance. To return to the terms offered in chapter 3: she might pass as willing in order to be willful.

Some diversity workers thus aim to maximize their distance from the figure of the institutional killjoy. Two members of an equality unit I spoke to informally talked about how they smiled when they arrived at their new jobs. The director of the unit said, "The first thing we did when we got here was smiled a lot, wore smart clothes and said yes to everything." Smiling becomes a strategy; to smile is to appear willing not willful, happy not unhappy, as friend not foe, familiar not strange. I referred in chapter 2 to Arlie Hochschild's work on how smiling becomes a form of emotional labor within the service sector. She considers how for the flight attendant smiling becomes "part of her work" and thus how workers can become alienated from their smiles (Hochschild [1983] 2003, 8). For the diversity worker, smiles might not have exchange value in quite this way: she is not required to smile in order to make customers happy. Rather, smiling becomes a strategy because the worker is alienated from the organization by virtue of the kind of work she is doing. She smiles in order to manage how diversity is perceived. She may certainly be alienated by this requirement to smile, but she senses that smiling is necessary in order to counter the perception of diversity workers as hostile or unfriendly.

Perhaps the word *diversity* is a smile (see Swan 2010a). The word *diversity* for some diversity workers thus has a practical appeal: if the term is less threatening, it can be a way of getting through people's defenses. As another practitioner describes, "I think it's really difficult: to use a term that's not acceptable is not to be able to do anything. In a way, you need to use a term that's not going to make people feel threatened if you're going to try and work with them." *Diversity* replaces other more unacceptable terms that can make people feel threatened. Another practitioner explains that she uses *diversity* because "it is not a scary word." I think the word *diversity* has become mobile partly as it does less: the words that travel more are the ones that do less (diversity), while the words that travel less do more (racism). Ironically, then, choosing words that do less becomes a strategy, almost as if to say, doing less is as much as we can do.

What happens when the words we use allow us to pass over the reasons we use them? Some practitioners do not use *diversity* precisely because it is a more positive term: "Diversity obscures the issues. . . . It can—diversity is like a big shiny red apple, right? And it all looks wonderful, but if you actually cut into that apple there's a rotten core in there and you know that it's actually all rotting away and it's not actually being addressed. It all looks wonderful, but the inequalities aren't being addressed."

When I listened to this practitioner I was reminded of Betty Friedan's (1965) critique of the image of the happy housewife whose beaming smile hides an infection. We can think of the labor of creating shiny surfaces; we can think of what those shiny surfaces allow us not to see. Diversity too is a form of institutional polishing: when the labor is successful, the image is shiny. The labor removes the very traces of labor. When something is shiny, so much is not reflected, just like the happy family discussed in chapter 1. The creation of a shiny surface is how an organization can reflect back a good image to itself. Diversity becomes a technique for not addressing inequalities by allowing institutions to appear happy. For some practitioners, the positivity of the term *diversity* makes it useful as a way of getting people to the table; for others, the positivity is a problem as it allows the reasons you might want people to get to the table to be obscured. While some practitioners participate in the polishing, others try to tarnish the image. I would describe the key difference here as one of strategy: that is, they are different ways of trying to unblock a blockage.

SENDING THINGS OUT

Strategies are what diversity workers develop because of a blockage in a system. What I learned from being a diversity worker as well as talking to diversity workers is how what you introduce to unblock a system can be used to reblock the system. This is why it is important to theorize from our own embodied work: we learn from what happens to what we introduce. I think of the process a bit like this: you throw something out, and you witness what happens to what you have thrown. This witnessing allows you to develop and refine your understanding. The process might not always be so refined. You might be thrown by how things are thrown. In other words, we change how we think, or even what we think, because of the changes that are not brought about by what is sent out.

What we learn from how ineffectual a strategy can be is this: that institutions might name things or say yes to something in order not to bring some things into effect. We too as diversity workers might labor for something (a new policy, a new document), and these things can provide yet more techniques whereby institutions appear to do something without doing anything. This is difficult: our own efforts to transform institutions can be used by institutions as evidence that they have been transformed.

One of my first experiences of this mechanism: I was a member of a working group that was set up to write our university's race equality policy in 2001. Writing the policy happened to coincide with the arrival of a new vice chancellor at the university. He set up some meetings with members of the university, which took the form of an official address. I was surprised at one of these meetings when the vice chancellor, with a letter in his hand, referred to the race equality policy that we had written. With an extravagant smile, and waving the letter in front of us (somehow the physicality of this gesture mattered), he talked about the content of the letter, which took the form of a congratulation (or which he gave the form of a congratulation), informing the university that it had been given the top rank for its race equality policy. "We are good at race equality," he said, pointing to the letter. It was a feel-good moment, but those of us who wrote the document did not feel so good. A document that documents the inequality of the university became usable as a measure of good performance.

Indeed, as I conducted my research into diversity within universities, I became aware of how diversity can be used by organizations as a form of public relations. As I have already noted, most of the interviews I conducted took place after the Amendment to the Race Relations Act (2000), which required all public sector organizations to write and disseminate race equality policies and action plans. This act was followed by many others, and then finally by the Equality Act (2010), which required all of these distinct policies to be brought together in a single document: the Single Equality Scheme. So over the period of a decade, most of the work of diversity workers was about writing documents. At various points, the Equality Challenge Unit, which oversees equality in the higher education sector, measured or ranked these documents, as I have discussed, moments of measuring that can be used by institutions that did well as a sign they are doing well.

But what is being measured by these documents being measured? I put this question to a diversity practitioner, who answered, "We are good at writing documents." I reply, without thinking, "Well yes, one wonders," and we both laugh. We are wondering whether what is measured through these documents is the degree of competence in writing documents. Organizations are able to translate their writing competence into an equality competence. As this practitioner further describes:

> I was very aware that it wasn't very difficult for me and some of the other people to write a wonderful aspirational document. I think we all have great writing skills and we can just do that, because we are good at it. That's what we are expert at. And there comes with that awareness a real anxiety that the writing becomes an end in itself. The reality is being borne out by, say, for example, we were commended on our policies and when the ECU reviewed our Implementation Plans last year, there were a number of quite serious criticisms about time slippages, about the fact that we weren't reaching out into the mainstream, and the issues hadn't really permeated the institution and the money implemented in certain specific areas. And it wasn't that there was hostility; it was much more of this kind of marshmallow feeling.

Being good at writing documents become a competency that is also an obstacle for diversity work, as it means that the university gets judged as good because of the document. It is this very judgment about the document that blocks action, producing a kind of "marshmallow feeling," a feeling that we are doing enough, or doing well enough, or even that there is nothing left to do. Marshmallow, a soft, white, gooey, sticky substance, seems a good substance to express how things stop happening by becoming too comfortable.

Many practitioners and academics have expressed concerns that writing documents or policies becomes a substitute for action: as one of my interviewees puts it, "You end up doing the document rather than doing the doing." Documents become all diversity workers have time to do. Documents then circulate within organizations, often referring to each other, creating a family of documents. They create a paper trail, a trace of where they have been. In some sense the point of the document is to leave a trail.

Diversity work: a paper trail.

The very orientation toward writing good documents can block action, insofar as the document then gets taken up as evidence that we have "done it." As another practitioner describes, "Well I think in terms of the policies, people's views are, 'Well we've got them now so that's done. It's finished.' I think actually, I'm not sure if that's even worse than having nothing, that idea in people's heads that we've done race, when we very clearly haven't done race." The idea that the document is doing something is what could allow the institution to block recognition of the work that there is to do. The idea that the document does race means that people can think that race has been done when it has not. The idea that we are doing race is thus how we are not doing race.

One of the consequences of equality becoming embedded in audit culture is that equality itself becomes a good performance of the organization, or a way the organization can perform well. When an equality policy is ranked as good, this rank is taken up as a sign of equality, which is how signs of inequality disappear from view. Equality and diversity are used as performance indicators to present the best view of the organization. Diversity is thus increasingly exercised as a form of public relations: "the planned and sustained effort to establish and maintain good will and understanding between an organisation and its publics."[2]

In an interview I had with staff from a human resources department, we discussed a research project that was collecting what is called in the equalities sector "perception data," that is, data about how external publics perceive an organization. This project was funded as part of the university's equality policy. What did they find?

> Okay, yes. It was about uncovering perceptions about the [university] as an employer. . . . [The university] was considered to be an old boys' network, as they called it, and white male dominated, and they didn't have the right perceptions of the [university] in terms of what it offers and what it brings to the academia. I think most of the external people had the wrong perceptions about the [university].

This is another way that diversity involves image management: diversity work becomes about generating the right image for the organization by correcting the wrong one. Here the perception of the institution as white is treated as wrong; to make the perception right you change the image. Diversity becomes about changing perceptions of whiteness rather than changing the whiteness of organizations. And we can see a key difficulty here: even if diversity is an attempt to transform the institution, it too can become a technique for keeping things in place. The very appearance of a transformation (a new, more colorful face for the organization) is what stops something from happening.

A new policy can be agreed upon without anything changing. A new policy can be agreed upon as a way of not changing anything. Another practitioner spoke to me about what appeared to be an institutional success story: a decision was made and agreed upon by the university's equality and diversity committee that all internal members of appointment panels for academics should have had diversity training. This decision could be described as good practice. It was made properly by the committee that was authorized to make the decision (the equality and diversity committee), which included members of the Senior Management Team (SMT). The minutes were then sent for approval to council, which alone had authority to make the recommendation into policy:

> When I was first here, there was a policy that you had to have three people on every panel who had been trained. But then there was a decision early on when I was here that it should be everybody, all panel members, at least internal people. They took that decision at the equality and diversity committee, which several members of SMT were present at. But then the director of human resources found out about it and decided we didn't have the resources to support it, and it went to council with that taken out and council were told that they were happy to have just three members, only a person on council who was an external member of the diversity committee went ballistic—and I am not kidding, went ballistic—and said the minutes didn't reflect what had happened in the meeting because the minutes said the decision was different to what actually happened (and I didn't take the minutes, by the way). And so they had to take it through and reverse it. And the council decision was that all people should be trained. And despite that, I have then sat in meetings where they have just continued saying that it has to be just three people on the panel. And I said, but no, council changed their view and I can give you the minutes, and they just look at me as if I am saying something really stupid. This went on for ages, even though the council minutes definitely said all panel members should be trained. And to be honest, sometimes you just give up.

It seems as if there is an institutional decision. Individuals within the institution must act as if the decision has been made for it to be made. If they do not, it has not. A decision made in the present about the future (under the promissory sign "we will") can be overridden by the momentum of the past. The past becomes like the crowd discussed in part I: a momentum becomes not only a direction, but a directive. A command does not have to be given to ensure things go that way, and indeed a command would not stop things from going that way. Perhaps a yes can be said because the weight of the past will not allow that yes to acquire the force needed to bring something into effect. I have called this mechanism non-performativity: when naming something does not bring something into effect or (more strongly) when something is named in order not to bring something into effect. When yes does not bring something into effect, that yes conceals this not bringing under the appearance of having brought.

A yes might even be more utterable when it has less force; or a yes might be uttered by being emptied of force. In other words, it might be easier for an institution or individuals within an institution to say yes because there is nothing behind that yes. I return to this example in chapter 6 because it has so much to teach us about institutional walls.

PUSHY WORK

I have been describing how the world might appear in a certain way when you are appointed to transform that world. Diversity workers thus have an oblique relation to the institution. Institutions too are straightening devices: when things are in line, they recede. Think of tracing paper: when everything is lined up, you can only see one set of lines. By virtue of her appointment, a diversity worker begins to witness the mechanisms that generate one set of lines, or an institutional line. No wonder things then appear wonky. She appears wonky.

We learn from what happens to the things that are sent out. For example, we learn that even when diversity work leads to the adoption of new policies, they are not necessarily enacted. Within the organization there is a gap between words and deeds, between what organizations say they will do, or what they are committed to doing, and what they are doing. Even if words become substitutes for action, these words can still be useful. One practitioner talked of how she used "statements of commitment" as principles that "the university is meant to be acting upon." So if organizations are saying what they are doing, you can show they are not doing what they are saying. Diversity workers often live in this gap between words and deeds, trying to make organizations catch up with the words they send out.

Diversity work: mind the gap.

Another way of saying this: organizations are not behind many of the policies introduced as a result of the efforts of diversity workers. *Behind* here refers to a substantive commitment.

Think with bodies. Bodies think.

The more a body gets behind an action, the less conscious effort is required to bring something about. When you are committed, say, to a particular stroke in tennis, the momentum of getting behind the action is sufficient to complete that action (and indeed, more effort would be required to stop the completion of the action than it would to complete the action). The fact that diversity workers have to keep prompting, reminding, and pushing, demonstrates the lack of institutional commitment to what they are trying to bring about. As a result, changes that are more structural or substantial (and I would argue that any changes relating to appointment procedure are structural, as they are the mechanisms through which a collective body is reassembled) are fragile or precarious: such changes of procedure might never become, or might cease to be, operative or functional.

Diversity workers thus have to keep pushing, even when policies have been adopted that they themselves have brought about. A policy can be treated as a stranger to the organization even when the organization has adopted that policy. One of the practitioners I interviewed was not called the equality or diversity officer at her university. She was a human resources manager, and diversity and equality were among her many duties. The person who had been in this post previously had been called the equity officer. Why the new job title? She explained to me the reason for this decision: "Our general manager did not want me to be seen as the equity person." Becoming "the equity person" can be a problem, as it can mean that equity stops and starts with a person. When one person becomes the equity person, other people do not have to become equity people. The logic being used here was that of mainstreaming: equality and diversity were now treated by her university as what all those employed by the university should be doing. There was no longer going to be an officer or an office for equality and diversity; what they were "trying to do was share it across the board."

Mainstreaming did not work. This practitioner gave no more detail than necessary to convey why it did not work: "We haven't been able to give as much attention as we would have liked to it." Unless equality and diversity are made to be what you attend to, they tend not to be attended to. Many practitioners I spoke to were skeptical of how mainstreaming is used as a cost-cutting exercise, a way of not giving resources to support equality and diversity (I have noted that appointments can be made without support mechanisms, but appointments might still be necessary to create a support mechanism). As another practitioner described, mainstreaming is used by managers to imply "it doesn't need people who are experts like us and everything's okay. That's not the case; we know that, particularly on race, that's not the case." Diversity and equality are not mainstream and to treat them as if they are mainstream simply means the message will not get through. Without an institutional push, without pushers, nothing happens. Diversity and equality tend to fall off the agenda unless someone forces them onto the agenda, where that someone is usually the diversity or equality practitioner. Of course, as soon as something is forced onto the agenda, then it is not mainstream. You do not have to force what is mainstream; something is mainstream when it is part of the organizational flow (it is the way things are going). Mainstreaming thus fails to describe the kind of work that diversity work involves: having to push for, or drive forward, agendas that organizations often say they are for, but show they are not behind.

Diversity and equality require offices and officers who keep pushing; otherwise things do not happen. As I noted in chapter 3, if you are going the wrong way in a crowd, you have to push harder than any of those who are going the right way. The effort required to do things is unevenly distributed. To push is thus to push against a direction. This is why pushing has a unique kind of temporality as well as affective quality (I would think of pushing as a straining temporality, you have to strain for a future). When you push, you are often pushing for something; a possibility can be what we are pushing for. If you don't push, it seems, at least sometimes, a possibility is what recedes. For some possibles to become actuals would require more of a push than others. The necessity of pushing is a consequence of what has become hard or hardened over time, as I explore in more detail in chapter 6. You have to push harder to dislodge what has become harder.

Some work is more difficult than other work because some things are more difficult to dislodge than other things. Diversity work is pushy work because you have to push against what has already been built. We have to make adjustments to an existing arrangement in order to open institutions up to those who have been historically excluded by them. It is the very necessity of making adjustments that teaches us how organizations are built. Access is pedagogy. Adjustments have to be made to spaces and buildings because they assumed certain bodies; the pavement might have to be adjusted to support the passing through of those in wheelchairs; a podium might have to be adjusted to support those who are not the right height; a timetable might have to be adjusted to support those with child care responsibilities, and so on.

Diversity work is about rebuilding institutions in order to make them more accessible. As Tanya Titchkosky (2011) has observed, access is not simply a bureaucratic procedure, but shows how spaces are orientated toward some bodies. Access can be the formal requirements you might need to meet to enter a world. But accessibility and inaccessibility are also a result of histories that congeal as habits or shared routines. And often these histories are about the narrowing or restriction of what bodies do. Say, for example, it is routine to have long meetings, seated at a table. The routine assumes a body that can be seated in this way; it assumes a body that does not require breaks. Note here that accessibility in a fuller sense might require a diversification of styles of behavior or conduct. Accessibility would be about loosening a set of requirements.

There is an intimacy then between the requirement to push and the narrowness of a restriction. You have to push to make room for those who are not accommodated by this restriction. Those who are given an opening by a restriction thus encounter diversity workers as pushing in. The figure of the feminist killjoy (and the diversity worker as an institutional killjoy) can thus be related to another figure: that of the pushy feminist. Feminists have to push if we are to do our work. We have to keep pushing even when it seems we have brought something about. Feminists are diversity workers in this first sense: we are trying to transform institutions by challenging who they are for. We have feminist centers and feminist programs because we do not have feminist universities: that is to say, because sexism, gender inequality, and sexual harassment continue to structure university environments. We have feminist centers and programs because we need to push harder to get through what has become harder. A feminist job is also "a banging your head against a brick wall job." Our job description is a wall description.

As I described in the previous section, the tools you introduce to address a problem can be used as indicators that a problem has been addressed. In my college, we developed a new feminist center in part as a response to the problem of sexism, sexual harassment, and gender inequality. In a meeting, the very existence of the center is held up as evidence of the college's own commitment to equality and feminist values. A program developed in response to a problem is assumed to resolve a problem. When the problem is not resolved, the resolution becomes the problem.

The resolution becomes the problem. In subsequent chapters I describe the work we have been doing around sexual harassment and my eventual decision to resign from my post as professor in protest against the failure to address the problem of sexual harassment. How did the college respond to my statement of resignation? They released their own statement, which names the college's own commitments, values, and equality credentials: "We take sexual harassment seriously"; "Inclusivity is a defining theme"; "We are one of the leading providers in the UK of taught programmes focusing on gender, sexuality, race and ethnicity." The statement refers to a conference organized by feminist activists Anna Bull, Tiffany Page, and Leila Whitley as evidence of how it has addressed the problem of sexual harassment. As they note in their response to the statement: "It was because no one else was willing to organise an event on sexual harassment that we took it upon ourselves."[3] An event that was claimed as evidence of what the college was doing came about because of what the college was not doing. Feminist work in addressing institutional failure is appropriated as evidence of institutional success. The very labor of feminist critique ends up supporting what you critique. The work you do to expose what is not being done is used as evidence of what has been done.

We keep pushing

Up against it

Feminists in the academy have pushed over decades for changes to curricula. We have shown how the university often equals men's studies. Universal = men. Gloria Wekker, in her important critique of whiteness as "a cultural archive," shows that whiteness becomes a reference point in women and gender studies through how race and racism are disavowed and displaced onto an elsewhere: certain bodies and words are not admitted into the field or the classroom (2016, 75–76). As a result, women and gender studies can exercise their own universal. Universal = white. A universal can be a combination of different forces; we can specify a combination in the following formula. Universal = white men. In making this equation, we are showing how a universal not only universalizes *from* particular bodies, but is an invitation *to* those very bodies, providing a space in which they can be accommodated. The universal: how some pass through. In chapter 6 I show how "white men" is thus an institution: a body that has come into being over time. We might think here too of Sylvia Wynter's powerful archaeology of the emergence of Man. She shows how European man is "overrepresented" as if he were "that of the human" (2006, 119). Katherine McKittrick, in her account of Wynter's work, describes how this "figure of man" becomes the "measuring stick against which all other beings are measured" (2015, 3). When we give this figure its history, it no longer performs the same disciplinary function.

One might expect that decades of strong critiques of how subjects are formed as disciplines would have transformed the very nature of those disciplines.[4] In my department I have always taught a course on race, which foregrounds how race emerges through histories of European imperialism.[5] I teach the work of black writers and writers of color, especially black feminists and feminists of color. Every year I have taught this course, black students and students of color have come to my office to tell me that was the first time that they had been taught materials that they could relate to their own experiences. This is in a department shaped by the intellectual traditions of British cultural studies and in particular the legacy of black British theorist Stuart Hall. Here whiteness is still business as usual; education as usual. We are still doing diversity work here because the foundation upon which the house has been built creates strangers; those who are passing by at the edges of social experience; those who, when they meet themselves in the materials, feel grief for not having met themselves before.[6]

And over the past few years many students have relayed to me that they have had a hard time accessing feminist theory or doing feminist projects in their own departments (even departments known to have large numbers of feminist faculty). Some students have said to me that feminism itself tends to be seen as passé. This sense of feminism as "past it" is how feminism ends up not being taught; there is a fantasy of feminist digestion, as if feminism has already been taken in and assimilated into a body and is thus no longer required. The fantasy of feminist digestion is a little bit like diversity: a fantasy fold (Ahmed 2012, 163). A fantasy of being folded in is how some bodies are kept out.

In other words, a fantasy of inclusion is a technique of exclusion. Recently when I have examined more curricula in cultural studies more closely, I have been struck by just how many courses are organized around or even as a white male European genealogy. Looking more deeply, it seems that this is more the case than it was before; that some curricula have become less diverse over time. It seems once the pressure to modify the shape of disciplines is withdrawn, they spring back very quickly into the old shape. We have to keep pushing; otherwise things will be quickly reversed to how they were before. Pushing might be necessary to stop a reversal. Even when a new policy is adopted, or new books are put on the syllabus, we know we have to keep pushing for them; an arrival can be fragile, precarious. If we don't keep pushing for some things, even after they have been agreed upon, they might be dropped rather quickly. In order for some things that have appeared not to disappear, we have to keep up the pressure; we have to become pressure points.

This was also my experience of working in women's studies: we had to keep pushing for things to stay up. Women's studies as a project is not over until universities cease to be men's studies. It is not surprising that women's studies has unstable foundations. To build women's studies is to build in an environment that needs to be transformed by women's studies; the point of women's studies is to transform the very ground on which women's studies is built. We have to shake the foundations. But when we shake the foundations, it is harder to stay up.

When our labor creates something fragile, we have to be careful not to break what we make. I return to the fragility of women's studies in chapter 7. But note how labor can be required to keep hold of the very things we ourselves have brought about. We have to keep pushing: to keep up, to keep it up. Perhaps we are willing to do this. Or perhaps we become exhausted and we decide to do something else instead. The history of the spring-back mechanism is impossible to separate from the history of our exhaustion as diversity workers. Which is also to say: the very necessity of having to push for some things to be possible can be what makes them (eventually) impossible. If we cannot sustain the labor required for some things to be, they cannot be. Something might not come about not because we have been prevented from doing something (we might even have been officially encouraged to do something), but when the effort to make that thing come about is too much to sustain.

CONCLUSION: DIVERSITY WORK AS WILLFUL WORK

When there is resistance to what you are trying to do, you might have to become willful to keep trying. Diversity work could thus be described as willful work. You have to persist because they resist. And diversity workers tend to be judged as willful: as if we are imposing our own will by the very expectation that some things can or should be modified. We learn from this: willfulness is, as ever, how we know. That we notice the modification of spaces required to make them accessible reveals how spaces are already shaped by the bodies that inhabit them. What is already willed is not encountered as willful. The modifications that are required for spaces to be opened to other bodies are often registered as impositions on those who were here first. Diversity workers end up challenging what gives security, warmth, place, and position. They become institutional killjoys, whatever they intend, however much they appear willing, however they speak or dress; to do diversity work is to receive that kind of assignment. If when we do diversity work we are trying to modify something that has been in existence for some time, then diversity work is judged as not only coming from the outside in but as brought about by outsiders (even when diversity workers have been officially appointed to do this work). The experience of resistance to diversity work becomes intrinsic to what makes this work "work." You speak the happier languages of diversity because of what you encounter. You might smile more the more you encounter resistance. You have to find other ways to get through. You have to become more inventive the more you are blocked.

We have to keep pushing if we are to open up spaces to those who have not been accommodated. Or those who are not accommodated have to keep pushing even after they have apparently been accommodated. For example, even when universities have access policies, it is often still left to students with disabilities to find out about those policies, to ask about access arrangements at each and every event.[7] The very effort required to find out about access can end up making events inaccessible. Access can become inaccessible. Diversity becomes work for those who are not accommodated by an existing system, whether or not they aim to modify that system. This is what I am referring to as the second sense of diversity work. And it is to this sense that I now turn.

5 / BEING IN QUESTION

A norm is something that can be inhabited. I think of a norm as rather like a room or a dwelling: as giving residence to bodies. In this chapter, I explore diversity work as the work we do when we do not quite inhabit the norms of an institution. Not to inhabit a norm (or not quite to inhabit a norm) can be experienced as not dwelling so easily where you reside. You might be asked questions; you might be made to feel questionable, so that you come to feel that you do not belong in the places you live, the places you experience as home; you might turn up and not be allowed in or find it too uncomfortable to stay. Indeed, I will explore how norms are often maintained through how those who do not quite inhabit norms are treated. Norms can be produced by organizations (as a set of formal rules or arrangements), but are also at work in everyday situations into which bodies are thrown. Indeed, not to inhabit a norm (or not quite to inhabit a norm) is often an experience of being thrown.

Diversity work is often the work we have to do because we are thrown. This chapter develops my account of diversity work by thinking about how existence as such becomes a form of political labor. To be in question is to try to be; to be in question makes being trying. In particular, I explore how being in question is often about passing: in order to pass through (a street, a neighborhood, an organization), you have to pass as something you are assumed not to be.

WHERE ARE YOU FROM?

We are all in a profound sense temporary residents. We arrive in a world only to depart again. Life is coming and going, and what happens in between. We pass through a world. When we are passing through, some of us are stopped and asked questions. To pass through, you might have to pass in another sense: to pass as something. We might be stopped when we fail to pass. Those who are not stopped might be assumed to be residing somewhere properly; they become permanent residents, even though there is nothing permanent about their residence.

We can begin with questions. We can be wrapped up by them. How many times have you been asked this question: where are you from? Here is just one time.

I am walking down a street in Cardiff. And I am stopped by someone; he is walking the other way. How interested he seems. In what, am I what? "Hey, where are you from?" The question is asked with a smiling curiosity. I shift around on my feet. It is a familiar question, but it is an uncomfortable familiarity. I know what the question is asking of me. I resist giving the answer I am being asked to give. "Australia," I say. No, I mean originally. "I was born in Salford." The questioner's face creases with irritation. "Where are your parents from then?" He knows I know what he is asking. I give in, wanting to move on. "My father is from Pakistan." That's it. The conversation is over. I have given the right answer, the answer he was waiting for, even hoping for.

To be asked to account for yourself; to give an account of yourself; to feel you have to account for yourself. How do questions fall? On whom do they fall? Moments like this, for many of us, are repeated over time. I am still asked these kinds of questions, though far less often than before, and rarely from those whom I encounter on the fast everyday of the street. More often now, it's a question that gets asked when I say my surname, or by someone I encounter more regularly, but just do not know on a first-name basis.

To be questioned, to be questionable, sometimes can feel like a residence: a question becomes something you reside in. To reside in a question can feel like not being where you are at. Not from here, not? Or maybe to become *not* is to be wrapped up by an assertion. To be asked "Where are you from?" is a way of being told you are not from here. The questioning, the interrogation, can stop only when you have explained yourself. For me to explain myself, to explain where I am from, is not only to give an account of not being from here (being from Australia as not being from here would not suffice; that I am born here in the United Kingdom would not suffice), it is an account of how I ended up brown. Brownness is registered as foreign; brown as elsewhere.

Where else? Ien Ang's wonderful chapter "On Not Speaking Chinese" describes conversations that unfold from the question "Where are you from?," often followed by "Where are you really from?" She suggests that such questions are "typical" for nonwhite people living in Europe (Ang 2001, 29). These questions only appear to be questions; they often work as assertions. When you are stopped, a right to stop you is asserted. In being assertive, such speech acts render you questionable, as someone who can be questioned, as someone who should be willing to receive a question. A body can become a question mark. And we learn from how questions can function as assertions. Some do not get stopped, some can move along, because how they appear is consistent with an expectation of what or who is here. A here can be made into an assertion, not only by who is held up but by who is not.

Being made into a stranger: what do I mean by this? In chapter 1, I referred to an experience I had of being asked by the police, "Are you Aboriginal?" Recalling this experience helped me to think about how the stranger is not anybody but somebody; how the figure of the stranger points to some bodies. The stranger as an anonymous figure is exercised in stranger danger campaigns. The word *anonymous* derives from the word *name*: a stranger is unnamed. But only some unnamed others will be stopped; only some unnamed others will be judged as not having a legitimate purpose. To be identified as a stranger is to be identified as not being from here, or not being entitled to be here; you are identified as someone who endangers who is here. A condensing of this argument: *not from* as endangering *from*. Or being judged as dangerous is a way of making somebody not from.

To become a stranger is not to pass through. To pass through often requires passing out of the figure of the stranger. My own stranger story shared in chapter 1 is really a passing story. If I was at first identifiable as a stranger (there had been burglaries in the area), if I was stopped and asked questions, I was able to move on. Why, how? When they asked me whether I was Aboriginal, I replied that I was not. If I had been Aboriginal, and had identified myself as being Aboriginal, I would not have been allowed to move on. The question would have led to further interrogation. In other words, being able to start up again was a form of racial privilege: if I was brown, I was a brown settler. Being a brown settler is still being a settler.

Race is a complicated address. The second policeman then asked, and the question had the intonation of a quip, "Or is it just a suntan?" Here color becomes *it* (it is all about it). Color becomes something that has to be explained or explained away. The question is an explanation. A tan explains color as domesticated color. A tanned woman would be a woman who acquires her color in the way other Australians do: her color is not a stain on her being; her color is not foreign; her color is even an expression of national character, of what we do in our leisure time.

Sometimes we cease to be in question by giving an explanation that is not our own. So I was able to pass through, to start up again, by being also to pass as white (the suntanned woman is one who acquires her color) and thus to pass into white space. To be a white woman with color is to be bronzed rather than brown. I remember so many comments when I was growing up about being suntanned, often superficially admiring or positive comments: Oh how lucky you are to brown so easily, how lucky you are; how I wish, look at me, with my burned pink red white skin.

How I wish, wish, wish

Smiling

When admiration is given as compensation, it is not admiration. The effort not to be sorry can be a way of being sorry.

Oh dear

But lucky you, dear

Such comments should be grouped together as polite racism, a genre that works to deflect attention from race as if race as such is an embarrassment, something that could not or should not be brought up in polite society. Such speech acts could thus be translated: your color is not a stain on your being; we will give you the benefit of the doubt by assuming you are white underneath, or at least we will pretend you are white underneath because it would be harder, hard, not to pretend.

Whiteness: when color is something that is acquired

Becoming brown not being brown

Becoming not being

In chapter 2, I referred to "presumed heterosexuality," a goodwill presumption that you are heterosexual unless you assert otherwise. Polite racism works to create presumed whiteness. It is deemed more polite to assume you are white. Qualify: it is more polite to assume you are white unless you look black. Racial ambiguity becomes treated as promissory: presumed whiteness assumes the desirability of distance from blackness. Such comments thus also imply:

I don't see you as brown, but tanned like me, which usually means, I don't see you. When people claim they don't see race, it often means they don't see those who are assumed to bring race with them (white: not of color; race: of color). "I don't see race" thus translates as: I don't see those who are not white as not white, which translates as: I don't see not white. In order not to disappear, you have to make your brownness into a willful assertion. Again: some have to become willful just to appear.

More is at stake in how I was able to pass by or pass through in this encounter. I also think by speaking in the voice I have, with the voice I have, I identified myself as being middle class, as being someone who belongs in this neighborhood, as someone they were policing for, not against. This is what intersectionality can mean in practice: being stopped because of how you can be seen in relation to some categories (not white, Aboriginal; not middle class), being able to start up because of how you are seen in relation to others (not Aboriginal; middle class, white).[1]

Intersectionality is messy and embodied. In a wonderful dialogical article, Ruth Frankenberg and Lata Mani reflect on postcoloniality as a politics of location that is shaped by multiple historical trajectories. A location is unstable; an individual history is shaped by longer histories of colonialism. In her riff, Lata Mani (writing as an Indian feminist working in the United States) addresses two moments of arriving at her university after hours. In the first, a white male professor opens the door and refuses her entry: "He cannot let anyone in off the street god knows what you might do" (Frankenberg and Mani 1993, 296). In the second, a Filipina woman is at work cleaning the corridor: "She looks up at me, smiles and without a word opens the door for me" (296).

Anyone: riff-raff.

Someone: smile, come in.

Intersectionality: stopping, starting, anybody, in, somebody, out.

In one moment, you are not allowed in because of how you are seen (you are a stranger; you are brown; you could be anybody). In another moment you are allowed in because of how you are seen (you are a professor; you are brown but of a higher class; you are somebody). Depending on who encounters whom: you are in or not in. And of course it is the professor, not the cleaner, who holds, as it were, the door to the institution; who decides who can reside there, who can be legitimately employed there. Depending on who encounters whom; passing comes up when you do not pass through. When we are talking about passing, we are talking about doors. For some to pass through the door, to enter a room, requires being given permission by those who are holding that door. A door is not just a physical thing that swings on hinges, but a mechanism that enables an opening and a closing. Some have to pass when this mechanism is working.

By *some* I mean: not all. It does not work to say "we are all passing," even if we are all in some sense passing through because we are all, as I suggested earlier, temporary residents. We might say, for instance, all women are passing as women: we pass into or through the category "woman" by being assigned her or assigning ourselves as her. But if you do not constantly have your legitimacy thrown into question, if you are not asked whether you are a woman, constantly, repeatedly, if you do not have the door shut in your face when you try to enter that room, then you do not have to pass as woman in the same way. Passing is what you have to do because or when your legitimacy is in question. Trans women may have to pass in a way that some cis women do not: because of this constant questioning of legitimacy. To pass would not necessarily mean here to pass as women, as if trans women are not women: although the perception of trans women as not women has material life consequences. Juliet Jacques (2010), drawing on Julia Serano (2007), explores precisely this problem: how the passing narrative casts trans women as deceivers or as fraudulent (see also Jacques 2015, 182–89). But sometimes, as Jacques herself notes, passing might be what you have to do to avoid being harassed. To pass as cis is to pass through without being detected: or to try to. Passing might then require a certain kind of confidence: the creation of an impression of having a right to be where you are.

You experience a requirement to justify your existence in the manner of your existence. Diversity work can end up being about a manner of being. Diversity work can end up being about manners.

BEING A QUESTION

Sometimes, whether or not you are asked a question, you feel questionable. Maybe you have been questioned too many times; you come to expect it; you begin to live your life as a question. You feel like a question mark; you feel marked by questions. Sometimes you might be asked questions because of who you are with; or how you are with who you are with. So many times, I have been asked when I enter a local shop with my girlfriend, "Is she your sister?" Who is she? Is it a way of saying, what is your relationship? A relationship can be questionable. Sister: a way of seeing or not seeing lesbian? Sister: a way of evoking an intimacy without naming it, sister as euphemism? A lesbian couple were asked by their newly arrived neighbors, "What are you?" A relationship can appear like a willful object, something that obtrudes, stands out.

When you are heterosexual you might not be asked to explain how you became heterosexual. When you come out as lesbian, gay, or bisexual, you might be asked to give an account of yourself. The sciences of sexology institutionalized this demand: How can we explain perversion? What are the origins of perversion? Who are the perverts? Are you a pervert? Or maybe we could say: in becoming a pervert, you become the one who is questionable, the one whose biography becomes testimony. Every bit of you can become a revelation.

When you deviate from a straight line, it is the deviation that has to be explained. In *Queer Phenomenology*, I shared an anecdote about being asked a question, this time by a neighbor. Let me share this anecdote again.

I arrive home. I park my car and walk toward the front door. A neighbor calls out to me. I look up, somewhat nervously. I have yet to establish good relations with the neighbors. I haven't lived here very long, and the semipublic of the street does not feel easy yet. She mumbles some words, which I cannot hear, and then asks, "Is that your sister, or your husband?" I don't answer and rush into the house.

There are two women, living together, a couple of people alone in a house. So what do you see? The first question reads the two women as sisters. By seeing us as siblings, the question constructs us as alike: like sisters. In this way, the reading both avoids the possibility of lesbianism and also stands in for it, insofar as it repeats the familiar construction of lesbian couples as siblings: lesbians are sometimes represented as if they could be sisters because of their family resemblance. The fantasy of the likeness of sisters (which is a fantasy in the sense that we search for likeness as a sign of a biological tie) takes the place of another fantasy, that of the lesbian couple as being alike, and so alike that they even threaten to merge into one body. Once when I shared this anecdote at a conference, a woman in the audience remarked, "But that is amazing—you're a different race!" While I wouldn't put it quite like that, the comment spoke to me. My girlfriend is white. I am brown. Seeing us as alike or as like sisters meant overlooking signs of difference.

The move from the first question to the second question, without any pause or without waiting for an answer, is fascinating and even now still fascinates me. If not sister, then husband. The second question rescues the speaker, by positing the partner not as female (which even in the form of the sibling risks exposure of what does not get named), but as male. The figure of "my husband" operates as a legitimate sexual other, the other half, a sexual partner with a public face. Or the question could have been a more playful one, in which the figure of the husband was not necessarily a reference to "male": that is, *the husband* could refer to the butch lover. The butch lover would be visible in this address only insofar as she took the place of the husband. Either way, the utterance rereads the oblique form of the lesbian couple, in the way that straightens that form such that it appears straight. Indeed, it is not even that the utterances move from a queer angle to a straight line. The sequence of the utterances offers two readings of the lesbian couple, both of which function as straightening devices: if not sisters, then husband and wife.

It is a long time since that moment. But when we walk down the street, questions still follow us. Or should I say, questions follow her, and me, as part of us, one of two. "Are you a boy or a girl?" they ask her, this time, a question that drips with mockery and hostility. A question hovering around gender: not being housed by gender, being unhoused by gender. Some of these questions dislodge you from a body that you yourself feel you reside in. Once you have been asked these questions, you wait for them; waiting to be dislodged changes your relation to the lodge. Gender could be redescribed in concrete terms of accommodation.

You might not be at home in an existing assignment. In order to be at home, you might have to become insistent. If you are transgender and/or gender nonconforming, you might have to insist on being "he" or "she" or "not he" or "not she" when you are assigned the wrong pronoun; you might have to keep insisting because you are not heard when you indicate your preferences. To be in a same-sex relationship can also involve experiencing the pronoun as a struggle, one that is both personal and political: when your partner is assumed to be "he" or "she," you have to correct the assumption, and the very act of correction is heard as a requirement, an imposition or a demand on others. Heard as a requirement: there is a history abbreviated here of how the modifications required for some to be are heard as making demands on others. This is how political correctness is used: as the imposition of an order that regulates the behavior of others. For some to be is to become an imposition or restriction on the freedom of others. It is exhausting, this labor, which is required because certain norms are still at work in how people are assumed to be and to gather. We also learn: the desire for a more normal life does not necessarily mean identification with norms, but can be a desire to avoid the exhaustion of having to insist just to exist.

If you do not inhabit existing norms, it can be uncomfortable. I often think through the politics of comfort through chairs: furniture is always good to think with. Think of how it feels to be comfortable: say you are sinking into a comfortable chair. Comfort is about the fit between body and object: my comfortable chair might be awkward for you with your differently shaped body. Comfort is about an encounter between more than one body; the promise of a sinking feeling. Heteronormativity functions as a form of public comfort by allowing bodies to extend into spaces that have already taken their shape. Those spaces are lived as comfortable, as they allow bodies to fit in; the surfaces of social space are already impressed upon by the shape of such bodies (like a chair that acquires its shape by the repetition of some bodies inhabiting it: we can almost see the shape of bodies as impressions in the surface). Spaces extend bodies and bodies extend spaces; the impressions acquired by surfaces function as traces of such extensions. Gill Valentine (1996, 49) shows how the "heterosexualisation" of public spaces such as streets is naturalized by the repetition of different forms of heterosexual conduct (images on billboards, music played, displays of heterosexual intimacy, etc.), a process that often goes unnoticed by heterosexual subjects. Streets record the repetition of acts, and the passing by of some bodies and not others.

Heteronormativity also becomes a form of comforting: one feels better through the warmth of being faced by a world one has already taken in. One does not notice this as a world when one has been shaped by that world, and has even acquired its shape. Norms may not only have a way of disappearing from view, but can also be that which we do not consciously feel. If you do not inhabit heterosexuality, when faced by the comforts of heterosexuality you may feel uncomfortable (the body does not sink into a space that has already taken its shape). Queers might be asked not to make others feel uncomfortable, by not displaying any signs of queer intimacy. You might be asked to tone it down, or you might decide to tone it down to avoid creating discomfort. The availability of comfort for some bodies may depend on the labor of others, and the burden of concealment.

Who are you, what are you, explain yourself. A question can have a mood: a pointed sharp utterance thrown at you can throw you. And a question can be addressed to you, as if you yourself are in a mood, or are moody. Someone might say, "What's up?" Or they might say, "What's wrong?" Maybe this question comes out of intimacy: she asks, "What's up?" because she can tell something is wrong by the intonation in your voice, by your expression. But not always: we can get it wrong about whether something is wrong. If the question can find a feeling, it can give form to a feeling. You might not experience anything as being up; you might not feel down. And then: being asked what's up, as if something is up, can bring you down. Nothing, you say grumpily. And then you enact the truth of the judgment by contradicting the judgment; to find as to form.

When you are asked what's wrong, it might refer to your disposition; your face and your body are judged as declaring something wrong. And you might be declaring something wrong. But the question "What's wrong with you?" is not always asked with reference to mood or disposition. A question can be a situation. Maybe you are in a hospital, a place you go when something is wrong with you. Rights and wrongs can be health issues. In becoming ill, you have to give an account of yourself. This is what's wrong with me.

A question can be what does not fall. Maybe when a wrong becomes a question, a right becomes an idea. You are wrong because you are not right; something is not right. A right body might be fully functioning; a right body is upright; an able body. A new baby arrives: to confirm everything is right, toes and fingers are checked.

All present

She is all present

All the fingers, all the toes: a perfect normal child; the right child. As Rosemary Garland-Thomson notes, with reference to Andrew Solomon's work, a disabled child might become a foreigner or stranger to a family. The disabled child becomes the wrong child: "This does not mean that disabled people are unloved or unaccepted within families or communities, but it suggests another way that congenital or early-onset disability can be understood as some version of wrongness, often a benevolent wrongness, because it violates the anticipated continuity of sameness as non disabled status within families. In other words, the seeming wrongness of congenital disability lies in the narrative that the family has got the wrong child, a changeling for the non disabled child who was expected" (2014, n.p.). An expectation of a nondisabled child makes the disabled child the wrong child. When your being is wrong, you are wronged. Garland-Thomson also notes how disabled subjects are perpetually asked the question, "What's wrong with you?" The question that asks what is wrong makes a wrong into an account. Part of the experience of disability is the requirement to give an account of oneself as an account of how things went wrong. An answer might be: I was born this way. Garland-Thomson notes that even those with congenital disabilities become disabled when they are not accommodated by an environment. This is how histories become concrete, as I discuss in more detail in chapter 6. If environments are built to enable some bodies to do what they can, environments can be what stops bodies from doing: a *cannot* is how some bodies meet an environment.

How one answers the question "What's wrong?" matters. A wrong that is made personal (what's wrong with you) can be shown to be a matter of how a person inhabits an environment (it is wrong for me). It might be that we cannot avoid questions: this is what it means to be in question. The political struggle then becomes: to find a better way of answering the questions, ways of questioning the questions, so that the world that makes some beings into questions becomes what we question.

INSTITUTIONAL WORK

We embody diversity by appearing in a way that is inconsistent with the norms of an institution. In formalizing an arrangement, institutions create a residence for some bodies more than others. You can become a stranger within an institution, or a "space invader," to borrow Nirmal Puwar's (2004) evocative term. Diversity work is then the work you do because you do not fit with a series or arrangement. Rosemarie Garland-Thomson describes "a misfit" as follows: "A misfit occurs when the environment does not sustain the shape and function of the body that enters it. The dynamism between body and world that produces fits or misfits comes at the spatial and temporal points of encounter between dynamic but relatively stable bodies and environments. The built and arranged space through which we navigate our lives tends to offer fits to majority bodies and to create misfits with minority forms of embodiment, such as people with disabilities" (2014, n.p.). We have a misfit when there is an incongruous relation of body to thing, or body to world. In an earlier article, Garland-Thomson describes misfitting as "an incongruent relationship between two things: a square peg in a round hole" (2011, 592–93). When you try to fit a norm that is not shaped to fit your body, you create an incongruity. You become an incongruity. As I noted in the conclusion of chapter 4, accessibility becomes diversity work in the second sense: some have to work harder just to be accommodated.

I think of bodies and garments. Over time, a garment clings better to the body that wears it. A garment might even become clingy. A garment and a body are more attuned the more the garment clings to a body. Maybe an institution is like an old garment. It acquires the shape of those who tend to wear it; it becomes easier to wear if you have that shape. Privilege could be rethought in these terms: easier to wear. Privilege is an energy-saving device.

Less effort is required to be or to do. If you arrive with dubious origins, you are not expected to be there, so in getting there you have already disagreed with an expectation of who you are and what you can do, then an institution is the wrong shape; the jumper does not fit. You fidget to try to make it fit, but fidgeting shows all the more that it does not fit. Annette Kuhn describes how as a working-class girl in a grammar school, she feels "conspicuously out of place" ([1995] 2002, 111). And indeed, she describes this sense of being out of place by giving us a biography of her school uniform; how by the time her ill-fitting uniform came to fit, it had become "shabby" and "scruffy" (111). The word *wear* originally derives from the Germanic word for clothing. It then acquires a secondary sense of "use up, gradually damage" from the effect of continued use on clothes. Harder to wear: this is the second sense in which something can be wearing. It wears out; you are worn down.

When you try something on, you test the fit of a garment. Something is trying when it is subject to strain. No wonder: not to inherit privilege is trying.

It can be trying to embody diversity. Your body becomes a performance indicator. You become a tick in a box. You might be one of this many students from working-class backgrounds who get into the university; one of this many people of color hired by the university; one of this many women in senior positions; one of this many students or staff with disabilities. You might be familiar with being one of this many. Perhaps you have become a professor as a member of a minority. We might call you a passing professor. Pierre W. Orelus reflects on how as a professor of color he is often met with surprise. He writes, "After I formally introduce myself in class, I have undergraduate students who ask me, in a surprised tone of voice, 'Are you really the professor?' I sometimes overhear them asking their peers, 'Is he really the professor?'" (2011, 31). Really: Really? Are you sure? Orelus compares this mode of questioning, this sense of curiosity and astonishment, with the questions typically asked of immigrants. Being asked whether you are the professor is another way of being made into a stranger, a body out of place, subject to strain.

You have to make a declarative statement: "Yes, I am a professor." You might have to keep making that statement, because in declaring yourself a professor you might be speaking rather unlike a professor. A passing professor is most insistent.

Some have to insist on belonging to the categories that give residence to others. Another story: we are at a departmental meeting with incoming students. We are all talking about our own courses, one after the other, each coming up to the podium. Someone is chairing, introducing each of us in turn.

She says, this is Professor So-and-So. This is Professor Such-and-Such. On this particular occasion, I happen to be the only female professor, and the only professor of color in the room (the latter was not surprising as I was the only professor of color in the department). When it is my turn to come up, the chair says, "This is Sara." I am the only professor introduced without using the title "professor." What do you do? What to do? Diversity work is how we fill this gap or hesitation. If you point this out, or if you ask to be referred to by the proper name, you are having to insist on what is simply given to others; not only that, you are heard as insistent, or even, for that matter, as self-promoting (as insisting on your due). Maybe some have to be self-promoting because others are promoted by virtue of their membership in a social group. Not only do you have to become insistent in order to receive what was automatically given to the others, but your insistence confirms the improper nature of your residence. We do not tend to notice the assistance given to those whose residence is assumed.

Or maybe you notice that assistance when your own residence is not assumed. In chapter 1, I suggested that noticing puts you in a different world. Here I am suggesting: you notice something because your body puts you in a different world. Another time I walk into a room with a white male professor. I notice how the collective gaze falls on him. It feels like a landing. Plop, plop. You walk in together but you aren't seen as together. Maybe they assume you are an assistant, or a student. They see him as the professor, as they expect a professor to appear this way. He might have a beard, gray hair. Of course there is more to him than that; no doubt there are things they do not see. Quite right; that's the point. When he is seen as professor, there is a way he too is not seen. They are seeing what they expect to see; they are seeing one person and not another as professor. Here comes the professor; he is the professor; hello, professor.

Diversity work might be the work you do when you disappear from the room. You have to work to appear. Or diversity work might be the requirement to give an account of yourself: how you got somewhere. Or diversity work might be the work you do to avoid the necessity of having to explain your arrival. One way of avoiding the necessity of explaining your existence is what I call institutional passing. Institutional passing might include the effort not to stand out or stand apart (although the effort not to stand out can be what makes you stand out). Institutional passing might be what you end up doing when or even because you cannot pass for what you are not (because of the body you have, your history, or for whatever reason). Not being able to pass is often about visibility. You might be too visibly black to pass as white; too visibly disabled to pass as able-bodied; too visibly queer to pass as straight; too visibly trans to pass as cis. When you cannot pass for what you are not, you have to work harder to pass into or through the organization. You might pass by trying *not* to be that kind of minority, the one who belabors the point about being a minority. You might try not to make demands because you know they perceive you as being demanding before you even turn up; because you turn up.

Perhaps you pass by not speaking about yourself as a minority: as if by passing over being not, you would be less intrusive to those who are; or as if by passing over not being white, able-bodied, male, straight, cis, you would not be "not" in quite the same way. You allow others to pass over what makes you a stranger when you cannot eliminate what makes you a stranger. You might do this in order to survive, to pass through safely, let alone progress. One time I tried to set up a discussion group for black and minority ethnic staff (in policy speak abbreviated BME). Only one other person turned up. When discussing this fact with my colleague, he said that many BME staff sense that they have been given the benefit of the doubt by their white colleagues; they have to prove that they arrived on their own merits (and not because they are black or minority ethnic). If you are given the benefit of the doubt, you have to ensure your conduct justifies that benefit. You might have to establish a distance from the kind of minorities who think of themselves as minorities and who make "being a minority" what they profess or part of their profession. Institutional passing: survival within an institution, let alone career progression, might depend on not challenging norms or might even depend upon the extent to which we can increase our proximity to them (by conducting ourselves in the right way, proximity to whiteness often translates as proximity to a certain style of respectable middle-class conduct). You go up by appearing (more) like those who are up. It would be too easy to dismiss this work as assimilation. The idea that those who embody diversity should pay increasing costs for not inhabiting institutional norms would further the injustice of how those norms support and enable the progression of some more than others.[2] Put simply: some do not have to struggle for proximity to norms in order to ensure their own progression. You can inherit proximity; that's true, that too.

Sometimes passing is about trying to be less noticeable. We only have to try to be less noticeable when we are noticeable. To embody diversity is to be noticeable. As we know, diversity is often offered as an invitation. It might be a tagline: minorities welcome. Come in, come in! To be welcomed is to be positioned as not yet part, a guest or stranger, the one who is dependent on being welcomed (the word *welcome*, a "friendly greeting," derives from *will*, "one whose coming suits another's will"). Indeed a welcome can lead us into a precarious situation. The word *precarious* derives from *pray* and means to be held through the favor of another, or dependent on the will of another, which is how *precarious* acquires the sense of risky, dangerous, and uncertain. No wonder: an arrival can be precarious. If you are dependent on a door being opened, how quickly that door can be shut in your face.

We are back to that door, that mechanism that enables some to decide who is to be let in, who is not. But just because they invite you does not mean they expect you to turn up. What happens when a person of color turns up? Oh how noticeable we are in the sea of whiteness:

> When I enter the room, there is shock on people's faces because they are expecting a white person to come in. I pretend not to recognize it. But in the interview there is unease because they were not expecting someone like me to turn up. So it is hard and uncomfortable and I can tell that they are uneasy and restless because of the way they fiddle and twitch around with their pens and their looks. They are uncomfortable because they were not expecting me—perhaps they would not have invited me if they knew I was black and of course I am very uncomfortable. I am wondering whether they are entertaining any prejudice against me.

They are not expecting you. Discomfort involves this failure to fit. A restlessness and uneasiness, a fidgeting and twitching, is a bodily registering of an unexpected arrival.

I pretend not to recognize it: diversity work can be the effort not to notice the bother caused by your own arrival. There is pretense involved; this is not about pretending to be something you are not but pretending not to notice that you are not what they expect. If you cause discomfort (by not fulfilling an expectation of whiteness), you have to work to make them comfortable. You have to pass by passing your way through whiteness, not by becoming white, but by minimizing the signs of difference. Another woman of color describes: "I think with a person of color there's always a question of what's this woman going to turn out like. . . . They're nervous about appointing people of color into senior positions . . . because if I went in my sari and wanted prayer time off and started rocking the boat and being a bit different and asserting my kind of culture, I'm sure they'd take it differently." Some forms of difference are heard as assertive, as "rocking the boat." Some forms of difference become legible as willfulness and obstinacy, as if you are only different because you are insistent (on being different). The pressure not to assert your culture is lived as a demand to pass or to integrate. Note how this pressure can be affective: you experience the potential nervousness as a threat; you try to avoid the nervous glance by not fulfilling its expectation. Maybe you don't wear a sari; you don't want prayer time off, and so on. Or maybe if you do these things, because not doing them is not an option, then you find other ways of not rocking the boat.

Sometimes appearing as a stranger means you try to avoid appearing as a stranger. When you are caught up by an appearance, diversity work is emotional work. You have to manage your own body by not fulfilling an expectation of how you will appear. This quote is from a black male diversity trainer:

> The other point as well about being a black trainer is that I've got to rapport build. Do I do that by being a member of the black-and-white minstrel show, or do I do that by trying to earn respect with my knowledge? Do I do it by being friendly, or do I do it by being cold, aloof, and detached? And what does all this mean to the people now? From my point of view, it probably has nothing to do with the set of people that are in that room because actually the stereotype they've got in their heads is well and truly fixed.

Building rapport becomes a requirement because of a stereotype, as that which is fixed, no matter who you encounter. The demand to build rapport takes the form of a perpetual self-questioning; the emotional labor of asking yourself what to do when there is an idea of you that persists, no matter how you exist. Indeed, the consequences of racism are in part managed as a question of self-presentation: of trying not to fulfill a stereotype, which lodges in the minds of others as an idea of who you are, an expectation of how you will be. As he further describes:

> Don't give white people nasty looks straight in their eyes; don't show them aggressive body positions. I mean, for example, I am going to go and buy a pair of glasses because I know the glasses soften my face and I keep my hair short because I'm going bald, so I need something to soften my face. But actually what I am doing—I am countering a stereotype; I'm countering the black male sexual stereotype and yes, I spend all my time, I counter that stereotype, I couch my language, behavior, and tone in as English a tone as I can. I am very careful, just very careful.

In chapter 2 I suggested that smiling becomes necessary to soften an appearance when you are perceived as too hard. Passing here is about softening your appearance. You have to work not to appear as aggressive because you are as-sumed to be aggressive before you appear. The demand not to be aggressive might be lived as a form of body politics, or as a speech politics: you have to be careful what you say, how you appear, in order to maximize the distance between yourself and their idea of you. The experience of being a stranger in the institutions of whiteness is an experience of being on perpetual guard: of having to defend yourself against those who perceive you as somebody to be defended against. Defenses do not always work; I think we know this.

Diversity work: when you have to try to make others comfortable with the fact of your own existence. Institutional passing can also require working on one's own body in an effort to be accommodating. The effort to rearrange your own body becomes an effort to rearrange the past. This past is not only difficult to budge; it is often what those to whom you appear do not recognize as present.

Institutional passing can involving minimizing signs of difference from in-stitutional norms. Or institutional passing can involve maximizing signs of difference from a set of expectations about what those who are different from norms are like. Institutional passing would then include the work you do to pass through by passing out of an expectation: you try not to be the angry per-son of color, the troublemaker, that difficult person. You have to demonstrate that you are willing to ease the burden of your own difference. The killjoy too appears here as the one that we must give up; institutional passing as appear-ing to fulfill the happiness duty, softening our appearance, smiling because or when we are perceived as too harsh. We smile as compensation, almost as if we are apologizing for existing at all. Of course if we pass as happy, we are not happy. And sometimes we refuse to give up the killjoy; we claim her, stake a claim to her; we might even profess to be her, or create a profession out of her. We learn from the conditions under which she can make her willful appear-ance: sometimes we cannot afford to make a profession out of being a killjoy, whether or not we are assigned her.

CONCLUSION: QUESTIONING BEING

Questions can hover around, a murmuring, an audible rising of volume that seems to accompany an arrival. Perhaps we come to expect that murmur; per-haps we too murmur; we become part of the chorus of questions; we might come to question ourselves. Do I belong here? Will I be caught out? Do I fit in here? "I am" becomes "am I?"

Perhaps any of us can feel the weight of questions that are taken on and in as one's own. We can seek to ask these questions, whatever we are asked. Education aims to throw life back up as a question, after all; these moments of suspension, before things are reassembled, are the moments of being thrown. To throw things up is to be opened up. And we can be thrown in so many ways: by what we encounter, by whom we encounter. Perhaps privilege offers some protection from being questioned or becoming questionable: a buffer zone as a zone without questions. And perhaps the modes of questioning I am describing here relate to how a body is identified in relation to a group whose residence is in question. This is how you can inherit a question, how you can become questionable before you even arrive.

If we have a body that is expected to turn up, we might be less likely to be caught by what comes up. Cultural studies as a discipline begins with the lived experiences of not residing, of not being received well by where you end up, experiences of working-class kids ending up in elite institutions, experiences of diasporic kids ending up in the same institutions. When you don't fit, you fidget. How quickly the fidgeting body appears to be not residing in the right place. Eyebrows are raised. Really; really? Are you sure?

What I am calling diversity work involves transforming questions into a catalog. A catalog does not assume each question as the same question, but it is a way of hearing continuities and resonances. It is a way of thinking of how questions accumulate; how they have a cumulative effect on those who receive them. You can be worn down by the requirement to give answers, to explain yourself. It is not a melancholic task; to catalog these questions, even if some of the questions are experienced as traumatic, difficult, or exhausting. To account for experiences of not being given residence is not only a sad political lesson, a lesson of what we have had to give up in order to keep going. After all, think of how much we know about institutional life because of these failures of residence, of how the categories in which we are immersed become explicit when you do not quite inhabit them. When we do not recede into the background, when we stand out or stand apart, we can bring the background into the front: before we can confront something we have to front up to how much depends on your background.

A questioning can become the source of political excitement and interest. Think about this: when you don't sink, when you fidget and move around, then what is in the background becomes in front of you, as a world that is gathered in a specific way. Discomfort, in other words, allows things to move. Every experience I have had of pleasure and excitement about a world opening up has begun with such ordinary feelings of discomfort, of not quite fitting in a chair, of becoming unseated, of being left holding onto the ground. If we start with a body that does not sink into the chair, the world we describe will be quite different. Perhaps we are speaking here of the promise of reorientation.

Or disorientation

Blink

Descriptions of a world from the point of view of not sinking into a world make things into questions. When we are in question, we question. Perhaps we wonder about things, to return to my discussion in chapter 1, when they do not recede. You know that vase that appears on the mantelpiece. You notice it when it is missing. It becomes striking in its absence; by not being in the right place, you can be struck by its being. What happened to the vase? Where is the vase? It is the beginning of a story: something is missing; you perceive something.

So much political work begins with moments of disorientation. Disorientation involves failed orientations: bodies inhabit spaces that do not extend their shape, or use objects that do not extend their reach. At this moment of failure, a here becomes strange. Bodies that do not follow the line of whiteness, for instance, might be stopped in their tracks: this does not necessarily mean you are stopped from getting somewhere, but it does change your relation to what is here. The world does not recede when you become the stranger, the one who stands out or stands apart. Things might even become oblique for you, even if the feeling of being a stranger has become a familiar feeling. Disorientation can thus move around; it involves not only bodies becoming objects, but also the disorientation in how objects are gathered to create a ground, or to clear a space on the ground. If your arrival can disturb the whole picture, it can be disturbing for the one who arrives.

Frantz Fanon proceeded in his devastating critique of Western ontology (the study of being), a critique that begins with a description of an everyday encounter between a black man and a white child in Paris. To become a black man is to be "sealed into that crushing objecthood," sealed by whiteness (Fanon [1967] 2008, 109).

Sealed by whiteness

Whiteness as seal

From Frantz Fanon, we learn about the experience of disorientation, as the experience of being an object among other objects, of being shattered, of being cut into pieces by the hostility of the white gaze. White, Fanon showed, becomes the universal. Or as Lewis Gordon describes, "White people are universal, it is said and Black people are not" (1999, 34). Black: not universal. Not universal: particular. Not white: particular. To be particular can be to inherit a requirement to tell your particular story. They want to hear from you, about you. If you speak, you are heard as speaking about yourself, whatever you say. To be particular can be to be lodged in a body. We speak back, if we begin with this requirement, if we seize hold of how we are held, willfully. This is a promise: those lodged as particular can dislodge the general. We can dislodge a lodge by showing how we are lodged, how we are sealed into the object or thing, not subject, not human; not universal. We have many histories, many points of arrival, those of us who somehow find themselves not. A not can be the basis of a rebellion. Being not, not being, being in question; it can be an affinity, one that is behind us. An affinity can be the startle of being in question, of being as a question.

To be in question is to question being.

6 / BRICK WALLS

Thus far I have considered diversity work in two senses: the work we do when we aim to transform the norms of an institution, and the work we do when we do not quite inhabit those norms. These two senses often meet in a body: those who do not quite inhabit the norms of the institution are often those given the task of transforming these norms.

A meeting point is often a laboring point. If you are not white, not male, not straight, not cis, not able-bodied, you are more likely to end up on diversity and equality committees. The more nots you are, the more committees you might end up on. Not being not can mean being less likely to end up doing this kind of work. Given that diversity work is typically less valued by organizations, then not being not can mean having more time to do more-valued work. And I think this is really important: so much of what we have to do, because of what or who we are not, is not recognized. When we are diversity workers in both senses this both tends to be obscured as if doing diversity is just about being diversity, or as if being is all we have to do. In fact, as I showed in chapter 5, for diversity workers being is never "just being." There is so much you have to do to be.

In chapter 2, I referred to one practitioner's description of diversity work as a "banging your head against a brick wall job." Walls often come up when we are doing diversity work. Practitioners regularly use wall expressions to describe their work. In this chapter, I want to reflect on walls, brick walls, institutional walls; those hardenings of histories into barriers in the present:

barriers that we experience as physical; barriers that are physical. We often use wall expressions to talk about the obstacles that prevent us from realizing a desire or completing an action (an obvious example would be the expression used by marathon runners: "hitting a wall"). Throughout this chapter I will be showing how taking walls seriously, as a metaphor, but also as more than a metaphor, is a way we can offer a materialism that shows how history becomes concrete. Walls allow us to think about how obstacles can be physical, in the world, and yet how these obstacles are only obstacles for some bodies. If the two senses of diversity work meet in our bodies, they also meet here: at the wall.

HARD HISTORIES

I want to start by working closely with the description of diversity work as a "banging your head against a brick wall job." What are brick walls doing in this saying? When we use this expression, we are not saying there is an actual wall in front of us. There is no spectacle, no towering thing; nothing that we can point to and say "there it is." We can start with what is implied by what we are not addressing: the brick wall is a metaphor. The expression suggests that doing diversity is like banging your head against a brick wall. The metaphor seems to be pointing to a quality of feeling: this is what diversity work feels like.

But still we can ask: what does this metaphor mean? When I wrote *On Being Included*, the copyeditor suggested I take *tangible* out of my discussion of walls because the walls I was referring to were metaphorical walls, not literal or actual walls. The wall, in being used as a metaphor, is not real in the sense of a tangible thing, what is perceptible through touch. But the metaphor (something is like something) of the wall seems to matter to convey how these institutional processes become something that can be touched. A wall is what you come up against. It is a physical contact; a visceral encounter. When I write this, I might not at first be talking of literal walls. A wall is an effect of coming up against.

The likeness is the effect.

Now we are talking.

I want to return to one of the examples discussed in chapter 4 as an example of coming up against a brick wall. In this case, a new policy is adopted by an organization that requires all academics on interview panels to have diversity training. The practitioner spoke of the different ways the policy was almost stopped from being implemented. A policy also has to get through an organization: it has to be written as a proposal, discussed in committees, recorded in the minutes as agreed, and passed on to a higher committee before it can become policy. In this case, eventually, after considerable work from multiple actors, a policy is agreed to by a higher committee, the one that can authorize the decisions made by other committees. And still nothing happens. It is as if no one has even heard of the policy. In this example, a lot of things could have stopped something from happening. It could have been the removal of the policy from the minutes; it could have been that no one from the diversity committee that agreed to the policy was on the higher committee; it could have been that no one on the higher committee noticed this removal; but it was none of these things. It was simply this: those employed by the institution acted as if this policy had not been agreed upon even though it had.

We need to understand these mechanisms. We need to make the impasse or blockage the occasion for more thought. From this example, we learn that the passing of something, an agreement, can be how something is stopped. Doing diversity work has taught me that agreeing to something is one of the best ways of stopping something from happening. Agreeing to something is an efficient technique for stopping something because organizations can avoid the costs of disagreement.

A brick wall refers not only to what is stopped but to how something is stopped. A wall is a defense system: if a blockage is unblocked here, it can reappear elsewhere. Being an institutional plumber can often feel like you are lagging behind what you are following. I suspect there is a connection here between the sense of being behind the organization and that killjoy feeling of being stuck on fast forward: as if you have to rush to catch up with others. You do have to rush: what blocks you seems to be just ahead of you. The wall refers to what keeps its place or stays in place; what is stationary. However, the mechanisms for stopping something are mobile. For something to be immobile (for an institution not to be moved by the efforts to transform it), the means for defending against movement move.

The wall is a finding. Let me summarize that finding: what stops movement moves.

We learn from this: that when you notice movement (and movement is often what catches our attention), we are not noticing what stays put.

I can still hear voices saying, but isn't the brick wall a metaphor? It is not that there really is a wall; it is not an actual wall. This is right. The wall is a wall that might as well be there, because the effects of what is there are just like the effects of a wall. And yet not: if an actual wall was there, we would all be able to see it, or to touch it. And this makes an institutional wall hard. You come up against what others do not see; and (this is even harder) you come up against what others are often invested in not seeing. After all, if the diversity worker had not attempted to change the existing policy, the wall would not come up. The wall comes up in response to the effort to modify an existing arrangement. When no attempt at modification is made, a wall is not necessary; nothing needs to be blocked or stopped.

Diversity work is hard because what you come up against is not revealed to others. I have been speaking here of diversity work as hard in the sense of difficult. But the brick wall is hard in other senses. In physics, hardness refers to the resistance of materials to change under force. The harder something is, the more force we have to apply. When we use the description "it is a banging your head against a brick wall," we are referring to coming up against something that is hard. Let's talk about actual walls. A wall is hard; it matters that a wall is made from hard matter. Let's say the wall is made from cement. Cement is a binder: it is a substance that sets and hardens and can combine other materials together. Through cement, bricks can be stuck together firmly to become walls. Hardness is necessary for the wall to function or to be functional. A wall has a job to do. A wall too has a job description.

You can witness the hardness of a wall. Say you throw something against the wall: a little object. You can tell how hard the wall is by what happens to what is thrown against it: a wall might be scratched at the surface by encountering the object. And this too is what diversity work can feel like: scratching at the surface, scratching the surface. The object might splinter and break by the force of what it comes up against. Hardness here is a quality of something revealed through an encounter between things. Diversity work certainly involves an encounter between things: our bodies can be those little objects hurled against walls, those sedimented histories. Watch what happens. Ouch. And maybe it happens, time and time again. Banging your head—we sense the point of this phrase as the sore point of repetition. The wall keeps its place, so it is you that gets sore. I come up against a wall if I try to change something that has become harder or hardened over time. Literally I mean: a wall as material resistance to being changed by force. The materiality of resistance to transformation: diversity workers know this materiality very well. We live this materiality.

Materiality: if we are hit by something, we become conscious of something. Of course we learned from *Mrs. Dalloway* that you can be hit by something before you become conscious of something. If we are hit by something, again and again, our body might register this impact as an expectation: that the wall will come up. Diversity workers become conscious of the brick wall as that which keeps its place *after* an official commitment to diversity has been given. Timing matters. It is the practical effort to transform institutions that allows this wall to become apparent.

This practical effort, let us be clear here, is somebody's effort: it is the effort of a diversity worker; of her blood, sweat, and tears. That I can share this story is also a consequence of the efforts of a diversity worker. I used to think that as a researcher I was generating data on diversity work, but I have come to realize diversity work generates its own data. We are thickening our descriptions of institutions by showing how institutions are thick; thick in the sense of a deep or heavy mass.

The story of a diversity policy that does not do anything is a tantalizingly tangible example of what goes on so often. But even if the story makes something tangible, it shows us how some things are reproduced by stubbornly remaining intangible. After all, the diversity worker has to labor to convince others of the existence of the policy even though she has paper evidence of that policy ("I can show you the minutes"). She has evidence; she can point to it; but it is as if she has nothing to show. We learn from this: intangibility can be a product of resistance; it could even be described as an institutional achievement.

Diversity work: you learn that tangibility is quite a phenomenon. In recent years, for example, I have been involved in an effort to challenge the problem of sexual harassment in universities. And this has been an experience of coming up against wall after wall. As Leila Whitley and Tiffany Page (2015) have shown, there is a problem in locating the problem of sexual harassment. A wall can come up to prevent students from making complaints in the first place. Often students are actively discouraged by explicit argument or implicit narratives: if you complain, you will hurt your career (this can work as a threat: you will lose the very connections that enable you to progress); or if you complain, you will hurt the professor (whose reputation will be damaged); or if you complain, you will ruin a center or collective (often aligned with something critical and progressive). Another wall comes up once complaints have been made. Testimonies are heard as an injury to the professor's reputation, as what stops him from receiving the benefits to which he is entitled. Complaints about sexual harassment are not made public as a way of protecting the organization from damage. Even if the complaints are successful, even if a contract is terminated (which is rare) or someone leaves rather than face a tribunal, it can be as if what happened never happened. No one is allowed to speak of it; no one speaks of it. A wall can be the effort to stop a complaint from being made. If that complaint is made, then a wall can be what happens to a complaint; how it is stopped from going through the whole system.

Indeed so often just talking about sexism as well as racism is heard as damaging the institution. If talking about sexism and racism is heard as damaging institutions, we need to damage institutions. And the institutional response often takes the form of damage limitation. This is so often how diversity takes institutional form: damage limitation.

You encounter the materiality of resistance to transformation when you try to transform what has become material. Sexual harassment is material. It is a network that stops information from getting out. It is a set of alliances that come alive to stop something; that enable a complaint to be held up or to become confidential, so that it never comes out into the public domain. And notice here: so many complex things are going on at the same time. It is not activity that is coordinated by one person or even necessarily a group of people who are meeting in secret, although secret meetings probably do happen. All of these activities, however complex, sustain a direction; they have a point. Direction does not require something to originate from a single point: in fact a direction is achieved through consistency between points that do not seem to meet. Things combine to achieve something that is solid and tangible; bonds become binds. If one element does not hold, or become binding, another element holds or binds. The process is rather like the cement used to make walls: something is set into a holding pattern. The setting is what hardens. Perhaps when people notice the complexity, or even the inefficiency and disorganization, they don't notice the cement. When you say there is a pattern, you are heard as paranoid, as if you are imagining that all this complexity derives from a single point.

A pattern is experienced as weight. We learn from this: to try to bring someone to account is to come up against not just an individual but histories, histories that have hardened, that stop those who are trying to stop what is happening from happening. The weight of that history can be thrown at you; you can be hit by it. The word *harass*, remember, derives from the French *harasser*, "tire out, vex." When you speak of harassment you can end up being harassed all over again. Harassment is a network that stops information from getting out by making it harder to get through. It is how someone is stopped by being worn down. What happens to a policy can happen to a person. A policy disappears despite there being a paper trail, despite the evidence, or perhaps even because of the evidence. People disappear too, because of what they make evident, of what they try to bring into view. Sometimes these are the choices: get used to it, or get out of it. No wonder if these are the choices, many get out of it.

Sexual harassment works—as does bullying more generally—by increasing the costs of fighting against something, making it easier to accept something than to struggle against something, even if that acceptance is itself the site of your own diminishment; how you end up taking up less and less space. It is because we perceive this wall that we end up having to modify our perception (perhaps this is what it means to get "used to it"). You might feel you cannot afford to become alienated from those around you; not only might you lose access to material resources (references, scholarships, courses to teach), but you might lose friends, connections that matter. Maybe you too begin to feel that the wall is inside your own head. I return to this idea of an inside wall in chapter 7. It is happening all around you, and yet people seem to be getting on with it. You can end up doubting yourself, estranged from yourself. Maybe then you try not to have a problem. But you are left with a sickening feeling.

Because all around you there is a partial sighting of walls, a partial sighting that is at once a justification: oh he's a bit of a womanizer; oh yeah I was warned about him; oh yeah that was the booze talking; there might even be a smiling, a joking, there might even be a certain kind of affection. This affection is structured as an appeal to students whose concern is bordering on disclosure: let it go; let him off. A culture is built around this affection, which is to say: harassers are enabled by being forgiven, as if their vice is our virtue. And those who know it is wrong even when they try to persuade themselves otherwise, even when they try to minimize a mountain of abuse, can feel all the more wrong, can feel the full force of it, when the wall finally does come into view: she is not okay; I am not okay; this is not okay; "How could I let this happen?"

Guilt; shame; they can leak out, getting everywhere. Perhaps sometimes we just can't do this; it means being prepared to be undone, and we just don't know if we are ready to put ourselves back together again, as I discussed in chapter 1. I also explored in that chapter how to expose a problem is to pose a problem. We can now see how, if to expose a problem is to pose a problem, then the problem you expose is not revealed. The exposure becomes the problem. It is not surprising then that those who don't come up against walls experience those who talk about walls as wall makers. And we are back to the feminist killjoy. It is never long before she makes an appearance. The feminist killjoy is understood as a wall maker. The wall maker is the one who makes things harder than they need to be; she makes things hard for herself. Just recall the words of the diversity practitioner: "They just look at me as if I am saying something really stupid." We can imagine the eyes rolling when she points out the policy, when she tries to say, to show, that she has institutional support.

A wall comes up in the reframing of walls as immaterial, as phantoms, as how we stop ourselves from being included, how we stop ourselves from doing something, from being something. To think about materiality through institutional brick walls is to offer a different way of thinking the connection between bodies and worlds. Materiality is about what is real; it is something real that blocks movement, which stops a progression. But this something is not always something that can be apprehended. It might be an arrangement of things, a social as well as physical arrangement, that stops something from happening or a body passing through or information from getting out. It might be the force of momentum that carries something forward, that picks up more and more things, so that more and more weight is acquired, so that things tend that way, bodies lean that way, almost independently of individual will. I return to this *almost* in the final section of the chapter. This means that what is real, what is in concrete terms the hardest, is not always available as an object that can be perceived (from some viewing points), or an object that can touched (even by those who are seated at the same table). What is the hardest for some does not even exist for others.

A LIFE DESCRIPTION

Diversity work in the second sense also involves coming up against walls. When we fail to inhabit a norm (when we are questioned or question ourselves whether we are "it," or pass as or into "it") then it becomes more apparent, like that institutional wall: what does not allow you to pass through.
    A job description can be a wall description.
    A life description can be a wall description.
I have already noted how when diversity workers talk about walls, the walls become phantom walls, as if we bring the walls into existence by talking about their existence. When something is not really in our way, we are in our way. We have to show what we know: walls are not just perceptions. But perception

A life description

does still matter. Some perceptions are walls. What you are perceived as being can be what stops you from being.

Let's return to my discussion of stranger danger from chapters 1 and 5. There are techniques, bodily as well as disciplinary techniques, whereby some bodies are recognized as strangers, as bodies out of place, as not belonging in certain places. These techniques are formalized in Neighborhood Watch programs in which the stranger is the one whom citizens must recognize in order to protect themselves: their property, their bodies (Ahmed 2000, 2004). Recognizing strangers becomes a moral and social injunction. Some bodies are in an instant judged as suspicious, or as dangerous, as objects to be feared, a judgment that is lethal. There can be nothing more dangerous to a body than the social agreement that that body is dangerous. We can simplify: it is dangerous to be perceived as dangerous.

There are so many cases, too many cases. Just take one: Trayvon Martin, a young black man fatally shot by George Zimmerman on February 26, 2012. Zimmerman was centrally involved in his Neighborhood Watch program. He was doing his civic neighborly duty: looking out for what is suspicious. As George Yancy has noted in his important piece "Walking while Black," we learn from Zimmerman's call to the dispatcher how Trayvon Martin appeared to him. Zimmerman says, "'There's a real suspicious guy.' He also said 'This guy looks like he's up to no good or he's on drugs or something.' When asked by the dispatcher, he said, within seconds, that, 'He looks black.' Asked what he is wearing, Zimmerman says, 'A dark hoodie, like a gray hoodie.' Later, Zimmerman said that 'now he's coming toward me. He's got his hands in his waist band.' And then, 'And he's a black male'" (Yancy 2013, n.p.). If some questions are assertions in disguise, some assertions are just that: assertions. Note the sticky slide: suspicious, "up to no good," coming at me, looking black, a dark hoodie, wearing black, being black. The last statement makes explicit who Zimmerman was seeing right from the very beginning. That he was seeing a black man was already implied in the first description, "a real suspicious guy." He is up to no good: his hands are in his waistband; a gun might as well appear because he is here. The unarmed black man is seen as armed whether or not he is armed. He is seen as armed; seen as arm. The wayward arm makes another appearance. You become arm when your whole body is perceived as a potential weapon. Unarmed; armed; arm.

Let me repeat: there can be nothing more dangerous to a body than the social agreement that that body is dangerous. And later, when Zimmerman is not convicted, there is a retrospective agreement with that agreement: that Zimmerman was right to feel fear, that his murder of this young man was self-defense because Trayvon was dangerous, because he was, as Yancy describes so powerfully, "walking while black," already judged, sentenced to death, by the how of how he appeared. Racism is a matter of perception, as Claudia Rankine (2014) has shown so convincingly: a black body is magnified, appears larger, a demon; immigrants appear more, a swamp, a spread. The law makes this perception, however wrong, a right; a right to kill as the right to perceive the other as a wrong or to perceive the other wrongly. Racism makes a wrong a right. If racism is a matter of perception, perception matters.

The stranger is a dark shadowy figure. I use the word *dark* deliberately here: it is a word that cannot be untangled from a racialized history. To use this word as if it can be disentangled from that history is to be entangled by that history. The very perception of others is thus an impression of others: to appear as a stranger is to be blurry. The blurrier the figure of the stranger, the more bodies can be caught by it. Racism is a blunt instrument. Stop and search, for example, is a technology that makes this bluntness into a point: Stop! You are brown! You could be Muslim! You could be a terrorist! The blunter the instrument, the more bodies can be stopped. To explore how bodies are perceived as dangerous in advance of their arrival thus requires not beginning with an encounter (a body affected by another body) but asking how encounters come to happen in this way or that. The immediacy of bodily reactions is mediated by histories that come before subjects, and which are at stake in how the very arrival of some bodies is noticeable in the first place. The most immediate of our bodily reactions can be treated as pedagogy: we learn about ideas by learning how they become quick and unthinking. There is nothing more mediated than immediacy. You can be stopped by a perception. You can be killed by a perception.

Strangers become objects not only of perception but also of governance: bodies to be managed. You can be managed out of existence. Gentrification is a public policy for managing strangers: a way of removing those who would be eyesores; those who would reduce the value of a neighborhood; those whose proximity would be registered as price. We learn from this. There are technologies in place that stop us from being affected by some bodies; those that might get in the way of how we occupy space. We might not even have to turn away from those who would get in the way.

Walls are how some bodies are not encountered in the first place.

Walls are how other bodies are stopped by an encounter.

Indeed an exploration of the role of walls in politics might first explore walls as borders: a walled nation, a walled neighborhood. As Wendy Brown (2010) notes, walls built from concrete and barbed wire function as barricades. Walls are put up by governments as a mechanism to control the flow of human traffic. Brown demonstrates how walls as a stark image of sovereign power are reminders of a failed sovereignty. A border is instituted most violently when it is under threat.

A wall comes up to defend something from someone; walls as defense mechanisms.

A wall becomes necessary because the wrong bodies could pass through.

Even in the case of physical walls that make concrete the intent to bar and to block, walls are differentiated: some bodies are allowed to pass through, which means that the wall does not come up in the same way even if a wall is there, literally, actually. A wall is not encountered as a wall: it is an open door, a passage through. A wall remains functional: for the body who is allowed through, the function of such a wall is to stop others from getting through. As Leila Whitley (2014) explores, for those who pass through without a door being opened, without legitimate documents, a body becomes a border. A body can be a document: if your papers are not in the right place, neither are you.

Whitley shows how those who manage to get through without the right papers experience the border as imminent, always potential, as that which could come up at any time. When you know you could be stopped at any time, a wall is anywhere and everywhere. A border then would not be what you leave behind when you cross a border; a border would go with you wherever you go. I return to another way in which bodies can become walls in chapter 7.

Some bodies might appear wrong even with the right papers; histories of racism are condensed in the very figure of the stranger as the one who does not pass by receding into whiteness, as I noted in chapter 5. A wall can be how you are stopped from residing somewhere. Or a wall can be what you experience once you get here.

We could think of whiteness as a wall. You know that experience: you walk into a room and it is like a sea of whiteness. A sea: a wall of water. It can feel like something that hits you. It is not just that you open the door and see whiteness but that the door feels as if it is slammed in your face, whether or not it is. It is not always that you are not allowed in. You might even be welcomed; after all, you would promise to add diversity to an event. But you would feel uncomfortable. You would stick out like a sore thumb. So you might leave the situation voluntarily, because it would be too uncomfortable to stay. When you leave, you leave whiteness behind you.

For those who are not white, whiteness can be experienced as wall: something solid, a body with mass that stops you from getting through. Whiteness can be like that crowd I discussed in chapter 2: many as momentum, many as movement. Things are fluid if you are going the way things are flowing. If you are not going that way, a flow acquires the density of a thing, something solid. What one body experiences as solid, another might experience as air.

A wall; no wall. There; nothing there.

Flight, bright, light, white.

There; nothing there. No wonder "there" can become despair.

Heavy, slow, down, brown.

When you speak of whiteness, it can then seem like you are making something from nothing. We speak of whiteness. We keep speaking of whiteness. Walls come up. Walls keep coming up. One time after I gave a talk on whiteness, a white man in the audience said, "But you're a professor?" You can hear the implication of this *but*: but look at you, Professor Ahmed, look how far you have gone! How easily we can become poster children for diversity, how easily we can be held up as proof that women of color are not held up. Being a diversity poster child: it can make the world you come up against recede as if you bring it to an end; as if our arrival and progression makes whiteness disappear.

> Look at you: look, look!
>
> A diversity poster child.
>
> I am supposed to smile.
>
> I don't smile.

Your own body becomes used as evidence that the walls of which you speak are not there or are no longer there; as if you have eliminated the walls through your own progression. You got through, so they are not there. The figure of the wall maker discussed in the previous section is transformed into the wall breaker: as if by progressing and professing we bring the walls down.

When women of color become professors, this is not the only kind of reaction we receive. When a colleague of mine, a feminist of color, became a professor, someone said to her, "They give professorships to anyone these days." In one case you fulfill the fantasy of meritocracy, a singular brown body becoming shiny happy evidence of inclusion. In the other, the very fact of your arrival erodes the value of what it is that you enter, tarnishing something shiny. A wall can come up by how she becomes evidence that there are no walls (see: she was not stopped by being brown or female); or by how her progression becomes deflation (see: if she can become a professor, anyone can).

No wonder, when you bring up walls, some people just blink. It is another way in which you might encounter startle: the startle of what you bring up as well as the startle of turning up. And we are not simply talking here about a difference of view; some people see the world in one way, others in another way. When you bring up walls, you are challenging what lightens the load for some; you are questioning how space is occupied as being for some. You become a threat to the easing of a progression when you point out how a progression is eased.

Coming up against walls teaches us that social categories precede a bodily encounter, deciding how a body appears in an instant. This is where things get real. We have a way of responding to the arguments that gender and race are not material while class is material, an argument articulated so often that it feels like another wall, another blockage that stops us from getting through. The walls are precisely evidence of the materiality of race and gender; though of course this is a materiality that only some come up against. Many of the recent arguments against intersectionality, identity politics, and so on (this is not my *and so on*: this is not my sticking together of words as a way of sticking together certain bodies, but one I have encountered in some recent writings by some Marxist writers, and by *some* I mean some) as being somehow less material than class can be understood as an enactment of privilege, the alignment of body to world. Race might seem immaterial or less material if you are white; gender might seem immaterial or less material if you are a cis man; sexuality might seem immaterial or less material if you are straight; (dis)ability might seem immaterial or less material if you are able-bodied, and so on. Class too can be understood in these terms: class might seem to be immaterial or less material if you benefit from class privilege, those networks and buffer zones; those ways a body is already somehow attuned to a bourgeois set of requirements.

If walls are how some bodies are stopped, walls are what you do not encounter when you are not stopped; when you pass through. Again: what is hardest for some does not exist for others.

ACADEMIC WALLS

In this section I want to think more about academic walls. Universities too have walls, and I am not only speaking of the mandate to become the police, to become Neighborhood Watch; to look over and at students with suspicion, to count the bodies of international students—are they all present; they are all present—although we can and must include that mandate.[1] It is through doing diversity work within the academy that I began to understand how walls are mechanisms; to understand how things keep their place. The diversity work I am describing in this section primarily relates to pointing out sexism and racism within citational practice (and by this I include not only who is cited in written texts but who is speaking at events). In my introduction to this book I described citations as academic bricks through which we create houses. When citational practices become habits, bricks form walls. I think as feminists we can hope to create a crisis around citation, even just a hesitation, a wondering, that might help us not to follow the well-trodden citational paths. If you aim to create a crisis in citation, you tend to become the cause of a crisis.

When we speak about what we come up against, we come up against what we speak about.

Another way of saying: walls come up when we talk about walls.

Diversity work is often about making points; we might call these sore points. You make public what you notice. You might point out that apparently open or neutral gatherings are restricted to some bodies and not others. You often become a sore point when you point out such restrictions, almost as if, without pointing them out, they would not exist. In simple terms: when you notice a restriction, you cause a restriction.

For example, when you make an observation in public that the speakers for an event are all white men, or all but one, or the citations in an academic paper are to all white men, or all but a few, a rebuttal often follows that does not take the form of contradiction but rather explanation or justification: these are the speakers or writers who just happen to be there; they happen to be white men. You say: this event has a structure. The response becomes: this is an event, not a structure. It is as if by describing the event as having a structure, you are imposing a structure on the event. Even by describing a gathering as "white men," you are then assumed to be imposing certain categories onto bodies, reducing or failing to grasp the heterogeneity of an event; solidifying through your own description something that is fluid.

When you describe stabilization as worldly, a restriction in who gathers that is in the world, you are treated as stabilizing a world as if it is a thing. So much is invested in not noticing how social and institutional gatherings are restricted. There is what we might call a goodwill assumption that things have just fallen like that, the way a book might fall open at a page, and that it could just as easily fall another way, on another occasion. Of course the example of the book is instructive; a book will tend to fall open on pages that have been most read. As I explored in chapter 2, tendencies are acquired through repetition. A tendency is a direction: it is a leaning that way, a falling that way, a going that way. Once a tendency has been acquired, a conscious effort to go that way is no longer necessary. Things fall that way almost of their own accord. The reproduction of the same thing is precisely what does not have to be willed. No wonder there is so much investment in not recognizing how restrictions are structured by decisions that have already been made. These restrictions are precisely what do come into view. And no wonder diversity work is so trying: it takes a conscious willed effort not to reproduce an inheritance.

In the previous chapter I referred to diversity work as a cataloging of incidents.

A wall is a catalog.

A history of what comes up.

One time I pointed out that the speakers for a gender studies conference were all white. Someone replied that my statement did not recognize the diversity of the speakers. When perceiving whiteness is a way of not perceiving diversity, diversity becomes a way of not perceiving whiteness.

Another time I suggested an exercise on Twitter: go to the index of a book near to hand and count how many of the references are to men and to women. I did my exercise with a book that happened to be on my desk at the time (I was reading it for my project on utility). Out of hundreds of citations to individuals in the index, I could find only a few references to women. Two of these were telling: a woman referred to as the partner of a male artist; a woman referred to as a daughter of a male god.

Sexism: women as existing only in relation to men; women as female relatives. I tweeted this finding, and the author replied that I had described the patterns right as "they were in the traditions that influenced" him. It is interesting that justifying sexism is one of the few times that passivity (x is in what I read, so x is in what I write) becomes a masculine and academic virtue. Sexism is justified as what is received because it is assumed as in what is received. Sexism becomes a received wisdom. Sexism, in other words, by being accepted as in the pattern or in the traditions is rendered not only acceptable but inevitable.

Sexism: the elimination of a gap between inheritance and reproduction. One time I pointed out the whiteness of the field of new materialism. Someone invested in that field replied to me that it might be right to describe the field as white but that this whiteness was "not intended." Citational privilege: when you do not need to intend your own reproduction. Once something has been reproduced, you do not need to intend its reproduction. You have to do more not to reproduce whiteness than not to intend to reproduce whiteness. Things tend to fall how they have tended to fall unless we try to stop things from falling that way. An intending is required given this tending, given this tendency.

Another time I had a conversation with someone on Facebook about the masculinist nature of a certain field of philosophy. They responded with a "well of course," as if to say, well of course it is like that. It is the philosophy of technology. I have begun calling these kinds of arguments disciplinary fatalism: the assumption that we can only reproduce the lines that are before us. Disciplinary fatalism rests on the gender fatalism discussed in chapter 1, "boys will be boys" becoming "boys studying toys will be boys studying toys." We can note here how fatalistic arguments make something inevitable: it will be this way. They then record the consequence of their arguments as evidence of the argument: it is this way. The techniques that justify something as intrinsic are intrinsic to making something be what it is. A momentum is almost enough to keep things going that way; the force of a momentum is supplemented by justifications, denials, prompts, persuasions, which all participate in sustaining a direction. A momentum lessens the effort required to bring something about (just as it increases the effort required not to bring something about, as I described in chapter 4). Individual effort is still required, perhaps at those moments of deviation, when the rightness of a path is questioned. A hand might then appear to stop things from going astray.

Another time I was invited to speak at a conference on phenomenology. I was sent the calls for papers, which referred to twelve white men and one white woman. I pointed out this citational practice, and the person who invited me was very apologetic; he said my point made him "feel somewhat ashamed." Perhaps we learn from this response how feminism becomes dismissible as moralizing: as if the point of making feminist points is to shame others, to make them feel bad. The discourse of moralizing is about how feminist ideas are received, not how they are sent out. After all, you can feel bad as a way of doing nothing, and we send out these letters because we want something to be done.

The histories of racism as well as sexism are littered with good intentions and bad feelings; they seem to bind together in a certain way, as if to say: by feeling bad, I mean well.

This invitation was not unusual: I have had numerous invitations to be a speaker at events when the calls for papers refer only to white men (or all but one). You can be invited to reproduce what you do not inherit. The wall breaker is about to make another appearance here. Whiteness can be reproduced by the assumption that by inviting you (somebody not white), they will bring an end to it. Whiteness: by invitation only. We do not bring an end to it. The genealogy remains the same despite or even through the extension of an invitation to somebody who is not part of that genealogy. Inviting those who are not white to insert themselves into whiteness can be how whiteness is reinserted.

If we question the genealogy, we learn the techniques for its reproduction. In his e-mail response, the person who invited me wrote that he knew of feminists and scholars of color working in this area and gave an explanation of why he did not cite them: "I believe my predominant mentioning of white men and the deficits in their theorizing is—in an unreflected way—owed to the circumstance that I do try to also cater to my more conservative colleagues, who I feel might need a kind of reassurance, achieved by citing people they are well acquainted with." Sexism and racism as citational practices are also a catering system; justified as a form of reassurance, a way of keeping things familiar for those who want to conserve the familiar. They are a way of keeping acquaintance, a friendship network, a kinship network, something that white men do on behalf of other white men, to reassure them that the system in which they reproduce themselves will be reproduced.

A system in which we are acquainted is a system of acquaintances.
Friendly, like.

White men: a citational relational. Perhaps thought as such becomes something that happens "between men," to borrow the title of Eve Kosofsky Sedgwick's (1985) important book on homosociality. I have had so many experiences within the academy of how intellectual life is assumed to be between men. Another time a male professor writes an e-mail in which he mentions a new woman colleague appointed to his center. He notes her credentials. And then he writes that she was a student of such-and-such male professor. He then adds for emphasis, "Yes, the" such-and-such male professor, who was taught by another such-and-such male professor, and was friends with another such-and-such male professor. Yes, the: the letter was gushing about men, passing over the woman quickly to get to the main point/men point. She is mentioned only in relation to men: and the relationship between men (which reads like a closed circle, or a closing of a circle: male teachers, friends, colleagues) is established as the primary relationship.

Sexism: how women are introduced only to be passed over.

Another time I was interviewing a practitioner. She shared with me a story. She had been looking at the new web page of the senior management team at her university. They had just put up photographs of each member of the team. Her friend looked over her shoulder and asked, "Are they related?" Are they related? What a good question. Well perhaps they are not related in the sense of how we might usually use the word *related*. They are not related. Or are they? Each member of the team could be one of a kind. The homogeneity of an appearance registered by or in this question points to another sense of being related: being as relation. They were all, as it happens, white men. To use this expression is not to summarize a relation; the relation is itself a summary (how the institution can be built around a short series of points). The photograph gives us a summary of a summary: this is who the organization is; this is who the organization is for. Of course an image can change without changing a thing. This is why diversity is so often a poster: as I discussed in chapter 5, you can change the whiteness of an image in order to keep the whiteness of a thing.

When we talk of white men, we are describing something. We are describing an institution. An institution typically refers to a persistent structure or mechanism of social order governing the behavior of a set of individuals within a given community. So when I am saying that white men is an institution, I am referring not only to what has already been instituted or built but the mechanisms that ensure the persistence of that structure. A building is shaped by a series of regulative norms. White men refers also to conduct; it is not simply who is there, who is here, who is given a place at the table, but how bodies are occupied once they have arrived.

In one course I taught, each year I taught it, some students assigned to my seminars would not turn up. Instead, they turned up in the class of the white male professor, taking his class even though they were assigned mine. I was so intrigued by what the explanation would be that I asked one of these students when she came to my office hour why she went to his class. "He's such a rock star," she sighed wistfully. And then, as if to give substance to her admiration, as if to explain this admiration in more educational or at least strategic terms, she added, "I want to go to America to do a PhD." She did not need to say more. Her ambition was offered as an explanation of a decision. She estimated that if you had a reference signed by white men, you would increase your own chances of moving up or moving forward in academic life. She had already digested an institutional diet, which is at once a social diet; higher = him. Note an estimation of a value that will be added is enough to add value.

White men: the origins of speculative philosophy, one might speculate.

Speculate, accumulate.

Another time, two academics, a brown woman and a white man, are presenting a shared research project. They are equal collaborators on the project; but he is a senior man, very distinguished, well known; perhaps he too is an academic rock star. He jokingly refers to her as "his wife" at the end of the presentation. He is describing how he sees their relation by joking about their relation: the husband, the author, the originator of ideas; the wife, the one who stands behind him. Maybe she provides helping hands; maybe she makes the tea. She doesn't of course; she provides ideas; she has ideas of her own. Her intellectual labor is hidden by a joke; how it is hidden is performed by the joke.

When it is not funny, we do not laugh.

I pointed out in chapter 2 how if you don't participate in something you are heard as being antagonistic toward something, whether or not you feel antagonistic. When you talk about white men, you are heard as making an accusation against him. Well, maybe I am talking about him: a pronoun is an institution. Him: for some to become him is to pass into them, a singular pronoun, a general body. To refer to white men is to refer to what as well as who has already been assembled in a general sense. This is not to say that white men are not constantly being reassembled; you can meet up in the present; you can have a future meeting, because of how the past splinters into resources.

Maybe a brick is a chip off the old block. Reproduction and paternity are understood by this expression, "a chip off the old block," in terms of likeness: like from like. And if a chip comes from a block, a chip might also become a block from which another chip will come: like to like. Diversity workers have to chip at that block, or chip off the block.

Chip, chip.

Sharp.

Splinter.

I will come back to this expression "chip off the old block" in chapter 9. Diversity work teaches us about this block; how organizations become reproduced around and from the same bodies. One practitioner I interviewed called the mechanism "social cloning," referring to how organizations recruit in their own image. I attended a diversity training session. A fellow participant talked about how members of her department would ask whether potential job candidates would be "the kind of person you can take down to the pub." To become relatable is to restrict a relation; people you can relate to because they are at home not only in meeting rooms or the seminar rooms, but in social spaces, spaces that have their own histories. Norms might become more regulative the more casual the spaces.

When rules are relaxed, we encounter the rules.

Flinch.

How then is "white men" built or how is "white men" a building? Another practitioner relayed to me how they named buildings in her institution. All dead white men, she said. We don't need the names to know how spaces come to be organized so they can receive certain bodies. We don't need the names to know how or who buildings can be for. If citations are academic bricks, bricks too cite; bricks too can be white.

Whiteness: reassembled, brick by brick.

Another time, I pointed out that a speaker list for an event included only white men. I should add that this conference took place at Goldsmiths, where I work, and these kinds of "only white male" or "only but one" events happen regularly here, I suspect because of the kinds of bodies that tend to be organized under the rubric of critical theory. Someone says in reply that I sounded "very 1980s" and that he thought we had "got over" identity politics. Not only might we want to challenge the use of identity politics as a form of political caricature, but we might want to think this over. Feminist and antiracist critique are heard as old-fashioned, as based on identity categories that we are assumed to be over. Some words are heard as dated; and those who use these words become those who lag behind.

This is how: it can be deemed more old-fashioned to point out that only white men are speaking at an event than to have only white men speaking at an event. I suspect that criticality—the self-perception that in being critical we do not have a problem or that in being critical we are over it—is often used and performed in these academic spaces. I have called critical racism and critical sexism this: the racism and sexism reproduced by those who think of themselves as too critical to reproduce racism and sexism.

Words like *racism* and *sexism* are heard as melancholic: as if we are holding on to something that has already gone. I have heard this viewpoint articulated by feminists: that focusing on racism and sexism is an overly negative and old-fashioned way of relating to the world, a bad habit or even a knee-jerk feminist response to traditions that we should embrace with more love and care.[2] If feminist critiques of racism and sexism are knee-jerk, we might need to affirm the intelligence of feminist knees. Even within feminism there is a sense of: we would do better, go further, if we could put these words and the very critical impulse behind us. Perhaps a critical impulse, the impulse to critique something, becomes another version of willfulness: as if she opposes things because she is being oppositional, as if her critique has become an automatic pilot, as if she cannot help herself. We learn as well then: theory is a social landscape like any other. It is probably true that you would travel further the less you use words like *racism* and *sexism*. Feminist work that does not use these words is more likely to travel back into wider academic discourse. Some words are lighter; other words weigh you down. If you use heavy words, you slow down. Heavier words are those that bring up histories that we are supposed to get over.

There are now many strategies for declaring racism as well as sexism over. In *On Being Included* (Ahmed 2012) I called these strategies "overing," strategies that imply these histories would be over if only we would get over them. Overing thus becomes a moral injunction. You are asked to get over it, as if what stops it from being over is that you are not over it. For example, one argument I hear often, whether made or implied, is that race and gender are human issues, so that being posthuman means in some way being postrace and postgender, or that gender and race are about subjects, so the injunction to get over it becomes "to get over ourselves." We could call this oversubjectivity. The perception of feminists as having too much subjectivity (as overly subjective), which I discussed in chapter 3, becomes a requirement to give that subjectivity up; to give up.

A willfulness maxim is a refusal of this injunction: don't get over it if you are not over it. So yes: when histories have not gone, we might have to be willful to hold on. We will be judged as doing identity politics when we do not let go; when we labor over certain points, it will be assumed that it is because we are sore.

As I have already noted, when we describe how only certain bodies are speaking at an event, we are pointing out a structure. Pointing out structure is treated as relying on identity. Perhaps we are witnessing the effacement of structure under identity, not by those who are involved in what is called identity politics but by those who use identity politics to describe the scene of an involvement. Or, to put the argument even more strongly, when you point out structure, it is as if all you are doing is projecting your own identity onto the situation such that when you are describing who is missing, you are simply concerned with being missing yourself. White male genealogy is protected by the assumption that anyone who challenges that genealogy suffers from self-obsession. It is ironic, really, or perhaps not: you do not need to assert yourself when the genealogy does it for you. Also note how the two senses of diversity work become obscured here: as if you are only doing diversity because you are being diversity, because all you are doing is being a person of color or a woman concerned with her own exclusion (or both; being both is way too much being).

It is interesting how quickly and easily identity politics has become a charge, something that sounds intrinsically negative. Sometimes even mentioning race is enough to be judged as doing identity politics. Another time I respond on a Facebook wall to a blog that argues for the separation of ontology from politics. The blog included the following statement: "A great white shark eating a seal is simply an event that takes place in the world. It is simply something that happens. A person shooting another person is also, at the ontological level, simply an event that takes place." I write on a third party's wall: "Give more detail, show how things tend to fall: a white police officer shooting a black man and your ontological event is no mere happenstance." I gave some different details (a great white shark becomes a white police officer: I wanted the person-to-person encounter to echo the shark-to-seal encounter) to show how events can be "purely ontological" only if they are hypothetical, only if we strip subjects and objects of any attributes.

What follows? Much tangled discussion. My own use of the example of race is read by the blogger as an accusation against the blogger: "You rhetorically chose the example for a particular reason to try and position me as somehow indifferent to or supportive of racism." More responses: "We've become so accustomed to performing a shallow search for the most obvious or appealing or fashionable hook for explanations." And more: "The very clear position she took in responding to [blogger], namely that he was wicked for observing that shootings exist without immediately making appeals to identity politics." And more: "[Blogger] argued that the thing called 'a shooting' exists. That's not saying little, apparently, since it's so controversial. That was Ahmed's reaction, actually: no, you can't say that things exist; you have to choose my favourite political lens with which to talk about them." And more: "People like Sarah [sic] will tend to ignore other, perhaps more telling objects and trajectories because they have already *found* their necessary and sufficient cause through their over-determined political lens. Nothing really learned; we expected Sarah [sic] to come to that conclusion." One might comment here on flaming and the rather monstrous nature of any virtual conversations across blogs and walls. The use of racism as an example becomes an accusation made against someone (one of the most efficient techniques for not addressing racism is to hear racism as an accusation); a fashionable hook that stops us from searching for more complex causes; a political lens that distorts what we can see; a conclusion that is already made. Racism becomes a foreign as well as foreigner word: what gets in the way of description; what is imposed upon what would otherwise be a neutral or even happy situation (something that just happens).

A wall becomes a defense system. Sexism and racism are reproduced by the techniques that justify the reproduction. When these words are dismissed, we are witnessing a defense of the status quo: it is a way of saying, there is nothing wrong with this; what is wrong is the judgment that there is something wrong with this. The very systematic nature of sexism and racism is obscured because of the systematic nature of sexism and racism: so many of those incidents that wear us down, that we don't speak of, that we have learned not to speak of. We have learned to sever the connection between this event, and that, between this experience and that. To make a connection is thus to restore what has been lost (where loss should be understood as an active process); it is to generate a different picture. Apparently unrelated phenomena, things that seem "just to happen," to fall this way or that, become part of a system, a system that works. It is a system that works because of how it smooths progression.

We need to throw a wrench in the works, to stop the system from working. Or to borrow Sarah Franklin's (2015) evocative terms, we need to become a "wench in the works." Before we can do that, before we can be that, we have to recognize that there is a system. And we have to recognize that it is working.

Making feminist points, antiracist points, sore points, is about pointing out structures that many are invested in not recognizing. That is what an institutional brick wall is: a structure that many are invested in not recognizing. It is not simply that many are not bruised by this structure. It is also that they are progressing through the reproduction of what is not made tangible. When we are talking of sexism as well as racism, we are talking about systems that support and ease the progression of some bodies.

Sexism and racism can also ease the progression of some bodies through the distribution of labor. I remember reading an academic reference in which a young white male academic was described as "the next [male professor]." I have no doubt that such expectations can be experienced as pressure points. But think about the narrative of nextness: there is a waiting for the next such-and-such, such that when a body arrives who can inherit that position, he is given that position. And then: if you are perceived as the next such-and-such, you might be given more time to become him. Sexism and racism become systems of inheritance in which white men are freed up to take the place of other white men. More time to become him translates as more time to develop your ideas, your thoughts, your research. A way is cleared that enables or eases the progression of some bodies. And that way is cleared by requiring that others do less-valued work, housework; the work that is required for the reproduction of their existence. If your way is not cleared, you might end up part of the clearing system for others, doing the work they are released from doing. Sexism and racism enable some to travel faster. Sexism and racism slow other bodies down; holding them up, stopping them moving forward at the same rate.

CONCLUSION: THE MASTER'S RESIDENCE

I want to return to the Grimm story "The Willful Child" discussed in chapter 3. This story is also an institutional story. It is a story that circulates within institutions. It offers a warning, a threat: speak up and you will be beaten. The story is also an invitation to those who are at risk of identification with the wayward arm: become the rod as a way of avoiding the consequences of being beaten. Become the rod: too much violence is abbreviated here. But we witness the endless invitations to identify with those who discipline as a way of being disciplined without being beaten. No wonder: the willful child comes up whenever there is a questioning of institutional will. Whenever, say, she brings up sexism or racism, the willful child quickly comes after her: as if to say, speak up and her fate will be yours. There are many within institutions who cannot afford that fate; there are many who cannot raise their arms in protest even when the will of the institution is exposed as violence, even when that violence is directed against many. We need to give support to those who are willing to expose the will of the institution as violence; we need to become our own support system, as I explore in more detail in part III, so that when she speaks up, when she is, as she is, quickly represented as the willful child who deserves her fate, who is beaten because her will is immature and impoverished, she will not be an arm coming up alone; she will not be an arm all on her own.

In the conclusion to chapter 3, I assembled a feminist army of arms. Perhaps the arm in the Grimm story is also a feminist point. To make a feminist point is to go out on a limb. No wonder the arm keeps coming up. She makes a sore point. She is a sore point. We keep saying it because they keep doing it: assembling the same old bodies, doing the same old things. She keeps coming up because there is so much history to bring up. But when she comes up, this history is what is not revealed. Her arm is spectacular; when she makes these points, she becomes the spectacle. Her soreness becomes the spectacle. And no wonder: what follows her aims to discipline her. And no wonder: what precedes her aims to warn her. If we are to bring the walls down, we have to be willing to keep coming up, whatever precedes or follows.

When the arms come up, they come up against walls: that which keeps the master's residence standing. Arms in the labor and effort of what they come up against show us what is not over, what we do not get over. It can take willfulness to insist on this *not over* because the masters will not admit this world as their residence. To recognize the walls would get in the way of their standing, because it would make explicit that this standing (as intellects, say, as the originators of ideas, say) depends on histories that have sedimented as physical barriers to the progression of others. When we push against these walls, we are pushing against what does not appear to those who have been given residence. And when we do this kind of diversity work, trying to bring the house down by showing what stands up, like a statue that turns a violent past into a memorial,[3] there will be consequences. The judgment of willfulness will find us. Even to question what or who is standing is to become a vandal, a "willful destroyer of what is beautiful or venerable."[4] When the judgment of willfulness finds us, we find others through the judgment.

Arms: we need them to keep coming up. The arm that keeps coming up out of the grave, out of a death that has been and will be a collective assignment, can signify persistence and protest or, perhaps even more importantly, persistence as protest. We need to give the arms something to reach for. Or perhaps we are the ones being reached by the arms. After all, we know some of us are only here now on these grounds because arms in history have refused to keep laboring, to keep building or holding up the walls that secure the master's residence. We are here because the arms were striking; because the arms are striking. Arms in history, hands that clench into fists, arms as protest signs, arms raised as salute, arms that say, do not shoot. Some of us are only here now on these grounds because those arms in history have spoken, a history that is now, a history that is still.

We strike at what is still. Audre Lorde titled an essay with a proclamation: "The master's tools will never dismantle the master's house" (1984a, 110–13). In that unflinching "will never" is a call to arms: do not become the master's tool!

PART III **Living the Consequences**

IN THIS FINAL PART OF THIS BOOK, I explore how being a feminist is also about living the consequences of being a feminist, or living the consequences of describing oneself as a feminist. The reflections are about how we need feminism to handle what is directed toward us as feminists. Another name for this part could have been "Upping the Anti."

I have become used to this *anti*. I have lived with this *anti*. I was a lecturer in women's studies for the first ten years of my academic career. I used to listen to how people responded to women's studies, both within and outside the academy. It gave me lots of opportunity to hear how feminism is heard: responses would be mocking ("Ah is that where you teach women how to iron the clothes"; "Ah you can study *anything* in universities these days"; "Oh can I take the course—I fancy a bit of that") to hostile ("Oh a bunch of man-hating lesbians") and every now and then curious ("Oh, there is such a thing? *Women's* studies?").

Picking up the pieces of curiosity is a feminist gift. But you also have to work out how to handle the mocking and hostile responses. And when I am thinking of living a feminist life, one of the things I am thinking of is feminism as a handle or as a way of handling the same kinds of sexism directed toward us as feminists that led us on the way to becoming feminists in the first place. Feminism: what we need to handle the consequences of being feminist. Although fragility is the explicit theme of the first of the three chapters that make up this part, fragility will come up in different ways throughout all of the chapters. I want to consider the consequences of the argument I began the book with: that the histories that bring us to feminism are the histories that leave us fragile.

In this part of the book I want to think of the consequences of being a feminist not only in terms of being worn out or worn down by what we come up against, but also in terms of how we find the energy and resources to keep going. What I call feminist snap is about how we collectively acquire tendencies that can allow us to break ties that are damaging as well as to invest in new possibilities. I reflect specifically on lesbian feminism as not only where we come up against an anti, most personally, but also where and how we can be willful and creative; finding ways of relating to women as women is about finding other ways of relating.

I also want, in this part of the book, to allow my writing to express the quality of the experiences I am trying to describe. I am watching my sentences fall apart. I am putting them back together again.

7 / FRAGILE CONNECTIONS

It is difficult to describe what is difficult. I have been talking about walls, as a way of describing that which we come up against, those hardenings of history into physical barriers in the present. When we come up against walls, how easily things shatter. To be shattered can be to experience the costs of our own fragility: to break, to reach a breaking point. In chapter 8, I explore how we might aim for breakages, and how we might become inventive in dealing with them. Here, I want to consider fragility as the wear and tear of living a feminist life. Part of what makes diversity work "work" is the effort to find ways to survive what we come up against; to find ways to keep going, to keep trying, when the same things seem to happen, over and over again.

We can be shattered by what we come up against.
And then we come up against it again.
We can be exhausted by what we come up against.
And then we come up against it again.

No wonder: we might feel depleted. It is not that feelings are themselves being depleted, that the rather economic model of emotions that is evident, for instance, in some uses of the concept of compassion fatigue, in which is it is assumed that emotions, in being used, are being used up. By referring to "feeling depleted," I am addressing a material as well as embodied phenomenon: of not having the energy to keep going in the face of what you come up against. So much of the diversity work I discussed in part II taught us about the uneven distribution of energy, how some bodies become depleted because of what is required to go somewhere, to be somewhere, to stay somewhere.

We do have moments of relief; we work for those moments, or perhaps these moments are how we keep working. Sometimes, it is the relief of entering a room and not encountering what you usually encounter: all that whiteness. There have been a few moments in my academic career like this: when I have inhabited a sea of brownness. When you inhabit a sea of brownness as a person of color, you might realize the effort of your previous inhabitancy, the effort not to notice what is around you, all that whiteness. It is like how you can feel the weight of tiredness most acutely as the tiredness leaves you. You often become even more conscious of a feeling when it dissipates. When we leave the spaces of whiteness, which is where I have lived and worked and accounts for most of the spaces I have been in, we become even more aware of how wearing whiteness is.

When something is wearing, you do not always feel worn down. Feeling worn down can be a retrospective realization that you have been or are being worn down. It might be that in order to inhabit certain spaces we have to block recognition of just how wearing they are: when the feeling catches us, it might be at the point when it is just too much. You are shattered. Feeling worn down: I think feminist killjoys are familiar with this feeling, that sense of coming up against the same thing, whatever you say or do. We have, I think, in the face of this feeling to think about how to protect ourselves (and those around us) from being diminished.

In this chapter I explore how fragility itself is a thread, a connection, a fragile connection, between those things deemed breakable. I will be sharing some shattering stories. In a shattering story there is often a *too*, a *too* that often falls on what falls: fragility as the quality of being too easily breakable. I will start with some literary examples of objects breaking, ordinary breakages of ordinary things, as a way of opening up a reflection on histories that have become hard, histories that leave some more fragile than others. I will be reflecting on fragilities at different levels or scales: fragile things; fragile relationships; fragile shelters; and fragile bodies.

FRAGILE THINGS

I want to start with a breakage. When I first began writing about willfulness, I realized how often willfulness comes up in scenes of breakage. In this section, I draw on two descriptions of objects breaking that are offered in George Eliot's novels. I first wrote about these broken objects in my book *Willful Subjects* (Ahmed 2014). Eliot became my primary traveling companion in this book; it was not how I started the journey, with her work by my side, but it was how I ended up. I had begun with Maggie Tulliver, with how her will becomes the problem as well as the solution. I then reread Eliot as a novelist of the will or, as I think of her, a novel philosopher of the will. Then, only then, did these objects come into my field of vision; and it was through them that the book ended up being about willful objects as well as willful subjects. It is interesting, reflecting back, that it was broken things that caught my attention and that helped me to make sense of what was being depicted in Maggie's story. I have no doubt that it was by attending to willful things that I developed my understanding of how willfulness becomes an archive of shared experience. I return to what it means to think of willfulness as an archive in chapter 9. Here I want to pick up on the question of fragility, and what it means to relate to things as being breakable. A breakage is often accompanied by a story, a story of what breaks when something breaks, or an explanation of what is behind a breakage. This first description of an object breaking is from *Silas Marner*:

> It was one of [Silas's] daily tasks to fetch his water from a well a couple of fields off, and for this purpose, he had had a brown earthen ware pot, ever since he came to Raveloe, which he held as his most precious utensil, among the very few conveniences he had granted himself. It had been his companion for twelve years, always standing on the same spot, always lending its handle to him in the early morning, so that its form had an expression for him of willing helpfulness, and the impress of its handle on his palm gave a satisfaction mingled with that of having fresh clear water. One day as he was returning from the well, he stumbled against the step of the stile, and his brown pot, falling with force against the stones that overarched the ditch below him, was broken in three pieces. Silas picked up the pieces and carried them home with grief in his heart. The brown pot could never be of use to him anymore, but he stuck the pieces together and propped the ruin in its old place for a memorial. (Eliot [1861] 1994, 17)

This is such a beautiful description of how love can be bestowed on an ordinary thing; a brown earthenware pot. We learn: how what matters, matters. Silas is touched by his pot. If the pot lends Silas its handle, his palm receives the warmth of an impression. The pot is his companion; reliable; always in the same spot, always lending its handle. When the pot lends Silas its handle, his palm receives the warmth of an impression, warmth that gives direction.

The pot is mingled with other things that share this direction: the fresh clear water the pot helps to carry; the body carrying the pot; the path taken in the carrying of the pot from the well to the house. A relation of use is one of affection; we could think of the wear and tear of a handle and a hand as a trace of a common history. If the pot lends Silas its handle, in order that Silas can do something, or get something, the pot and Silas are in agreement, a willing agreement. When the pot is filled with the content of its agreement, its expression becomes that of willing helpfulness. When something cannot carry out what we will, it is no longer quite so agreeable, no longer willingly helpful. When the pot breaks, it is no longer in use, of use; it can take up its place by becoming memorial; a holder of memories, not water.

I will come back to this idea of becoming memorial in due course. I want to take another example of an object breaking, this time from *Adam Bede*. We are at home with a family. A child, Molly, is drawing some ale for her mother, Mrs. Poyser, but she is taking her time. "What a time that gell is drawing th' ale," says Mrs. Poyser (Eliot [1895] 1961, 220). Molly, we could say, is "too slow"; she is lagging behind an expectation. Molly then appears, "carrying a large jug, two small mugs, and four drinking-cans, all full of ale or small beer—an interesting example of the prehensile power of the human hand" (221). Perhaps a handy hand is like a willingly helpful pot: it is filled with the content of an agreement. But then Molly has a "vague alarmed sense" (there is a storm; her mother is impatient). When she "hasten[s] her step a little towards the table," she catches "her foot in her apron" and falls "with a crash and a smash into a pool of beer" (221). Whatever makes Molly fall, by falling she breaks the jug; leaving her "dolefully" to "pick up the fragments of pottery" (221).

We can deviate on this sadly clumsy note. Clumsiness might provide us with a queer ethics. Such an ethics attends to the bumpiness of living with difference, so often experienced as a difference in time; being too slow or too fast, out of time. Think of experiences of moving along a street with another. It is not going smoothly; you keep bumping into each other. You might experience the other person as being out of time; as being too slow or too fast, as being awkward or clumsy. Or we might turn toward each other in frustration, as we bump into each other yet again. Or you might experience yourself as being clumsy, as the one who is too slow, or too fast, whose job it is to pick up the pieces of a shattered intimacy. Bumping into each other is a sign that we have not resolved our differences. The resolution of difference is the scene of much injustice. Things might be smoother because some have had to adjust to keep up with others. Corporeal diversity, how we come to inhabit different kinds of bodies, with differing capacities and incapacities, rhythms and tendencies, could be understood as a call to open up a world that has assumed a certain kind of body as a norm. The bumpier the ride could be an expression of the degree to which one style of embodiment has not determined an ethical or social horizon. Rather than equality being about smoothing a relation, perhaps equality is a bumpy ride.

Back to the jug: once the jug has broken, and some bumps can lead to breakages, what happens? Mrs. Poyser remarks, "It's all your own willfulness, as I tell you, for there's no call to break anything." Yes, willfulness comes up in a scene of breakage. Mrs. Poyser suggests Molly's willfulness is what causes Molly to be wrong footed. Willfulness is here a stopping device: it is how a chain of causality is stopped at a certain point (for the child to become the cause of the breakage, we would not ask what caused the child to fall). And yet, willfulness seems to be catching: "Mrs. Poyser had turned around from the cupboard with the brown-and-white jug in her hand, when she caught sight of something at the other end of the kitchen; perhaps it was because she was already trembling and nervous that the apparition had so strong an effect on her; perhaps jug-breaking, like other crimes, has a contagious influence. However it was, she stared and started like a ghost-seer, and the precious brown-and-white jug fell to the ground, parting for ever with its spout and handle" (Eliot [1895] 1961, 220). Mrs. Poyser, we might say, catches Molly's alarm. An alarm is a chain reaction.

Willfulness comes up to explain a breakage, to stop a chain reaction. But when Mrs. Poyser breaks this jug, she does not blame herself. She first offers a certain kind of fatalism: she says, "What is to be broke *will* be broke" (220, emphasis in original), a way of using will as a simple future auxiliary verb, but one that has a certain predictive force (what happens will happen, whatever will be will be). Gender often operates as a form of willing fatalism (what is to be boy will be boy or, more simply and more usually, as I discussed in chapter 1, boys will be boys); gender as a sentencing to death, a bond of fate, a fatal bond. But even if this break seems like fate, Mrs. Poyser blames the jug: "The jugs are bewitched, *I* think. . . . There's times when the crockery seems alive an' flies out o' your hand like a bird" (222). When the jug appears willful (in the precise sense as too full of its own will, as not empty enough to be filled by human will), it not only causes its own breakage, it breaks the thread of a connection. Note the beginning of another connection, between a girl and a jug, a fragile connection, between those assumed to cause a breakage. In chapter 3, I explored willfulness as a feminist history. Perhaps this history involves other bits and pieces, shattered pieces, of broken things. I will come back to this connection between the girl and the jug as a way of picking up some of these shattered pieces.

We might note as well a link between deviation and breakage: to deviate from a path is to lose the potential to carry out will. When we talk of a path in this context, we are talking of the unfolding of an action in time; a path is what we have to take to reach something. To be on a path is to be in a moment of suspension: the hand has left its resting place; it is carrying something toward something, but the task has yet to be completed. The hand has not yet reached its destination. A break is not only a break of something (a pot, a jug); it is the shattering of a possibility, a possibility of completing an action or of reaching a destination. As I noted in chapter 2, happiness is often understood as a destination, as what we are reaching for when we reach for something, as what we get if we are going the right way. No wonder the killjoy emerges from a scene of breakage: in preventing an action from being completed, she gets in the way of the happiness assumed as in the way; she stops happiness from becoming actual.

FRAGILE RELATIONSHIPS

Fragility: the quality of being easily breakable. Fragility: when being breakable stops something from happening. Relationships can break too; we know this. Have you ever been with someone, someone whom you are trying to love, trying not to give up on, and they say something that you find unbearable? You can hear glass shatter; that point when you realize what you had is something that cannot be reassembled. If you put the pieces back together, you would be left rather like Silas, with a memorial, a holder of memories. You would be left rather like Silas, with an empty container, a reminder of what was once but is no longer.

When my own parents broke up, a friend of the family came around to talk to my mother, who was the one who had been left. He said, "This is what happens when you marry a Muslim." The words were uttered pointedly, cutting the atmosphere like a knife. Relationships and families breaking up: it happens. Shit happens. But in a mixed relationship, one whose legitimacy is already insecure, a breakup acquires a certain meaning: a breakup becomes what we were heading for right from the beginning. This is what happens when: as if *when* leads only to this. For a white woman, an English Christian woman, to marry out, to marry a brown man, a Pakistani Muslim, leads her only to this point, this ending, a relationship that "could only end in tears," becoming, retrospectively, always tearful.

When things were going smoothly, this friend said nothing. When things broke, race came up. We learn making from breaking. What we might call background racism might be part of the situation in which we find ourselves; racism hovers in the background when things are working, which is how race can come up so quickly when things stop working.

A wall: reassembled at the point of shattering.

Maybe it begins with a prediction made by others: that's going to be difficult; that's not likely to work out. Maybe you feel the pressure to make things work to show that they can work. For queers to make things work can be a pressure as well as a project. I noted in chapter 2 how it can be presumed that a queer life is an unhappy life, a life without those things that would or should make you happy. You can feel this presumption as a pressure to prove that a queer life can be a happy life. You know that if there is a breakup, it can fulfill an expectation that such relationships are less lasting, less secure; fragile. There is a kind of queer fatalism at stake here: that to be on a queer path is to hurtle toward a miserable fate, queer as a death sentence; queer as self-shattering. And then if things do shatter (as things do tend to do), you have fulfilled an expectation that this is where being queer led you.

From the example of mixed and queer relationships, we learn how some are assumed to be inherently broken, as if their fate is to break, as if a break is what we were heading for right from the beginning. A break becomes the realization of a quality assumed to belong to something; breaking as the unfolding of being. And this is difficult: the assumption of fragility can make something fragile. The more careful you are, the more your hands tremble. The word *care* derives from the Old English *cearu* suggesting sorrow, anxiety, grief. In chapter 1 I noted how becoming careful relates to a sense of oneself as breakable. Perhaps to become careful, to be full of care, is to become anxious about the potential to break something else. You can become clumsier when you are trying to be careful not to break what easily breaks. If you are already known as the clumsy one, you might become even more afraid of breakage, because you know that if there is a breakage, you will be judged as the one who is behind it. The more you try, the more you seem to slip up.

Fragility can be a regulative assumption that generates the quality assumed to belong to a thing. A consequence can be recruited as a cause. It might be assumed you caused your own damage because you left the safety of a brightly lit path. Gender norms too can work like this: when femininity is registered as fragility, when that fragility is used to explain what happens to her, or what she can or cannot do, a consequence of power is recruited as the cause. She is treated with caution and care because she is fragile; because she is treated with caution and care, she is fragile. Politics is what happens in between these *becauses*.

And a wall can come up again. A wall can become something that feels internal, like a voice inside your own head that makes you stumble. I brought up this possibility of an internal wall in chapter 6: how when those around you don't perceive something even though it happens right in front you (such as sexual harassment), it can lead you to doubt what you perceive; it can lead you to try to modify your own perception. That doubt is then turned inward: a wall can be an obstacle that is created because you doubt yourself. Even if this wall feels internal, it does not begin there. You might have been told: You can't do that. You won't be able to do that. This lack of confidence might be attached to you being a girl, or you just being the being you are; not good enough, not smart enough, or just not, not enough; or too much; it is too much for you; you are too much; that too. You might be defiant in the face of this lack of confidence. I can do that. I will be able to do that. But if those words are repeated—you can't do that; you won't be able to do that—they can become a wavering of your own will, a doubt; an uncertainty. Confidence too can shatter. A conviction "I can" transformed into a question: can I? When she is in question, she begins to question herself. And maybe as you begin to question yourself, you don't put yourself behind yourself to protect yourself from the possibility of not being able to do what you had thought you could do. And then you don't. And then you think, "I can't." Your effort acquires the quality of the fragility that is put into the world by an expectation. You waver, you fall. And you confirm the expectation. A confirmation can be the hardening of an idea: it becomes a thing. You encounter that thing; you become that thing. And the wall that tells you you can't go there becomes harder, until you don't go there, in case you can't, and then you can't. If politics is what happens in between these *becauses*, politics is what happens to you. I will return to how fragility can become a structural question, a question not only of a life but of a lot, in chapter 9.

What happens to you: we need to handle what we come up against. But what if the handle is what breaks? Fragility: losing the handle. When the jug loses its handle, it becomes useless. We sense the terror of its fate; the fragments swept up and away. And when we say we are losing the handle, we often mean we are no longer able to grasp hold of what we need to persist. The handle provides a connection. The figure of the feminist killjoy recalls that of the broken jug: she too flies off the handle, an expression used to indicate the suddenness of anger. The origin of this expression is said to be from the speed of an axe head parting company from its handle during a downstroke. When a feminist flies off the handle, she is held responsible for her sad parting from company. I want to repeat almost word for word a sentence I used earlier in describing fragile things so we can hear a resonance. It is a slight alteration of how I described the moment when Mrs. Poyser blames the jug for breaking the jug. *She not only causes her own breakage, she breaks the thread of a connection.* Feminism as self-breakage: history enacted as judgment. Or feminism as a tear in the social fabric; history enacted as loss; a tear; a tear. To give a cause to breakage is to create a figure, one that can contain the damage by explaining the damage. The feminist killjoy is such a figure. To be a container of damage is to be a damaged container; a leaky container. The feminist killjoy is a leaky container. She is right there; there she is, all teary, what a mess.

When we speak, no wonder: it can feel like everything shatters.

We can become the point from which things cannot be reassembled.

It is not that we always want or will this to happen. Sometimes we might not want relationships to shatter because they matter. And this can be another crisis: when the requirements to keep a connection that matters going require giving up on something else that matters. Say my good friends are laughing at a joke. The laughter picks everyone up; the room is brimming with it. I might start laughing too, before I even hear the joke. But when I hear the joke, and when I register what has been said, I might find that I do not find it funny at all; or even that I find it offensive. Sometimes we keep laughing out of fear of causing a breakage. We might, in other words, decide not to become a killjoy in certain moments, because the costs would be too high: we would break what we need to hold on to, a relationship that we care about, a person we love, a world we cannot let go of. Of course, sometimes being a killjoy is not up to us: it can be decided for you; you can receive the assignment without saying anything. Sometimes we stop laughing. And how quickly: things fall apart. Perhaps then feminism is how we pick up the pieces.

When I write about feminist killjoys, I know it might sound as if I am calling for her; as if her arrival for me is always a moment of political hope. That's not always how it feels, even if, for me at least, her failure to disappear is hopeful. Sometimes, when she appears on the horizon of our consciousness, it can be a moment of despair. You don't always want her to appear even when you see yourself in her appearance. You might say to her: not here, not now. You might not want to hear something as problematic because you do not want to hear someone as being problematic. Even though you know the problem of how exposing a problem is posing a problem, you can still experience exposing a problem as posing a problem for yourself. You might think, you might feel: I can't afford to be her right now. You might think, you might feel: she would cost me too much right now. When you have been a feminist killjoy, when she has been part of your embodied history, she can still appear willful to you, insisting on coming up, whenever something comes up. She can be tiring. You might experience her apparent exteriority as the alarming potentiality of interiority; of becoming her, of her becoming you. I return to how her arrival can be a crisis in my discussion of feminist snap in chapter 8. A feminist politics of fragility might be based not only on how to survive what we come up against but how to enable relationships to endure that can easily be threatened by what we come up against.

We can be shattered by the force of what we come up against, when our bodies are little objects thrown against the hard walls of history, to return to my description from chapter 6. We can damage relationships that matter. And that is one of the hardest things about coming up against walls: it can threaten some of our most fragile and precious, our best, our warmest connections. As I write this, I feel sad, so very sad. And this too is one of the risks of anger. There is so much to be against; we know this. But how easily anger can spill, can spill at those who happen to be nearby, who are the closest to us. How easily in being against something we can risk those who are with us, who are for us, who we are with and for; we can risk them because they are before us. Our anger, when generalized against the injustice of the world, can become directed toward those who happen to be nearest, often those who are dearest. The costs of struggling against injustices can be personal: indeed they are often personal; we can lose those who matter. We can get it wrong; we can be too sharp; we can regret having said something because the consequences of saying something were regrettable. Of course sometimes not: sometimes even when the consequences of saying something are regrettable, we cannot regret saying something, because not saying something would have been even more regrettable. There is time in these *sometimes*.

I have always resisted the idea that feminist killjoys mature, grow by growing up, and that maturity is about becoming less volatile. Maturity is without question the wrong term for my attempt to think through timing. The idea that maturing out of being a feminist killjoy assumes or hopes that feminism itself, or at least being that kind of feminist, the wrong kind, the one who always insists on making feminist points, the one who is angry, confrontational, is just a phase you are going through.

If being a feminist killjoy is a phase, I willingly aspire to be a phase.
The idea that you mature out of being a feminist killjoy, that in growing up you unbecome her, also implies a linear development and progression: as if being unaffected or less bothered is the point you should reach; what you should aim to reach. It associates maturity with giving up, not necessarily conviction as such, but the willingness to speak from that conviction.

A feminist life is not so linear. Some of us become angrier and more volatile in time. We don't always become feminist killjoys early on; she can catch up with you at any time. Once you are a feminist killjoy, however, I think the only option is to become more of a feminist killjoy. Becoming more of a killjoy is not about being more or less willing to speak your opposition. If anything, in having more experiences of killjoying, more of a sense of how wearing it can be, you learn from this experience of not getting through. Because you are becoming more of a feminist killjoy, you might become warier of the consequences of being oppositional; a consequence, after all, can be what we share with others. You become wary of being worn. You know the energy it involves: you know that some battles are not worth your energy, because you just keep coming up against the same thing. At the same time, or maybe at another time, you also know that you can't always choose your battles; battles can choose you. Sometimes the things you come to know seem to feel like another wall, another way of signaling that you have few places to go. Saying something, not saying something, your mouth an open question.

From my own experience of being a feminist killjoy over time, you do come to have more of a sense of time: when someone says something, you might be less quick to react. You give yourself time. Sometimes, now, you don't get wound up, even when someone is winding you up. There are still some things that, if said, would get through any of my defenses. There are some things I always want to react to too quickly, as I don't need time to react. I am not saying that taking time means that your response is better. It is just to say that sometimes, you have more room for a response. Perhaps we could call this room wiggle room.

In chapter 3, I reflected on how willfulness can be actively claimed as part of a feminist inheritance. But thinking through our own feminist fragility, how we can become fragile through feminism because of what we do not overlook, helps us to complicate that claiming: not to negate it, just to complicate it. There can be risks to becoming oppositional; to having a sense of oneself as always struggling against something. If you are used to having to struggle to exist, if you become used to having others oppose your existence, if you are used even to being thought of as oppositional, those experiences are directive. You can enact an expectation even in the struggle not to fulfill it. You can even become somewhat oddly invested in the continuation of what you are up against. This is not to say you really want what opposes you (although there is wanting at stake here: you want to oppose what you don't want). It is to say that if you spend time and energy in opposing something, an opposition can become part of you. It is not to say that the investment is what keeps something going at the level of the event or situation. I have experienced myself a sense of how possibilities can be closed down if I assume in advance an oppositional stance. You can get so used to struggling against something that you expect anything that comes up will be something to be against. It can be tiring being against whatever comes up, even if hearing a wrong ends up being right. And it is possible, of course, in expecting to hear wrongs not to hear them, because if you do hear them, they fulfill an expectation, becoming a confirmation of what you already know. We can stop hearing when we think we know. I suspect we all do this: hear with expectation, listen for confirmation, whether or not we think of ourselves as feminist killjoys or willful subjects; this is ordinary stuff.

And yet, we might in assuming our own oppositionality be protecting ourselves. We might not notice our own agreements, if they are histories that are still. This is why the figure of the killjoy is not a figure we can assume we always somehow are: even if we recognize ourselves in that figure, even when she is so compelling, even when we are energized by her. We might, in assuming we are the killjoys, not notice how others become killjoys to us, getting in the way of our own happiness, becoming obstacles to a future we are reaching for. So for example some feminists have made use of what I called in chapter 3 the "willfulness charge" to create an impression, that of being lonely radical feminist voices struggling against the tide of social opinion. They have used this impression of having to struggle against to articulate a position against trans people, who have to struggle to exist, a position articulated so vehemently that it could only be described as hate speech. When you assume your own oppositionality too quickly, you can inflate a minority into a majority, hear an injury as a lobby; interpret a fight for survival as the formation of an industry. I have called this dynamic, with reference to the Grimm story, "feel like an arm, act like a rod." What is assumed as willful feminism is instead willing transphobia.

Activism might need us to involve losing confidence in ourselves, letting ourselves recognize how we too can be the problem. And that is hard if we have a lifetime of being the problem.

FRAGILE SHELTERS

How can we think the consequences of our own fragility for how we build feminist shelters? It can be painstaking to build a shelter from materials left behind; from histories that make it difficult for some to survive. And yet we need to build such shelters to enable that survival. We are building precisely because of what has already been built, those walls that have hardened over time. Indeed, returning to my discussion in chapter 6, we can retell the story told by a diversity worker about her hard work in getting a policy agreed to that doesn't end up doing anything as another shattering story. In this story, it is she, the one telling the story, who is shattered. To be shattered in this sense means to be exhausted. The story of how a diversity worker is shattered is the story of how the wall keeps standing. In an informal conversation I had with diversity practitioners in 2013 a wall became a water cannon: "It's like water cannons. Sometimes the success story is to stay standing in the face of everything they throw at you. It doesn't always feel like a success. But it is a success." When to stay standing is a measure of success, you might have less time and energy to do other things. We can end up feeling used up. And also if we shatter because of what we come up against, but what we come up against is not revealed, it might seem as if we are shattering ourselves. Rather like Molly, it might be assumed we have tripped ourselves up, that we have wrong-footed ourselves; that our willfulness is behind our downfall.

When walls are not revealed it can appear as if we are shattering ourselves.

No wonder, if we are shattered, that we need places to go. It is not however that our experience of being killjoys means that we come together, however broken, to build a shelter that is warm, a shelter that would protect us from exposure to the harshness of the weather (although the idea of a killjoy shelter is appealing). If what we are building is on grounds that are not our own, it can be hard to build anything. My experiences of women's studies taught me about the fragility of feminist shelters. You have to work hard just for things to stay up. And I think that really affects the kind of work you do: you have less time to do things in the building when you are constantly doing building work. When you have to fight for an existence, fighting can become an existence. Women's studies is and will probably remain a fragile dwelling, with precarious and unstable foundations. This is because, as I noted in chapter 4, to build women's studies is to build in an environment that needs to be transformed by women's studies; the point is to transform the very ground on which we build. We want to shatter the foundations. It is not surprising that if we try to shatter the foundations upon which we build something, what we build is fragile.

Things falling apart: that was my experience of women's studies. One of the first signs that we were no longer going to be supported by the institution was when we were asked to move offices, from the front of the building to the back. Being put back out of the way: out of sight; out of touch. You sensed the direction things were going. You felt the precarity more and more, the gradual withdrawal of institutional support. In chapter 2, I mentioned the easing of pressure you might experience when you are going the right way as the lifting of a hand. A hand lifting can also be experienced as the withdrawal of support. When I felt that withdrawal, I became more and more desperate; I threw myself into the project of saving women's studies, of ensuring that it could retain its autonomy and that we could hold on to our undergraduate degree, which was one of the last single-honors women's studies degrees left in the United Kingdom. I think I exhausted myself as well as those around me. And in hindsight, not only having left but having left so much behind me, I realize that was the saddest thing: that I lost not only the building but my connections and relationships with my feminist cobuilders. There were lots of complicated institutional as well as personal reasons for this loss. There is no need to go into them; each of us would give a different account of them. But I have heard this story elsewhere and I have heard it often: that when a feminist project is not realized, when things shatter, as things do tend to do, then our relationships with each other often shatter too.

When we have to fight for an existence, it can shape our encounters with each other. There is no doubt we can experience each other as sharp and brittle. We come up against each other. This is why the feminist killjoy does not disappear when we are building feminist shelters. In fact, she appears very quickly. You can be a sore point within feminism. You can be a killjoy at feminist tables because of who you are, what you say, what you do; because of a history you might bring up just by entering a room. And no matter how difficult some of our experiences of being a feminist killjoy, they do not prepare you for the difficulties of being in feminist spaces and still encountering the problem of being the problem. And this is how many women of color experience feminist spaces. As I noted in chapter 3, when feminists of color talk about racism, we stop of the flow of a conversation. Indeed, perhaps we are the ones who interrupt that conversation. The word *interruption* comes from *rupture*: to break. A story of breakage is thus always a story that starts somewhere. To hear feminist of color contributions as interruptions is not only to render racism into a breaking point, but to construe feminism as a conversation that starts with white women. Feminism becomes a conversation that is not our own. Audre Lorde (1984a), bell hooks (2000), Sunera Thobani (2003), and Aileen Moreton-Robinson (2003) have all taught me to think about the figure of the angry black woman, the angry woman of color, as well as the angry indigenous woman, as another kind of feminist killjoy: a feminist killjoy who kills feminist joy. To talk about racism within feminism is to get in the way of feminist happiness. If talking about racism within feminism gets in the way of feminist happiness, we need to get in the way of feminist happiness.

As feminists, most of the time we do not inhabit feminist spaces, which is probably why encountering the same problems in feminist spaces that we encounter in the world at large is so exhausting. And depressing: the walls come up in the places we go to feel less depleted by walls.

I have often heard this refrain when I have presented my work in quite white spaces: But what about white people? Don't they have complex feelings too? One time, quite a while back in 1999, I was presenting a paper "Embodying Strangers," in which I referred to Audre Lorde's description, her quite extraordinary description, of racism on a New York subway. One white woman spoke in the question time with anger about how I hadn't considered the white woman's feelings, as if this was some sort of neutral situation and that to account for it we have to give an account from each point of view. Racism becomes the requirement to think of racism with sympathy, racism as just another view; the racist as the one with feelings, too.

In an unbalanced world, balance is unbalanced.

I think she spoke with anger because she heard my speech as anger. Another time, much later when I gave a lecture in 2011, I drew on bell hooks's description of how feminists of color seem to cause tension without saying anything. She gives us a scenario. I suspect she has been here many times; I have been there too, so I will share it again: "A group of white feminist activists who do not know one another may be present at a meeting to discuss feminist theory. They may feel bonded on the basis of shared womanhood, but the atmosphere will noticeably change when a woman of color enters the room. The white women will become tense, no longer relaxed, no longer celebratory" (2000, 56). It is not just that feelings are in tension, but that the tension is located somewhere: in being felt by some bodies, it is attributed as caused by another, who comes to be felt as apart from the group, as getting in the way of its organic enjoyment and solidarity. The body of color is attributed as the cause of becoming tense, which is also the loss of a shared atmosphere (or we could say, sharing the experience of loss is how the atmosphere is shared). As a feminist of color, you do not have to say anything to cause tension.

When I drew on this quote from bell hooks, a white woman came up to me afterward expressing not so much anger but hurt at hooks's description, and at my uncritical use of hooks's description, for the implication that all white women make women of color the problem. There was no *all* used in the example, but this does not mean someone cannot hear the example as *all*. When that is all they can hear, they hear you as saying *all*. And in being heard as saying *all*, whatever you say, you become a problem, all over again. I have been thinking of this: if histories that hurt bring us to feminism, what do we do when our own critiques become the cause of other people's hurt? Because hurt feelings, as both Audre Lorde (1984) and bell hooks (2000) teach us, can be a way of not hearing, a way of making something about oneself, a way of not listening to others.

One time I am speaking of racism in a seminar. A white woman comes up to me afterward and puts her arm next to mine. We are almost the same color, she says. No difference, no difference. You wouldn't really know you were any different from me, she says. The very talk about racism becomes a fantasy that invents difference. She smiles, as if the proximity of our arms was evidence that the racism of which I was speaking was an invention, as if our arms told another story. She smiles, as if our arms are in sympathy. I say nothing. Perhaps my arm speaks by withdrawing.

The withdrawal of an arm can be enough to create tension, as if by withdrawing your arm you are refusing a gesture of love and solidarity. Reconciliation is often presented as a gesture of goodwill, a handy gesture, where the hand is outstretched; the hand of the settler or occupier, say. If the outstretched hand is not shaken, something has been broken, the promise of reconciliation; the promise that we can get on; the promise that we can move on. It is the ones who do not receive that gesture as a gesture of goodwill who would be deemed to cause the breakage.

You can break a promise without making a promise.

If you refuse the gesture of sympathy, you become mean. In my own experience of pointing out racism, it is assumed not only that you cause other people hurt, but that you intended that hurt. Those who speak of racism become mean in the sense of stingy and unkind. Speaking of racism becomes a way of breaking a social thread, a fragile thread. Robin DiAngelo has called "white fragility" the "inability to handle the stress of conversations about race and racism" (2011, n.p.). White fragility works as a defense system.[1] If a consequence can be recruited as a cause, then a cause can be recruited as a defense: as if to say, we won't hear what we can't handle.

I noted earlier how an assignment of willfulness can be how a chain of causality is stopped at a certain point: the child becomes the cause of the breakage if we do not ask what causes the child to fall (such as the mother's impatience, such as the feeling of lagging behind an expectation, such as the bumpiness of corporeal difference). We learn more about causality not from hypotheticals (that old billiard ball) but from our immersion in a world with others. We learn how causality can be a social habit; how a chain of events is stopped at a certain point because it allows a subject to be identified not as causing damage but as damaged by another's cause. White fragility is this: a way of stopping the chain of causality, such that whiteness is defended against that which would trip it up, such that whiteness becomes that which would be damaged by a fall. We are learning here about the very mechanisms that lead us to a familiar place: when you speak about racism, you become the one who causes damage. Remember: diversity as damage limitation. Racism: damage to whiteness.

White fragility is how some words (such as racism) become identified in terms of their potential to cause a breakage. You are not supposed to utter words like this; they would break the thread of a connection. An emphasis on the potentiality to break can stop words from being sent out, as if the point of those words is to break the ones to which it is assumed they are directed. A history of fragility is also a history of meanness. Returning to objects that break, that become unable or unwilling to carry out what they are assumed to be intended for, those very objects are often called mean. Mrs. Poyser, if you remember her, when she breaks her jug, she also says, "It's them nasty glazed handles—they slip o'er the finger like a snail" (Eliot [1895] 1961, 220). When objects are not means to our ends, they become mean. Again we are back in the killjoy's territory: to be mean is to prevent the completion of a desired action; to stop what is desired (so often happiness, assumed to be desired) from becoming actualized. We have to hear how being judged as mean is to be judged as getting in the way of community: as shattering a possibility that we can be whole, that we can be as one.

FRAGILE BODIES

The word *fragility* derives from *fraction*. Something is broken. It is in pieces. A body can be broken. If we keep coming up against walls, it feels like we can shatter into a million pieces. Tiny little pieces.

Bodies break. That too. Though that is not all that bodies do.

Bones break. That too. Though that is not all that bones do.

Perhaps we need to develop a different orientation to breaking. We can value what is deemed broken; we can appreciate those bodies, those things, that are deemed to have bits and pieces missing. Breaking need not be understood only as the loss of the integrity of something, but as the acquisition of something else, whatever that else might be.

You are thrown.

Things can happen; accidents can happen. We can be thrown by what we come up against.

I have a story. Let me give you the bare bones of it.

One time, I was in New York at the gym and I was joking with somebody. I said, "I have never broken a bone; I don't think my bones are breakable." It was a joke, but it was a silly thing to say. And then not more than a week later I fell and broke something. I am not saying that this led to that; but it was an uncanny feeling of having in some way brought something about. That break did feel like fate. However that happened, this is what happened: I fell on the hard stone floor of the bathroom. An encounter with stones can break your bones. I managed to get myself up and into bed but woke up later that night, unable to move with a sharp searing pain. We had arrived in New York fairly recently, and I had no one with me—my partner was away—but luckily my mobile phone was by my side. I was able to ring for help. They had to break the door down to get me out and down five flights of stairs.

I had fractured my pelvis. For two months or so I used crutches and sometimes a wheelchair. Becoming conscious of breakability by breaking something was a worldly consciousness. I understood this disability to be temporary, as something I would pass through, which I have no doubt framed the situation. But despite the sense of passing through a disabled body, I learned how disability is worldly because I came up against the world; the different ways you are treated, the opening of doors, concerned faces, the closing of doors, rigid indifference. But most of all, I came to feel the little bumps on the street, little bumps I had not even noticed before. Those little bumps became walls that took a huge amount of energy just to get over or to get around.

Slow; heavy; down.

The little bumps I had not noticed before.

My mother is disabled; she became ill with transverse myelitis just after I was born. She has become progressively less mobile over time; now, she can barely walk, her knees rigid and hyperextended. When I was growing up, my mother's condition was kept a secret.[2] We were not told about it. We knew she couldn't do certain things; we thought even that she wouldn't do certain things, but we were never told why: there was secrecy; there was silence. It is a shame there was such shame. I remember experiencing her difficulties as impediments to my own existence: the sadness, say, of not having a mother come to a sporting event when other mothers turned up.

So often a broken history is also a history of secrets, of what is not revealed, including what is behind something, what could have helped to explain something: some difference, some deviation. When I fractured my pelvis, it did change how I related to my mother's situation. It is not that before I had no empathy with her pain: I wrote in *The Cultural Politics of Emotion* (Ahmed 2004) about how I learned about pain through becoming a witness to her pain. Bearing witness was not about grasping her pain; nor was recognizing her pain an adequate response. My mother's history of pain, disability, and illness was bound up with her own history as a migrant woman who had left behind her home, the place she grew up, her family, her connections, to come with her family to a new world. As Yasmin Gunaratnam has observed with reference to the pain experienced by migrants, "Some expressions of pain become discernible and others do not" (2014, 86). Others do not. I think my own experience of breaking allowed a break to become a connection, not even one discerned at the time: a retrospective realization of how a body is not given room to move by a world; how what for some are ordinary bumps for others are walls.

I learned too something about myself not only as a researcher and a writer but as a person: I began to ask myself why, despite having written about the intimacies of bodies and worlds, I had not reflected upon disability. I began to think more about my able-bodied privilege, which is not to say that I have thought about it enough: I have not. It is easy for me to forget to think about it, which is what makes a privilege a privilege: the experiences you are protected from having; the thoughts you do not have to think. Understanding privilege as an energy-saving device might be especially apt for thinking about able-bodied privilege: we are saved from knowing what we are saved from doing. I was able to put disability behind me despite having a disabled mother; or perhaps there is a *because* rather than *despite* here because there is pain there.

Disability was behind me and is still behind me; I do not have to pull it to the front (unless I do so as a deliberate act of self-reflection). I still remember one time overhearing a conversation between my mother and our elderly neighbor. My mother said something like, "Young people don't even have to think about putting one foot in front of the other." I remember when I heard this trying to think about putting one foot in front of the other. But I soon forgot about it. I can remember that I forgot.

A break: it can shatter a story we tell about ourselves. If so then: we can be shattered by a story.

You fracture more than a bone when you fracture a bone: you also experience a break from something; it is no longer as it was before; you are no longer as you were. Eli Clare, in his extraordinary book *Exile and Pride: Disability, Queerness, and Liberation*, describes how even when a broken bone has been healed, it is "different from the bone never broken" ([1999] 2015, 153; see also Oakley 2007). Clare shares many shattering experiences in this book, including experiences of sexual abuse and rape: "the ways my body had been stolen from me" (145). It is also a story in which experiences of being crip, being queer, being gender queer, being poor are all interwoven or entangled with these encounters with violence; a book that makes those knots a source of wisdom.

Writing about the physicality of his experience of cerebral palsy, Clare describes climbing up and down a mountain—"My feet simply don't know the necessary balance. I lurch along from one rock to the next, catching myself repeatedly as I start to fall"—alongside his experience of writing: "The faster I try to write, the more my pen slides out of control, muscles spasm, then contract trying to stop the tremors, my shoulder and upper arm painfully tight" ([1999] 2015, 7). Writing, climbing: they are activities, a body doing things, trying things. You might recall my suggestion that clumsiness is a queer ethics. Clumsiness can be a crip as well as queer ethics; we have to create room for bodies that do not obey commands, that do not move in straight lines, that lose their balance; a body that is less stable is less supported by a ground that is less stable. If a world is organized into straight lines, if there are narrow spaces available to move around in (along a corridor or between that table and that wall), if tools are intended for hands that can keep a firm grasp on things, then activities are harder for some to complete than others. Activities can bring you up against walls.

A body that wriggles about: deviating from an accepted path.[3]

Clumsiness: when a world is what you bump into.

And the wall appears in Clare's text as a place from which you can view a world that is alien: "I watched from the other side of a stone wall, a wall that was part self-preservation, part bones and blood of aloneness, part the impossible assumptions I could not shape my body around" (144). A stone wall: made out of a body that cannot be shaped by other people's assumptions, a body that has been stolen and has to be reclaimed before it can become a home (13). Clare describes how in this harsh and heavy world his most "sustaining relations" were with stones: "I collected stones—red, green, grey, rust, white speckled with black, black streaked with silver—and kept them in my pockets, their hard surfaces warming slowly to my body heat" (144–45). And it is the stones that Clare picks up and puts in his pocket which give him another sense of a body. From a shattering, a story can be told, one that finds in fragility the source of a connection. Picking up the pieces of a story is like picking up those stones; stones that are warmed by the heat of a body. A break can offer another claim to being, being in question as a break in being, recognizing breaking as making a difference in the present, shaping the present.

A break: a story we can tell about ourselves.

Gloria Anzaldúa once wrote, "I'm a broken arm" (1983, 204). She too was writing about fragility, about being brittle and bone; she was writing about being a queer woman of color.

Slow, heavy, down; brown.

I am a broken arm: we repeat history at the moment we fracture; or we become a fracture of a body. A broken arm is a queer kin to the willful arm discussed in chapter 3. A grim story: the arm is striking because it keeps coming up, despite the death of the child. An arm goes on strike when it does not work, when it refuses to be usefully employed. There are many ways to be striking. Something becomes all the more striking when it fractures; it becomes all the more striking when it does not enable you to move on or to get on with things. A body goes on strike when it gets in the way of what you want to accomplish. Your body can be what stops you. As Mia Mingus describes powerfully, "We can swing on a vine all day long yelling 'socially-constructed' but eventually I think we would hit a brick wall and I think that brick wall is our bodies" (2013, n.p.). Bodies too can be walls. Any social justice project has to have disabilities in mind, has to think from an experience of having, say, chronic fatigue syndrome, has to think of a body for whom getting up or getting going might be hitting a brick wall.

A wall can be what you wake up to.

Audre Lorde in *The Cancer Journals* describes in acute detail how it feels to wake up after a mastectomy, to wake up to the gradual realization through the fog of tranquilizers that her "right breast is gone," and of the increasing pain in her chest wall: "My breast which was no longer there would hurt as if it were being squeezed in a vise. That was perhaps the worst pain of all, because it would come with a full complement that I was to be forever reminded of my loss by suffering in a part of me which was no longer there" (1997, 37–38). We can feel an absence; we can sense what is missing.

The Cancer Journals also offers an account of the willfulness required not to wear a prosthesis in the place of a missing breast. Once when she goes to the doctor's office the nurse comments, "You're not wearing a prosthesis," to which Lorde replies, "It really doesn't feel right." The nurse responds, "You will feel so much better with it on," and then, "It's bad for the morale of the office" (60). Not to wear a prosthesis is not to cover over an absence; it is deemed to compromise the happiness of others. Here the broken body intrudes into social consciousness, becoming a reminder of illness and fragility that is unwanted. The killjoy appears again here: the one who gets in the way of the happiness of others by the way she appears. We learn then: bodies need to get in the way to open up a world to others. Yes, equality is a bumpy ride. Smoothing things over often means: eliminating the signs of injury to create a fantasy of a whole. Smoothing things over often means: eliminating those who are reminders of an injury.

CONCLUSION: THE FRAGMENTS ASSEMBLE

Perhaps those who are bad for morale can join forces. Audre Lorde's response to the demand to wear a prosthesis, to pass as a two-breasted woman, or a whole woman, is not only anger but a call for action: "What would happen if an army of one-breasted women descended on Congress and demanded that the use of carcinogenic, fat-stored hormones in beef-feed be outlawed?" she asks (1997, 14–15). An army of one-breasted women: What would happen? What could happen? A queer crip army would be assembled, made out of bodies without parts, or even parts without bodies. Carrie Sandahl (1993, 26) teases out the "affinities and tensions" between crip and queer. Crip and queer: both these words have hurtful histories; they are words that drip with insult. They are words that are claimed, becoming pointed; becoming ways of pointing to something, because they keep alive that history: negation as a political sensation.

This affinity might be carried by the words themselves, by how the words *crip* and *queer* become sites of potential insofar as they retain a negative charge. For Eve Kosofsky Sedgwick, what makes *queer* a "politically potent term" is how it cleaves to "childhood scenes of shame" (1993, 4). The potency of *queer* is the difficult history it keeps bringing up. Alison Kafer explores how *crip* is a charged word. Drawing on Nancy Mairs's essay on wanting people to wince at the word, she suggests, "This desire to make people wince suggests an urge to shake things up, to jolt people out of their everyday understandings of bodies and minds, of normalcy and deviance" (Kafer 2013, 15). *Queer* and *crip* are willful words that work by insisting on what they bring up; a charged history, a shattering history; they are shattering words.

The words, they come together; they have an affinity in what they refuse. A queer crip affinity might be possible when you share what you are not missing. A queer crip politics might allow the body deemed not whole to be revealed, a revelation that might be registered as a willful obtrusion into social consciousness ("bad for morale"). A queer crip politics might involve a refusal to cover over what is missing, a refusal to aspire to be whole. What I call the will duty often takes the form of an aspiration: even for bodies that are not able to be whole, they must be willing to aspire to be whole. There can be nothing more willful than the refusal to be aspirational.

We can refuse to miss what we are deemed to be missing.

We can share a refusal.

Does this mean that we can give ourselves a break? Does this mean that there is a way of relating to breaking that does not aim for restoration? Can the fragments reassemble in or from being shattered? Wear and tear: traces of time on the surface of your body, the warmth of affection, comings and goings, the sharpness of an edge, things we endure; a raised voice, brittle. Audre Lorde writes in *Zami*, "In order to survive the weather we had to become stone" (1984b, 160). Social forms of oppression, racism, the hatred that creates some bodies as strangers, are experienced as weather. They press and pound against the surface of a body; a body can surface or survive by hardening. Lorde then adds, "We bruise ourselves upon the other who is closest" (160). Lorde is writing here of relations between black women, of how easy it is because of how hard the world is, that black women can hurt each other. Those who have to harden to survive can hurt each other by what they have to do to be.

Hardness for Lorde is thus not the elimination of fragility; it is how we live with fragility. Sometimes we need a wall to protect ourselves. Sometimes we need to retreat when the world is intrusive. Sometimes we need to shatter that wall. A bruise can lead to a wall; a bruise can be a break. When a stone breaks, a stone becomes stones. A fragment: what breaks off is on the way to becoming something else. Feminism: on the way to becoming something else. Shattering: scattering. What is shattered so often is scattered, strewn all over the place. A history that is down, heavy, is also messy, strewn.

The fragments: an assembly. In pieces. Becoming army.

8 / FEMINIST SNAP

In this chapter I want to think about breaking points, as the very points we might aim to reach. When we say we have reached a breaking point, we often evoke a crisis, the kind of crisis I explored in chapter 7, when what you come up against threatens to be too much, threatens a life, or a dream, or a hope. A crisis can also be an opening, a new way of proceeding, depending on how we do or do not resolve that crisis; depending on whether we think of a crisis as something that needs to be resolved.

We can return to the happiness path discussed in chapter 2. A path can be a line we follow to get somewhere. A path once followed is behind us. When we think of a family background, we might tend to think of what is behind a child: a story of where she comes from. But a background can also be what a child is asked to aspire to; the happy family photographs that surround her become not only traces of where she and others have been, but suggestions for where she too may go, a future she too might have, should have. A background can thus orientate us toward the future. When the child reproduces what she inherits, she extends the family line. There is pressure to inherit this line, a pressure that can speak the language of love, happiness, and care. We do not know what we would become without these points of pressure, which insist that happiness will follow if we do this or we do that.

And yet, at certain points, we can refuse the inheritance, points that are often experienced as breaking points. In this chapter I explore what I call simply feminist snap, as a way of thinking more creatively and affirmatively about breaking points. Sometimes we have to struggle to snap bonds, including familial bonds, those that are damaging or at least compromising of a possibility that you are not ready to give up. It is not always certain or clear what is damaging; indeed, we learn from the figure of the killjoy that there is a politics to where damage is located. A snap can also be identified by others as damaging because of what or even who is broken when something snaps.

SNAPFUL

When I first saw the film *A Question of Silence*, I thought immediately that what was displayed was a collective act of feminist snap. I turn to this film in the final section of the chapter, thinking with it, alongside two other feminist films from the 1980s, *Nine to Five* and *Born in Flames*. The word *snap* came to my mind for what is shown in *A Question of Silence*, for what is so powerful about this film. That word has stuck with me since. Why this word? Let's take the full range of potential meanings and let's treat the word *snap* as verb, as doing something: to snap; she snaps.

To snap can mean to make a brisk, sharp, cracking sound; to break suddenly; to give way abruptly under pressure or tension; to suffer a physical or mental breakdown, especially while under stress; to bring the jaws briskly together, often with a clicking sound; to bite; to snatch or grasp suddenly and with eagerness; to speak abruptly or sharply; to move swiftly and smartly; to flash or appear to flash light; to sparkle; to open, close, or fit together with a click.

Snap is quite a sensation. To snap can be to make a sharp sound. As a feminist killjoy, I have been giving my ear to those who sound sharp. I will come back to the sounds of this sharpness; it matters. The temporality of snapping is also crucial: a snap is a sudden quick movement. The speed of snapping might be how a snap comes to be apprehended as a movement at all (the slower you move, the less a move seems like a movement).

I always think with the examples that come to mind; the sensations of being in the world with objects and others. And when I think of snap, I think of a twig. When a twig snaps, we hear the sound of it breaking. We can hear the suddenness of a break. We might assume, on the basis of what we hear, that the snap is a starting point. A snap sounds like the start of something, a transformation of something; it is how a twig might end up broken in two pieces. A snap might even seem like a violent moment; the unbecoming of something.

But a snap would only be the beginning insofar as we did not notice the pressure on the twig. If pressure is an action, snap is a reaction. Pressure is hard to notice unless you are under that pressure. Snap is only the start of something because of what we do not notice. Can we redescribe the world from the twig's point of view, that is, from the point of view of those who are under pressure?

We can begin to build a picture of how and why snap matters. I drew in part I on Marilyn Frye's (1983) recalling of the root of the meaning of oppression in *press*. Bodies can be pressed into shape; or are under pressure in being shaped. We learn as well: this pressure is not always something we can witness from the outside. You might experience that pressure only when you are under it, rather like you encounter the wall when you come up against it. The weightiest of experiences are often those that are hardest to convey to those who do not share the experience. If a snap seems sharp or sudden, it might be because we do not experience the slower time of bearing or of holding up; the time in which we can bear the pressure, the time it has taken for things not to break.

If the twig was a stronger twig, if the twig was more resilient, it would take more pressure before it snapped. We can see how resilience is a technology of will, or even functions as a command: be willing to bear more; be stronger so you can bear more. We can understand too how resilience becomes a deeply conservative technique, one especially well suited to governance: you encourage bodies to strengthen so they will not succumb to pressure; so they can keep taking it; so they can take more of it. Resilience is the requirement to take more pressure; such that the pressure can be gradually increased. Or as Robin James describes, resilience "recycles damages into more resources" (2015, 7). Damage becomes a means by which a body is asked to take it; or to acquire the strength to take more of it.

When you don't take it, when you can't take any more of it, what happens? The moment of not taking it is so often understood as losing it. When a snap is registered as the origin of violence, the one who snaps is deemed violent. She snaps. You can hear the snap in the sound of her voice. Sharp, brittle, loud; perhaps it is like the volume has suddenly been turned up, for no reason; the quietness that surrounds her ceases when she speaks, her voice cutting the atmosphere, registering as the loss of something; a nicer atmosphere, a gentler mood. And then: violence is assumed to originate with her. A feminist politics might insist on renaming actions as reactions; we need to show how her snap is not the starting point.

The killjoy gives us another handle at the very moment she seems to lose it. The feminist killjoy might herself be a snappy figure; feminists might be perceived as full of snap. Maybe there is a relation between willful and snapful. Snappiness as a quality is often defined in terms of aptitude. To be snappy is to be "apt to speak sharply or irritably." That certainly sounds like a feminist aptitude. Feminism: it has bite; she bites. We might even as feminists aim to develop this aptitude: by snapping, we acquire more snap. We aim to become snappier by snapping. This does not mean or make snappiness right or into a right. But perhaps snappiness might be required to right a wrong when a wrong requires we bear it; that we take it, or that we take more of it.

Snap: when she can't take it anymore; when she just can't take it anymore. Speaking sharply, speaking with irritation. Maybe we can hear her irritation; a voice that rises, a voice that sharpens. A voice can lose its smoothness; becoming rougher, more brittle. When her irritation speaks volumes, we might be distracted from what is irritating. Can we even distract ourselves?

Irritation is an intimacy of body and world. When I think of irritation, I think of contact dermatitis. What you come into contact with can irritate your skin. Irritation registers contact as intrusion. The surface of your skin might become rougher as well as itchy. You might scratch your skin because it is itchy; and there might be a sense of relief, but then it becomes itchier. You know this will happen, but you can't help doing this: because those moments of relief are too precious. The quality of an experience is that of rubbing against something other than yourself, but once you are rubbed up the wrong way, it can feel like your own body is against you, even in those moments of relief. To speak from irritation is to speak of being rubbed up against the world in a certain way. Sianne Ngai (2007) describes irritation as a "minor negative affect." That is such a good description. We all know that life is full of mild irritations. Perhaps irritation is a little like infection; things eventually come to a head. There is a point when it all comes out, a tipping point. There are a certain number of times you can be rubbed the wrong way, before you end up snapping. A snap might seem sudden but the suddenness is only apparent; a snap is one moment of a longer history of being affected by what you come up against.

Snap: a moment with a history.

If you are apt to be snappy, perhaps you are not happy. But perhaps this aptness is only a part of the story. Some get rubbed up the wrong way more than others; we know this. A feminist killjoy lives and works in a contact zone. She might acquire an aptitude for irritation not because of the nature of her speech or being, but because of how much she has already had to put up with. What she has to put up with becomes part of who she is. That she appears as a figure at all (remember, she is first received as an assignment by others) is often about a history of being rubbed up the wrong way. I described this in chapter 1 as "being wound up by someone who is winding you up."

We could think of feminist history as a history of snappy women. Perhaps we would be thinking of how what comes out of our own mouths is speaking this history. It might be that our tongues become snappy, speaking for us, in our struggle to speak back and to speak up. I think of *Jane Eyre*. Jane in the opening scenes of the novel, in the grim scenes of her childhood, struggles to speak back to her tyrannical aunt. Eventually Jane snaps. But she only speaks when her tongue seems to acquire a will of its own: "I say scarcely voluntary for it seemed as if my tongue pronounced words without my will consenting to their utterance" (Brontë [1847] 1999, 21). Our tongues can disobey for us; they can pronounce the words that announce a refusal to comply.

Perhaps feminists acquire willful tongues from the very act of speaking out. Perhaps we need willful tongues in order to resist being straightened out. Willful tongues: I think too of Gloria Anzaldúa's chapter, "How to Tame a Wild Tongue," from *Borderlands/La Frontera: The New Mestiza*. The chapter begins with a dramatic scene: a dentist who is cleaning the roots of her teeth says to her with "anger rising in his voice" that "we're going to have to do something about your tongue" and that he'd "never seen anything as strong and stubborn" ([1987] 1999, 75). Her wayward tongue evokes the willful arm of the willful child discussed in chapter 3. Her tongue keeps pushing out the "wads of cotton, pushing back the drills, the long thin needles" (75). All the materials the dentist, concerned with health and hygiene, puts in her mouth, are pushed right out again, as if her tongue is refusing to be cleaned, as if her tongue is spreading an infection. Gloria Anzaldúa describes many attempts to tame her tongue, to make her "speak English" (76). When she tries to tell the teacher how to pronounce her name she is heard as "talking back." To speak your own language is to become disobedient. Her tongue persists with a willful disobedience, refusing to be straightened out.

Feminism: a history of willful tongues. Feminism: that which infects a body with a desire to speak in ways other than how you have been commanded to speak. I think too of bell hooks's (1988) extraordinary text *Talking Back: Thinking Feminism, Thinking Black*. She explains how she renamed herself by adopting the name of her maternal grandmother as her pen name (9). Elsewhere, hooks describes how her grandmother was "known for her snappy and bold tongue" (1996, 152). Here a snappy tongue is affirmed as what black women inherit from each other; a maternal line as a snappy line. A snappy tongue gives the words for a black woman to pen her own name.

Snap can be a genealogy, unfolding as an alternative family line, or as a feminist inheritance. I often think of snap as what I have inherited from my Pakistani aunties. My sister talks of her daughter as having Ahmed genes, and I know what she means; she means she is another point on a line of snappy women. She means: like me, like you, like our aunties, this girl has snap. This girl has snap: maybe she too is a survival story. I think of my own family and the work that had to be done to keep things together, the work that women often did, to hold on when things are breaking up. We might, reflecting back to my discussion in chapter 7, be haunted by those breaks, even those that we did not live through ourselves. In my family's case, I think of Partition, how a country was broken up in the afterlife of colonialism; how borders became open wounds; how an infection can spread. Family stories were passed down about the trauma of Partition; a Muslim family leaving their home in Jalandhar, fleeing to Lahore, a long hard train journey, arriving, creating a new home from what had been left behind by those who, too, had fled.

We might inherit a break because it was survived. A survival can be how we are haunted by a break. When I think of this history of breaking, I think especially of my relationship to my eldest auntie, Gulzar Bano. I mentioned in the introduction how my own feminism was shaped by our many conversations. My auntie—who was most definitely snappy—did not marry. The family explanation is that this not marrying was because of Partition. A national break can be interwoven with a life story. Gulzar was deeply involved in women's activism as well as campaigns for women's literacy and education in Pakistan. She was a poet, too. Her words were sharp like weapons. When our lives don't follow the lines provided by convention, we still have people behind us, those who offer us lifelines, without expectation of return. Becoming close to my aunt, with her passion for feminism and for what she calls in our family biography "WOMAN POWER," helped me to find a different political orientation, a different way of thinking about my place in the world. In a conventional genealogy, the woman who does not have a child of her own would be an end point.

Snap, snap: the end of the line.

In a feminist and queer genealogy, life unfolds from such points.

Snap, snap: begin again.

SNAP THE BOND

Snapping at someone can also snap a bond to someone. Snapping might matter because a bond can be what gets in the way of living a life, perhaps living a feminist life. Not all bonds are destructive; some bonds we might need to sustain a feminist life. Recalling my discussion of willful womanism in chapter 3, sometimes we might need to be snappy to hold on to a bond that we are asked to give up. A familial bond can become a source of vitality and strength, even shelter, from the harshness of a world. Knowing the difference between bonds that are sustaining and those that are not is a challenge. A feminist life: living with that challenge. Sometimes we have a crisis because a bond we thought was sustaining ends up not being as sustaining as we thought.

We can have a bond not only to another person but also to an idea or ideal: a bond to a father can be a family bond, for instance, a way of investing in the very idea of the family. One of the pressures we live under is to preserve some bonds, at almost any cost. When my father "disowned" me (I shouldn't use this word, because it implies previous ownership, but it does help to convey something of the significance of snapping a bond), it was partly because my queer life choices represented for him a cut-off point.[1] He would probably say that he did not cut me off but that I cut myself off by virtue of the path I took, a deviation from the straight path. Probably, from his point of view, I was the one who snapped a bond, because of where I was going, because of what I was like; his final word to me was a letter about how I was "sick in the head," even if by the end of his communication his aim was to end our communication.

> Snap as a feminist sickness.
> She can't help herself.
> Sad; bad; mad; rad.

It makes a difference though, whether or not you experience yourself in the terms used to dismiss you. In some ways, I led him to these words, or at least I did not lead him away from these words. I did not fight to hold on to the fragile bond we had, which some might say a daughter is obliged to do. I did not even try to hold things together. I stopped doing the work of reconciliation because I wanted the bond to snap; I was exhausted by that bond; a bond can be a bind. I was tired of meeting up only to hear him say things that were harsh, critical, and judgmental; that weighed me down just as before he had weighed me down. One of the last times we met, he said women are not equal because babies need breast milk. I left the table, too infuriated for words, and the event was recalled by him and my stepmother as me "losing it." The choices were always limited: be silent or lose it.

I would prefer to lose it.

Obviously: this is the story of a relationship told from my point of view.

Obviously: the willful girl has a story to tell.

And now, when I tell people this story, they think I am telling them a sad story, a story of how a relationship between a father and daughter came to a sorry end; a story of the severing of a family bond. So often people are sorry; they are even sorry for me. But for me this part of the story is not the sad part. For me, this point, the snap, was not the sad point. It was rather a relief from pressure. In chapter 2, I noted how you can experience a relief from pressure by being willing to go in the direction you have been pressured to take. That's one way. You can also experience a relief from pressure by snapping a bond, by ending your connection to those who put you under pressure to go in a direction you are not willing to take. My relief was a relief not only from the pressure of a relationship that required me to go places I did not wish to go, but from the requirement to hold on to that relationship. To experience the end of a family relationship as not sad was to be alienated from the family all over again: alienated by virtue of how I was not affected. As I discussed in chapter 2, you can become an affect alien by not being sad when you are supposed to be sad.

Not only was I not sad, I experienced this snap as a lifeline, as a way of being pulled out of something that was difficult to survive. It gave me a freedom to get on with the life I wanted to live: a feminist and queer life. It meant leaving the family table behind, even if I keep carrying it with me, writing about it, that table memory, or that table as memory; even if other family tables would end up taking its place.

A snap is not a starting point, but a snap can be the start of something.

We can note from this example that it can be unclear who is snapping, or what is snapping. Even when things break, we do not always know what breaks. We do not always know what follows a break. If a snap is a stopping point, things start up again.

From our experience of snapping a bond, we might ask ourselves: what are the relationships we want to preserve? Lauren Berlant (2011) introduces the idea of "cruel optimism" to explain how we can end up holding on to what diminishes us; how we can stay attached to a life that is not working. To be in a relation of cruel optimism does not necessarily mean that we feel optimistic;

that we hold on to something because we hope that it could get us somewhere; although we can feel like this. Rather the bond itself is the scene of optimism; a cluster of promises that can surround an object (an idea, a thing, a person, a relation). Cruel optimism might be one way of explaining how we do not snap the bonds that are, at some level, compromising, maybe of our existence; maybe of our capacity to realize an idea of an existence.

All good concepts, sweaty concepts, have questions that surround them; they throw life up as a question. How do we know what diminishes us? How do we know when a life is working or not working? Who judges whether a life is working or not working? These are difficult questions, and our task is not to resolve them; they are life questions.

These are questions for us in living a feminist life. I know for instance that others might diagnose feminism itself as cruel optimism, as an attachment to a life that is not working. Indeed, for those who question feminist investments, a willingness to let a bond snap could be understood as a form of cruel pessimism, a failure to become attached to an idea of life that would have been less diminishing. In the context of academic culture, I think the one who points out sexism and racism in citational practice is often judged as suffering from cruel pessimism. If we snap this bond, we are assumed to be ending a line that would have been life sustaining as well as meaning making. When you do not extend a line, it might be assumed you are intending the end of a line in which others are deeply invested. You become a dead end. A snap can be judged as willful in the sense of when you put an end to it; you are assumed to be putting an end to what you need for your own continuation. You are putting an end to yourself. A snap can be judged as a way of depriving yourself of a connection, and thus a form of violence you direct against yourself.

Snap, snap.

She cuts: despite herself, in spite of herself.

Spiteful; ill will; malice.

She cuts off her nose in spite of her face.

We can hear what is at stake here: feminism becomes understood as how she harms herself. When she snaps the bond, snapping becomes self-harm. The feminist killjoy could be imagined as the scene of cruel optimism, which is all the more cruel as it rests on a pessimism: not only are her attachments judged as not working, as diminishing her own life as well as the lives of others, they stop her from being attached to, or reattaching to, a better script, one that would lead her in a happier direction. Feminists according to this scenario would need to snap their bond to the killjoy; they would need to give her up or let her go before she drains them (read us) of the energy required to get on with just getting along. Or the killjoy herself would be considered as a snap: as snapping the bond to the family, or to some idea of civil life, which is what stops her from keeping the peace, from reconciliation, from becoming more attuned or in harmony with others, what stops her from smoothing things over, from extending a line.

Snappy not happy.

From this we learn: it is not always self-evident which bonds are damaging. There are arguments and disagreements precisely because it is not always self-evident. As a feminist, I might need to make a case for a feminist life. I am willing this for; I am this for; I am for. I have to make a case: that living a feminist life is working; that this life is working. To make a case is not necessarily about giving that life a specific content, although it might involve emphasizing certain values, such as equality, not as something that we assume we have, but as the bumpy process of working out how to live with others. To make a case is not simply to argue for your own attachments as if they are preferable to others. I do not think it is good to be too confident in one's decisions and, thus, to be too confident in the shape of the life you live, a life that has acquired its shape because of decisions you have already made along the way. I think it is good to think of life as always potentially in crisis, to keep asking the question: how to live? A killjoy in crisis: there is value just in this; the value of opening up life to a decision, of realizing that life is open to a decision.

A case for a feminist life can be made in a moment of suspension: we suspend our assumptions about what a life is or should be. Just opening up room for different ways of living a life can be experienced by others as snap. You can become a killjoy just by saying: life does not have to be like this, or to be this.

Let's return to the word *happiness*. Happiness is such a weighty word, a moral word, because of how it has become attached to the good. If we go back, if we follow happiness back on the route to its root, we find that the word *happiness* derived from the Middle English word *hap*, meaning chance. Happiness shares its hap with the word *perhaps* as well as *happens* and *happenstance*. Happiness now sounds quite different from these words—these words seem lighter; they convey movement, blowing haphazardly, rather like straw in the wind.

How did happiness lose its hap? This was one of my primary questions in *The Promise of Happiness* (Ahmed 2010). I became very fond of the word *hap* once I happened upon it. And it is queer now to reflect that I happened upon hap because I was writing about happiness. Once I found the word, I fell for it.

When I go for a walk without knowing where I am going, I call it a hap walk. To affirm hap is to follow a queer route: you are not sure which way you are going; maybe you let your feet decide for you. You can be redirected by what you encounter along the way as you are not rushing ahead, rushing forward, to get somewhere. You wander, haphazardly at times, but then you might acquire a sense of purpose because of what you find on the way. How we take a walk is not unrelated to how we live a life. To proceed without assuming there is a right direction is to proceed differently. To say life does not have to be like this, to have this shape or this direction, is to make room for hap. To make room for hap can be experienced and judged as snapping a bond.

To affirm hap can be judged as snap.

To make a case for a feminist life can be about keeping open the question of how to live. This opening up can be experienced as a judgment: I have heard this. For instance, if you decide not to marry and have children, your decision can be narrated as somehow rejecting that life, or passing judgment on those who live that life, as if by not doing *x* you are saying *x* is wrong. Maybe sometimes you do speak of wrongs—you might say it is wrong to assume those choices are right or are the only right choices. But you can be heard as being judgmental or dismissive just by virtue of not following a well-trodden path. And in being heard thus, you are heard as harming not only yourself (the things you give up, the happiest days you will not have by virtue of the life you live) but others who gave things up to follow that path. It is then as if in giving up a life that you were expected to live (those casual conversations of futurity, the grandchildren it is assumed you would or should provide), you are giving up on others.

We thus learn the need for caution about harm: difference and deviation are often registered as damaging those who are different, those who deviate. So much conservation of power rests on the assumption that not to conserve the familiar forms of an existence would cause damage to what might be or who might be: the child who would be teased for being different. This child of the future, this child who would be teased, is called upon to bear the burden of what is risked if we were to become more inventive with family form, more inventive with life.

In some cases it is self-evident that a bond is damaging; a life is risked. Indeed, I would argue that judgments against certain lives borrow this self-evidence, and by doing so, they claim that certain lives are a form of harm. Antifeminist rhetoric often positions feminism as self-harm: as if to say that women harm themselves by experiencing certain relationships as being harmful. It is not despite but because this borrowing takes place that we need to recognize harm. Recognition, however, is often what we have to struggle for. It can be difficult for those who are in a harmful relationship to recognize harm because of harm.

A bond can be violent. What can make living with violence hard is how hard it is even to imagine or think the possibility of its overcoming; you might be isolated; you might be materially dependent; you might be down, made to think and feel you are beneath that person; you might be attached to that person, or believe that person when he says he will change; you might have become part of that person, have your life so interwoven with that person that it is hard to imagine what would be left of you if he left. The bonds we form are not exterior to ourselves; a bond is the loss of exteriority. Bonds are not something we can give up without giving up on part of ourselves, giving up on part of our own history. When you snap a bond it can appear to be an action directed toward someone else, but you can experience it as snapping at your own self.

And so: it can be hard to imagine what would be left of you if a bond was snapped. But in spite of that, the fear that there would be nothing left, there can be a point, a breaking point, when it is too much and what did not seem possible becomes necessary. She fights back; she speaks out. She has places to go because other women have been there. No wonder that leaving a situation of violence can feel like snap: a bond of fate has indeed been broken. Perhaps the slow time of endurance can only be ended by a sudden movement. Or perhaps the movement seems sudden only because, as I said earlier, we cannot see the slower times of bearing, what Lauren Berlant (2007) has called compellingly "slow death."

A breaking point can be experienced as the sadness of not being able to live the life you are living even if the life you are living is sad; moments when it is all too much, when a body, a life, a world becomes unbearable. A snap signals that a life that one has been bearing is a life one is no longer willing to bear. A snap can be directed at one's own past bearing. You can snap because you are exhausted by having not snapped thus far and by what you have had to put up with. You can't bear what you have borne for too long.

A snap can tell us when it is too much, after it is too much, which is how a snap can be feminist pedagogy. Sometimes you snap when an effort to do what you have been doing is too much to sustain. In chapter 6 I discussed my involvement in an effort to address the problem of sexual harassment in universities. I recently resigned from my position as a professor without another academic position to go to. What I had been asked to bear became too much; the lack of support for the work we were doing; the walls we kept coming up against. That I could resign depended upon having material resources and security. But it still felt like I was going out on a limb: I did not just feel like I was leaving a job, or an institution, but also a life, an academic life; a life I had loved; a life I was used to. And that act of leaving was a form of feminist snap: there was a moment when I couldn't take it anymore, those walls of indifference that were stopping us from getting anywhere; that were stopping us from getting through. Once the bond had snapped, I realized that I had been trying to hold on to something that had already broken. Maybe my relationship to the institution was like Silas's relationship to his pot: if I had tried to put the shattered pieces back together, they would become a memorial, a reminder of what could not be. Resignation can sound passive, even fatalistic: resigning oneself to one's fate. But resignation can be an act of feminist protest. By snapping you are saying: I will not work for an organization that is not addressing the problem of sexual harassment. Not addressing the problem of sexual harassment is reproducing the problem of sexual harassment. By snapping you are saying: I will not reproduce a world I cannot bear, a world I do not think should be borne.

That snap might sound quite violent, dramatic even. Resigning in feminist protest—and making public that you are resigning in feminist protest—does get attention. It can be a sharp sound; a sudden break. In my case, that break was supported by many of my feminist colleagues; but not by all. One feminist colleague describes my action as "rash," a word used to imply an action that is too quick as well as careless. Snapping is often a matter of timing. If a snap is a moment with a history, that history is the accumulated effect of what you have come up against. And just think: you have to do more, the more you do not get through. You have had hundreds of meetings, with students, with academics, with administrators. You have written blogs about the problem of sexual harassment and the silence that surrounds it. And still there is silence. To resign is a tipping point, a gesture that becomes necessary because of what the previous actions did not accomplish. The actions that did not accomplish anything are not noticed by those who are not involved in the effort. So the action that spills a history, so that it falls out, so there is a fall out, is deemed rash.

Well maybe then: I am willing to be rash.

It is not just the pressure you cannot detect when a snap sounds sudden; it is also a history of resistance, of not being willing to put up with something. Not all resistance is audible or legible. Snapping does not, however, always involve a conscious act of resistance. Snapping is not always planned. Indeed snapping can get in the way of the best-laid plan. Snapping can be about the intensity of a situation: when you are asked to do something and you experience that request as too much, this time, even if you have done it before. Something can become too much, before we even know it is too much. When we snap, we do not always know what we are doing. And when we snap, we do not always know where we are going. And yet we snap because of what we have been doing; we snap because where we have been is no longer where we can be. Perhaps snap involves another kind of optimism; we might call this an optimism without a future, an optimism that makes a break of something the start of something without knowing what this something is, or what it might be; an optimism that does not give a content to something, including what lies ahead.

COLLECTIVE SNAP

In this section I want to discuss three feminist films, all of which display feminist snap as a collective snap. I start with the film that inspired this chapter: *A Question of Silence* (dir. Marlene Gorris, 1982). I offered a very short reading of this film in my book *Willful Subjects* (Ahmed 2014), which is when I first introduced this idea of feminist snap, but I passed over much of the detail. Here I want to slow down. To hear snap, one must slow down; we listen for the slower times of wearing and tearing, of making do; we listen for the sounds of the costs of becoming attuned to the requirements of patriarchy.

It is a feminist plot: a female psychiatrist, Janine van den Bos, is employed to establish whether or not three women who brutally murdered a man, a boutique owner, are sane and can be held responsible for their actions. The three women are a housewife, Christine; a waitress, Annie; and a secretary, Anna. The film uses flashbacks: we begin after the event of the murder, with the arrest of the women, and then as they provide testimony to the psychiatrist, there are three flashbacks to the murder. We end with a courtroom scene, which I consider at length in due course.

The film might depict a moment of feminist snap: but we do not start with that snap, the moment when the violence endured by women gets redirected against a man in an outburst of rage. This moment, which is in fact a series of moments, a collection of snapshots, comes somewhere in the middle of the film. By going back into each of their lives, the film shows snap not as a single moment of one woman experiencing something as too much but as a series of accumulated gestures that connect women over time and space. The film gives snap a history. Each of the women has her own story, but they share what they are asked to endure: let us give the problem its name, patriarchy. The film works by juxtaposing scenes of being worn down, worn out; sexism as a worn thread of connection.

Through most of the film, Christine is willingly silent. As the psychiatrist says at the end, "She has made a decision to keep silent. She certainly can communicate. She doesn't see the point of it." We learn of her history of being worn down through her drawings, which show stick figures of nuclear families contained by boxes. We learn also of her history through her husband's testimony to Janine; her husband, who assumes she doesn't speak much because she "doesn't have much to say," and who reveals his own anger that she didn't keep the children quiet when he returned from work. Silence becomes an expectation: the assumption that women who work at home do not work, that their duty is to maintain a quiet household, organized around the protection of the time and space of the husband.

She says nothing. She becomes nothing. Or so he says.

In contrast, Annie the waitress is described by Janine as speaking too much. In one of the opening scenes of the film, she is at work. And the men she is waiting upon make sexist jokes; we sense those jokes are a routine (this one: that what women know about finance is "how to open their hands for cash" and that they "open their legs" in return). We get a sense that she is used to this; that she has come to expect this. When she (almost) snaps, they say, "Don't let it get under your skin." One man asks, "Where's your sense of humor?" She responds to the mockery of this question with humor: "I didn't bring it today." Maybe she does not snap because she has learned to laugh it off. Laughter can become a routine. But you have a sense of her weariness: the frustration of being laughed at, being laughed over.

And then there is the secretary, Anna, described by her boss as his right hand; smart, fierce, willful. They are at a meeting. They are seated at a table. She makes an intelligent suggestion. The men do not hear her. She is the secretary; she keeps their secrets; she is not supposed to contribute her thoughts. Another man says the same thing she just said. The other men rush to congratulate him for his good idea. Sexism: how women are passed over. Sexism: how women's ideas are attributed to men, as if an idea cannot be heard unless it originates from a male body. When she makes a sound (she stirs her tea with a spoon), she causes irritation; she becomes a disturbance. Then, only then, they turn to face her. Sexism: how women are heard only as interrupting the proceedings.

She says nothing but there is a close-up of her face: her expression is snap-ful; she recognizes what she is up against. We get a sense then that her snap-to-come is a delayed snap. A present snap can be an accumulated history; a history can be confronted in an act of snap. You enact a rage not only toward something or somebody in the present, but toward the past, all those past experiences of putting up with it. To snap is to say no to that history, to its perpetual reenactment.

And when Anna is talking to the psychiatrist, we get a sense of other histories of injustice, other ways that being for women or being women becomes restricted. Anna talks of her mother, how her mother wanted her to be married, wanted her to have children. We sense the mother mourning the loss of grandchildren; we sense that daughter mourning how her choices are mourned. We sense Anna's unhappiness at being the cause of her mother's unhappiness, her mother's unhappiness that her daughter is not normal. We hear how those words are another sad history; deviation as loss. Later, later, in one scene, Anna and Janine are close; we sense the possibility of lesbian desire; we sense another future, woven out of their intimacy. It is a future that might yet happen; post-snap who knows what might happen?

Many stories, each interwoven with each other, told together, creating a feminist tapestry. And the psychiatrist Janine is herself transformed by giving these women her ear: by listening to them, she becomes attuned to them; she begins to pick up what they hear. An ear can be attuned to snap, to what is out of tune, those jarring notes; those awkward stirring sounds of not being accommodated. The jarring jars against an idea of happiness. For the film began with a sequence showing Janine and her husband together at home; it is a kind of fantasy image, of an egalitarian relationship, an equal relationship. But as she begins to hear through the women who have snapped, who are postsnap, she becomes a silent witness to her own marriage, her own situation. It is not as happy or as equal as it seemed.

One time, again at a table—so much of life is assembled around tables—there is a dinner. And she and another woman—they are both wives—are listening to the men talking to each other, hearing how they are absent from the conversation; watching themselves disappear (remember Mrs. Dalloway, like Mrs. Dalloway). Janine cannot bear it anymore; she bangs the cutlery. Maybe it is an act of sabotage, maybe an accident: the men stop talking. She has their attention. Sharp, crash, bang. This sound, her sound: heard as disturbance. To become attuned to sexism, to begin to hear with a feminist ear how women are not heard, is to become out of tune with a world. When you find this world jarring, you are experienced as jarring. The men start talking again.

She has to smash it. To stop it she has to smash it.

A feminist ear picks up on what is being said, a message that is blocked by how what is being said is heard as interference. The sounds of no, the complaints about violence, the refusals to laugh at sexist jokes; the refusals to comply with unreasonable demands; to acquire a feminist ear is to hear those sounds as speech. But it is not just that feminist ears can hear beyond the silence that functions as a wall. I referred earlier to how working on the problem of sexual harassment led me to my own act of feminist snap. Once it is heard that you are willing to hear, more people will speak to you. While a snap might seem to make the tongue the organ of feminist rebellion, perhaps snap is all about ears. A feminist ear can provide a release of a pressure valve. A feminist ear can be how you hear what is not being heard.

Because: those who experience harassment come up against a wall of indifference. They have nowhere to go. Or if they do speak they are heard as complaining. The word *complaint* derives from plague, in a vulgar sense, to strike at the breast. A complaint: sick speech. Maybe she is heard as speaking from ill will: not only as being ill, but as spreading infection, as making the whole body ill. If diversity is damage limitation, as I described in chapter 6, then damage limitation takes the form of controlling speech, of trying to stop those who speak about violence from speaking in places where they can be heard. To contain damage is to contain those who have been damaged. When she is heard as complaining she is not heard. And those who are willing to hear will end up hearing more and more; you are providing a place to go. Something I learned from my own experience: resignation can be a feminist hearing. So many people got in touch with me after I spoke out about sexual harassment with their own stories of harassment and abuse in universities; with their own battles. Telling the story is part of the feminist battle. A feminist ear can be what we are *for*. The more wearing it is, the more we need to hear.

In *The Question of Silence*, the women are shown as worn down. But it does not just depict this wearing. These women happen upon each other because they happen to be in the same dress boutique at the same time. While they are doing an ordinary task they commit what appears to be an extraordinary act. One of the women is stopped by a male shopkeeper as she attempts to steal an item of clothing, to take what she has not bought, what is not rightfully hers. Maybe she is stealing as an enactment of what has been taken from her. Maybe

she experiences this event of being stopped as the injustice of not having recognized what has been taken from her. She is used to this injustice; she has
come to expect it; but this time she snaps.

She; they. The two other women move with sympathy; they, too, put items
of clothing in their bags. Rebellion becomes a feminist mirror; a way of reflecting each other. The women surround the man. They are silent; they are solemn. They are like magnets: drawn to each other. The loud jarring repetitive
music gives us the volume or pitch of their action. Surrounding these three
women who are killing a man they do not know (Anna later says to Janine that
this man "could have been any man") are four other women. They become
silent witnesses to this killing; they participate through or in their silence. We
become silent witnesses, too.

A feminist bond can be formed by what you hear. And Janine has given
her ear: we hear what she can hear, what is said, what is not said. When the
women are on trial in the courtroom, Janine shares her conclusion as an expert
witness. When she says the women are sane, that they are responsible for their
actions, the room is filled with shock. Her speech act is heard as hysterical, as
willful, as defiant even though she says what she says calmly, even though her
voice is reasoned, even though she gives her reasons. They cannot grasp the
reason of her reason. During the break in the session, her husband suggests
she is harming herself, her reputation, his reputation. He says she is being
carried away by idealism.

She knows what he is saying: stop or you will hurt me. She snaps. And
when they return to the courtroom, she speaks with even more conviction.
Her snap allows her to acquire an even more insistent voice. They are sane,
she says. They are sane, she repeats. The men are bewildered; they are enraged.
And then: the women start laughing at the patriarchal reasoning of the Law.
When the judge says, this situation could have been reversed; it could have
been a man killing a female boutique owner, Annie starts laughing. And then
the other women start laughing. They are laughing; the silent witnesses, too.
They laugh because the men don't get it; that fantasy of reversal shows how
they don't get it. The laughter is heard by the men as hysterical, because they
don't get it. How they are heard confirms what cannot be heard. And eventually Janine laughs too.

Another time we say snap: when we say or do the same thing at the same time.
Feminist snap: when laughter becomes a lead.

We learn from this film how laughter can be another kind of willful and rebellious noise.[2] To laugh compulsively, even violently, at the reasoning of Law, at

gender as reason, is to expose its violence. To expose violence is to become the origin of violence. However the women's laughter is heard, it is contagious for those who get it, which means getting that they don't get it. They leave the courtroom. Feminist snap: to snap a bond can be to make room for life by leaving the room.

Feminism often becomes part of a filmic landscape through snap: through the depiction of revenge against patriarchy, or against rape and sexual violence. Take *Nine to Five* (dir. Collin Higgins, 1980), which is a very different film than *A Question of Silence*. It is a comedy: and the use of comic inflection makes more palatable, or watchable, or bearable, the sexism and sexual harassment depicted. But like *A Question of Silence*, this film makes sexism a worn thread of connection between women; sexism as what you are supposed to get used to; sexism as how you are supposed to get used to being used. Sexism in this film appears in the figure of the male boss (Mr. Hart, who is described as a "sexist, egotistical, lying, hypocritical bigot") and the institutions of work that allow him either to use women's ideas as his own ("he stood right there and presented my ideas just as if they were his own") or to pass over women for promotion ("the company needs a man in this post"; "I lose a promotion because of one idiot prejudice") as well as to harass women and subject them to unwanted advances ("I've put up with all the pointing and the staring and the chasing me around the desk because I need this job"). And, again rather like *A Question of Silence*, the film is energetic because it does not just depict wearing. It shows snap. Indeed, it depicts multiple moments of snap that accumulate to form the basis of a collective rebellion, the removal of the patriarch from the office, and his replacement by a team of female workers who reorganize the workplace around feminist values (flexible time, job share, equal pay, child care on site).

Before we get to this feminist utopia, snap is evoked as well as enacted. When Mr. Hart tells one of the women, Judy, she will not be promoted, he says, "Don't go flying off the handle" (we have a handle on this expression), and then, "Save me the women's lib crap." How often the feminist killjoy is conjured up before she can make her appearance. And then, of course, she appears. We are waiting for her. There is room for her. All three women snap in more and less comic manners, through what they say ("And this is the last straw. I'm gonna get the gun of mine and turn you from a rooster to a hen with one shot") as well as what they do (pushing all the pencils and papers from his writing desk). In this film the more violent revenge is given the status of fantasy, and the mechanisms for the boss's eventual removal are, in plot terms, as much a result of happenstance as a consequence of a willed and willful act of feminist determination. But nevertheless, on the way, feminist snap, the cutoff points, generate a collective. A feminist collective in this sense is active: it is based on actions, on the refusal to put up with what women have been expected to endure.

Feminism: when we refuse to get used to it.

I found it striking that snap is explicitly evoked as danger. Judy says, "I swear one day he is going to push me too far and then I am really going to let him have it." And then, "I can't take much more of this." And then, "Inside I can feel the pressure building up. Sometime, somewhere I am going to snap and God help Mr. Hart because I won't be responsible for my actions." This prediction of a snap explains what would be necessary for snap. A revolution is premised on being irresponsible, or being judged as irresponsible, which is another kind of responsibility, one that is willing to live the consequences of snapping a bond. Being responsible for men, being responsible for maintaining the relationships that are diminishing, is what stops another kind of feminist optimism: the optimism that says this is not necessary, the optimism that says it is time to start again, the optimism that says we have had enough.

I want to consider one more feminist film from the early 1980s, *Born in Flames* (dir. Lizzie Borden, 1983), an independent documentary-style science fiction film. It is set in a future time after a socialist revolution has happened (a "war of liberation"), but the future looks rather like the present, or even the past; what is to come is already behind us. The documentary takes this form: we are introduced to many of the characters by snapshots attached to stories gathered by a surveillance team; the voice-over introducing each character as a suspect, as if to the police; different individuals who make up the Women's Army, who are protesting against this new regime. The film is dystopic: many of the promises of that socialist revolution are shown to have been empty; there is sexism; there is sexual harassment; there are cuts to services for women who are victims of rape; there is unemployment and poverty that disproportionately affects brown and black communities; there is disaffection; there is despair; there is depression; there is oppression.

It would be easy to hesitate on the differences of this film from our other two snappy films, but we can still attend to how they share a feminist lens. In this film there is also a concern with the exploitation of women workers, including secretaries (the film shows a scene of secretaries on a general secretarial strike—secretaries rebelling against their requirement to be what they call "office wives"). In one scene, women workers are united by being present as hands or as handy, a montage of hands that are doing work: sorting files, placing implements, picking up children, putting on condoms. One thinks here of women as hands, woman as his right hand; women as arms that are behind the Women's Army. As with our other two films, there is a sustained depiction of sexual harassment as an everyday reality that women are expected to bear as if this is just a part of life, how things are, how they will be; women attacked on the street, on the subway. I think, taken together, these three films show how sexual harassment is material: how it is a system that secures access to women's bodies; how it consigns women to some places and removes women from others.

But unlike the other two films, this film is assembled out of recognizable fragments of black feminist and feminist of color activisms, lesbian feminisms, queer feminisms. Characters speak a language that is familiar to those of us living a feminist life, the language of intersectionality, of intersecting oppressions; they give problems their names. It is quite uncanny to watch this film, to witness your own struggles potently formed into words uttered by characters you can relate to, from a film about the future made in the past. And because of how the film is set, the snap has a very precise point: it shows how any revolutionary struggle, any leftist politics, that dismisses sexism as immaterial, that makes women's lives secondary, will lead us to the same place. In one scene the president is speaking of the commitments of the party to equality and justice; we hear his address by watching him on television with others who are watching him on television. These words too can be non-performatives: said as a way of not doing something, said as a way of obscuring what is not being done. Zella Wylie, a senior black woman activist, rolls her eyes as he is speaking.[3] This is a different version of rolling eyes = feminist pedagogy. Here the eye rolling signals the collective recognition of the gap between what is said and what is done.

Feminist work: snap the gap.

In the film, the Women's Army is building up as a momentum; and the story of the film is the story of this buildup. One of the heroes of the film, Adelaide Norris, a young black lesbian, has a conversation with three white women who are part of the Socialist Youth Party, who in the film (at least in the beginning) speak the language of moderation, a language that identifies their feminist hopes with the hopes of the party. Adelaide points out that the inequalities they assume to be in the prerevolutionary past are the inequalities that are present for black working-class women like her own mother, like herself. What is past for some is present for others. Any feminism that leaves some women behind is not for women. Feminism requires fronting up to who has been left behind. The film gives voice to the myriad of ways that feminism as a revolutionary front is dismissed. The Women's Army is described as separatist, as having "selfish ends." We learned from how willfulness is used to dismiss feminism to hear what is at stake in these dismissals. When those who are behind question those in front, they are assumed to put themselves in front, to care only about themselves. To be concerned with the exploitation of women as workers is to be identified as separatist even if you are calling for women's freedom in calling for the freedom of all.

The Women's Army are also described as counterrevolutionary because they are impatient. *Impatient*: that's a word with a snappy history. Sometimes, if we recall Mrs. Poyser, we might become clumsy and fall because others are impatient with us, because we are too slow; falling as falling behind. But think of how we are told to be patient, to wait, when we make a demand for something. Patience refers to the willingness to bear suffering without irritation or the capacity to accept or tolerate delay. You are asked to be patient, as if what is wrong will not go on, as if with patience, things will only get better. Your impatience might even be deemed the cause of your failure to reach the happiness promised, as if by becoming impatient you have deprived yourself of what would have come your way, as if you have stolen your own future perfect.

Impatience: when you are not willing to bear. As Adelaide puts it, "It is already happening; it is here." We cannot wait because of what is here. *Born in Flames* teaches us how impatience can be a feminist virtue. We are not willing to wait. Not being willing to wait is not being willing to bear what you are told will lessen in time. Any revolution in which some are asked to wait their turn will end up in exactly the same place. We must not wait. We must demand justice and equality now. And feminist snap in this film is distributed through a series of actions and thus across a series of actors. A woman is harassed on the street or the subway: and women on bicycles with whistles come to her defense. Feminist snap can be planned and collective action. Snap requires its own support system. That action is called an attack on men by a media outlet; it is called dangerous by a commentator in the film because of its "vigilante sentiment." And perhaps that is feminist snap as political action work: vigilantism not only as lawlessness, or as taking the law into your own hands (the law as rod is precisely what we are fighting against), but also as a feminist vigil, as a demand to stay awake to, or to wake up to, the violence directed against women. Snap: you need to wake up to what is already happening.

The film shows how time matters because time is unevenly distributed as a way of relating to the past and the present. What is too sudden and too quick for some might be way too slow for others. And some things take more time to snap than other things. A line can be harder to snap because it has become stronger from being held on to for so long. A line can be policed; a line of police. I mentioned, in my reading of the Grimm story in chapter 3, how the police did not have to appear in the Grimm story because the police are the rods. Here the police appear with the rods. The escalation of violence that leads to the ending of the film (a bomb is placed on the top of the Twin Towers, an ending which of course history has rendered uncanny and difficult) is the death of Adelaide. The event that leads to snap building or a building of snap (snap as countermomentum) is the police killing of an unarmed black woman, a death they explain as her taking her own life: as suicide in a cell. The film: it feels like it is on a fast forward to the present, to how many are making movements out of the exposure of police brutality against unarmed black men and women.

The snap displayed in the film is the political work of getting that story out, that story of police brutality. The story of repression by the state is the story that is repressed by the state. The story of repression has to be pushed harder to get anywhere because it has to counter the story told by the state, a story that travels easily and quickly as the lines of communication are kept open for it. The state's story is hauntingly familiar to us. We know the story; it is the story of the willful girl. The state's story is of how those who die cause their own demise. The rod that beats her to death is made a right, because this story of the willful girl is told from the rod's point of view. It is the story of the willful girl for whom not obeying the party line is suicide. The story does not just depict her death; it sentences her to death. We learn: it is not just the content of the story of the willful girl that matters; it is the speed with which it can travel; saturating the world by canceling out the sounds of her scream, her *no*, which is heard as noise, as saying nothing. Feminist snap is required to counter the story by raising the sound of protest, making audible what is being done to her; a singular her, many hers. We have to gather to tell another story of what happened to her. We have to bring to the surface what is around the story: how she has to arm herself in response to the violence directed against her; we have to give an account of her death as murder, count her death as murder.

If feminist vigilantism can take the form of a feminist vigil, we might think of other senses of vigil. A vigil: to stay awake with a person who is dying; to mark or to mourn, to make a protest, to pray; to count our losses, to count her as loss, or, to borrow the name of a recent campaign in response to violence against black women, to say her name.[4] It is a call to arms: to mourn the wronged body. To mourn the wronged body is often deemed to mourn the wrong body. It is a call to arms, a call not to become the mourned body: as Adelaide Norris describes before her own untimely death, "Every woman under attack has the right to defend herself. . . . We must take on the whole armory and defend ourselves." Snap: how the violence that was already present now comes to the surface. Snap: the tenuousness of this now; it can be a body, her body; her body can be now, because when she ceases to be, she becomes a body.

As we know: so much violence does not become visible or knowable or tangible. We have to fight to bring that violence to attention. We need to be vigilant: watchful, careful; anxious. Feminist snap can be rethought of not only as an action but as a method of distributing information that can counter what is already known; sending stuff out that will enable a snap to be shared as a form of waking up to a world. It might involve what the film depicts: taking over media channels and interrupting an official broadcast (remember, *interrupt* comes from *rupture*: to break), or streaming music and messages on pirate channels that are on the move, music and messages that are designed to get under the surface of the skin; to pierce the seal, what I called in chapter 2 the happiness seal. You have to keep moving if you are being stopped. Feminist snap: how we tell a counter-story, the story that we must tell still, a story that if it is to be told requires sharp and sudden movements to get through or to get out because of what is still; how willfulness is still used by the state to justify her beating, her death. The telling requires snap: ways of ending the party line, ways of beginning another line, a lifeline that can pass messages like electricity through the whole body. Snap: when we revolt because the truth is brought home to us.

CONCLUSION: SNAP TO IT

I want to return to one line from *Nine to Five*: "Sometime, somewhere I am going to snap." It is a feminist hope: the realization of a feminist struggle. Snapping is necessary to break a bond, one that has been held up as necessary for life, for happiness, a bond that has been nurtured, cherished, by others. Snapping, a moment when the pressure has built up and tipped over, can be the basis of a feminist revolt, a revolt against what women are asked to put up with; a revolt that breaks things, that breaks things up; a revolt that is often understood as intending what it causes: mayhem. If it causes mayhem not to subordinate your will to the will of others, we must cause mayhem. We must do, if we do "do." From the shattered pieces, we start again. We pick up the pieces. We take care; we must take care, because history has sharpened their edges; sharpened our edges. We pick up the pieces; we start again. "Sometime, somewhere, I am going to snap." It is a feminist hope.

Snap becomes here a form of self-prophesy, a way of willing snap as feminist fate. Snap can also be how we try to get through to others. Snap then can be thought of as a feminist communication system. Take the expression "snap to it." It is an expression for when we have to break through something, to get attention, to pierce the seal of a haze or a daze. Maybe you have to snap your fingers.[5] Snap to it: how to create an impression strong enough, sharp enough, to get through the defenses. Snap here is not only about individual action, those moments when she doesn't take it anymore, when she reacts to what she has previously endured, though it includes those moments. Snap is also what is necessary for "it" to come to the surface as some tangible thing, as a situation that should not be patiently endured, as a situation that demands our collective impatience.

We will not wait. Any delay is intolerable.

I have in this chapter explored the heady contours of feminist snap through the lens of my own experience and with the examples of feminist films from the 1980s, films that provide snapshots or snap documents, and that reveal how feminist snap is collective labor. They are hopeful films. And all around us now are hopeful movements, snappy movements that call for us to snap to it, that demand our attention.

I think of a movement where I am, in the United Kingdom, which speaks out of the worn thread of connection that unravels in different ways across all of these films: sexism, sexual harassment, sexual violence. That movement is Sisters Uncut. It is a direct action movement that is addressing how austerity can be fatal for women, how austerity has meant the cutting back of domestic violence services, services that are lifelines for the many women experiencing emotional and physical violence at home.[6] As they put it in a snapful slogan: "They cut, we bleed." Direct action: putting bodies on the line, getting in the way, stopping the flow of traffic, putting red ink in the water of Trafalgar Square so the center of London appears flooded by blood. They cut, we bleed. Recalling the powerful vision of *Born in Flames*, Sisters Uncut show in how they do what they do that a politics that foregrounds sexism, sexual harassment, and sexual violence can be done through an intersectional lens; that such a feminist politics must also be about how stranger danger obscures the ongoing lived reality of domestic violence; and thus must also be about racism, including state racism, immigration, detention, poverty, unemployment, the erosion of the welfare state, all those structures that distribute vulnerability and fragility unevenly to populations. Their safer spaces policy states, "Sisters Uncut is made up of a diverse group of women and some of us experience many different kinds of oppression at the same time, such as sexism, racism, transphobia, ableism, classism and homophobia as well as others. These oppressions are not separate from each other. They intersect with each other, which can be frustrating, exhausting and painful."[7]

Frustrating, exhausting, painful: how we can experience intersections. Sisters Uncut also show how a feminist politics that centers on women can keep the category of women open to women. As they write in their safer spaces policy: "Our meetings should be inclusive and supportive spaces for all women (trans, intersex and cis), all those who experience oppression as women (including non-binary and gender non-conforming people) and all those who identify as women for the purpose of political organising. Self-definition is at the sole-discretion of that sister."[8]

At the discretion of sisters, we are sisters.
Sisterhood is snap.

9 / LESBIAN FEMINISM

I write this chapter out of a conviction: in order to survive what we come up against, in order to build worlds from the shattered pieces, we need a revival of lesbian feminism. This chapter is an explanation of my conviction.

Right now might seem an odd time to ask for such a revival. Lesbian feminism might seem to be passé precisely because lesbian feminism posed feminism as a life question. Many of the critiques of lesbian feminism, often as a form of cultural feminism, were precisely because of this attachment to life. Alice Echols, in her book *Daring to Be Bad*, which gives a history of radical feminism in the United States, describes: "With the rise of lesbian-feminism, the conflation of the personal with the political, long in the making, was complete and unassailable. More than ever, how one lived one's life, not commitment to political struggle, became the salient factor" (1989, 240). Note this *not*: the question of how we live our lives is separated from a commitment to political struggle; more than that, the focus on how we live our lives is implied to be a weak substitute for political struggle or a withdrawal of feminist energy from that struggle. We can hear a similar implication in Juliet Mitchell and Rosalind Delmar's argument: "The effects of liberation do not become the manifestations of liberation by changing values or for that matter by changing oneself, but only by challenging the social structure that gives rise to the values in the first place" (cited in Echols 1989, 244). The suggestion is not only that life change is not structural change but that focusing on how one lives one's life might be how structures are not transformed.

I want to offer an alternative argument by returning to the archives of lesbian feminism. When a life is what we have to struggle for, we struggle against structures. It is not necessarily the case that these struggles always lead to transformation (though neither does one's involvement in political movements). But to struggle against something is to chip away at something. Many of these structures are not visible or tangible unless you come up against them, which means that the work of chipping away, what I call diversity work, is a particular kind of work. The energy required to keep going when you keep coming up against these structures is how we build things, sometimes, often, from the shattered pieces.

Lesbian feminism can bring feminism back to life.

HETEROGENDER AS WALL

I write as a lesbian. I write as a feminist. This *as* is an individual claim but also a claim I make for others. To describe oneself as a lesbian is a way of reaching out to others who hear themselves in this *as*. But of course lesbian feminism means more than speaking as lesbian and speaking as a feminist; this *and* is too loose as a connecting device. Lesbian feminism also implies a stronger connection between these words. I think it is this stronger connection that makes lesbian feminism a site of so much anxiety, as explored by Victoria Hesford (2013) in her powerful analysis of the figure of the feminist as lesbian. This stronger connection is then heard as a charge against those feminists who are not lesbians as not being feminists. The charge of this connection could be heard not as a charge against something or somebody but as a charge with something. Perhaps we can recall the charge of willfulness: a charge that is electric. The connection between lesbian and feminist is not something that can be prescribed even if some of our histories include this prescription or even if lesbian feminism is heard as prescription (to be a lesbian you must identify as feminist; to be a feminist you must identify as lesbian). The connection is a connection to be lived: living as a lesbian is how I live a feminist life.

Throughout this book, I have been trying to bring feminist theory home by generating feminist theory out of ordinary experiences of being a feminist. The book could have been called *Everyday Feminism*.[1] Feminist theory is or can be what we might call, following Marilyn Frye, "lived theory," an approach that "does not separate politics from living" (1991, 13). We can think of life as data collection: we gather information. And being a lesbian, living one's life as a lesbian, gives us plenty of data. Lesbians collect information about the institutions that govern the reproduction of life: it is almost too much data; we don't have time to interpret all the material we collect. If living a lesbian life gives us data, lesbian feminism gives us the tools to interpret that data.

And by data I am once again referring to walls. In chapter 2, I offered a rethinking of heterogender as a traffic system, a way of directing human traffic. When a flow is directed, it becomes a momentum. In chapter 6, I began to rethink the materiality of power in terms of walls, the hardenings of history. We can rethink heterogender as another brick wall, one that is encountered by those who are not going in the right direction. When you are not going the right way, a flow is an obstruction. Lesbians know a lot about obstruction.

But it might seem now for lesbians that we are going with the flow. Hey, we can go; hey, here in the United Kingdom we can even get married. And if you talk about what you come up against now, those around you may blink with disbelief: hey, what's up, stop complaining dear, smile. I am not willing to smile on command. I am willing to go on a smile embargo, if I can evoke Shulamith Firestone's (1970, 90) "dream action" for the women's movement. Talking about walls matters all the more when the mechanisms by which we are blocked are less visible.

The everyday is our data.

A wall can be an atmosphere. A wall can be a gesture.

A queer experience: You are seated with your girlfriend, two women at a table, waiting. A straight couple walks into the room and is attended to right away: sir, madam, over here, sir, madam. Sometimes if you do not appear as you are expected to appear, you do not appear. There are many who do not appear under this word *couple*: sir, madam. The gaze slides over you, as if you are not there. This is not so much about being seen, as about being seen to, having your needs attended to: after all when the *sir, madam* becomes a question—"Is that sir, or madam?"—you are being seen, your body turned into a spectacle.

This queer experience might be better articulated as a lesbian experience or something women in particular experience: as if without a man present at a table, or a body visible as man, you do not appear. I have experienced much solidarity among women around these sorts of experiences: say you are pressed up against a busy bar, two women who do not know each other, and over and over again, the men are served first. You look at each other both with frustration but sometimes affection, as you recognize the other woman recognizes that situation as one in which she is perpetually thrown, recognizes being in that situation; you too, me too, she too, we too. When women are seated together you might not register as being there at all. For some, you have to become insistent to be the recipient of a social action; you might have to announce your presence, wave your arm, saying, "Here I am!" For others, it is enough just to turn up because you have already been given a place at the table before you take up that place. I have used *willfulness* to describe the consequences of this differentiation.

Of course more than gender is at stake in the distribution of attention. But gender is at stake in the distribution of attention. Feminist philosophers have taught us for over a century how man becomes universal; woman particular. Women become relatives, only registered as existing when existing in relation to men. We can now deepen the formulation I offered in chapter 6: women as female relatives. To become woman is to become relative: not only in the sense of kin (connected by blood or marriage) but also in the fundamental sense of considered (only) in relation or proportion to something else. We encounter the universal as a wall when we refuse to become relative. And note how we come to understand these distinctions (such as universal and relative) not as abstractions, but in everyday social life, which is to say, through being in a world with others. No wonder that by starting here, by starting with what gets thrown up in a concrete exchange, we generate concepts: sweaty concepts. We muscle in on a world from trying to be in a world.

Lesbian feminism gives us the tools to make sense of the sexism that becomes all the more striking when women exit from the requirements of compulsory heterosexuality (which is, in effect, a citational relational, a requirement to live a life by citing men). For her to appear, she might have to fight. If this is true for women, it is even truer for lesbians. Women with women at a table are hard to see (and by *table* here I am referring to the mechanisms of social gathering, a table as what we are assembled around). For a gathering to be complete, a man is the head. A table of women: a body without a head.

Data as wall.

You turn up at a hotel with your girlfriend and you say you have booked a room. A hesitation can speak volumes. This reservation says your booking is for a double bed. Is that right, madam? Eyebrows are raised; a glance slides over the two of you, catching enough detail. Are you sure, madam? Yes, that's right; a double bed. You have to say it, again; you have to say it, again, firmly. In chapter 1, I introduced a formula: rolling eyes = feminist pedagogy. Another formula:

Raised eyebrows = lesbian feminist pedagogy.

Really, are you sure? This happens again and again; you almost come to expect it, the necessity of being firm just to receive what you have requested. Disbelief follows you wherever you go, still. One time after a querying—are you sure madam, are you sure, madam—you enter the room: twin beds. Do you go down; do you try again? It can be trying. Sometimes it is too trying; it is too much; and you pull your two little beds together; you find other ways of huddling.

A history can become concrete through the repetition of such encounters, encounters that require you to put the whole of your body, as well as your arms, behind an action.[2] Maybe these actions seem small. Maybe they are small. But they accumulate over time. They can feel like a hammering, a chip, chip, chip against your being, so that eventually you begin to feel smaller, hammering as hammered down.

Actions that seem small can also become wall.

AN ORDINARY BATTLE

An ordinary is what we might be missing when we feel that chip, chip, chip. An ordinary can be what we need to survive that chip, chip, chip. Susan Griffin remembers a scene for us, a scene that has yet to happen:

> I remember a scene. . . . This from a film I want to see. It is a film made by a woman about two women who live together. This is a scene from their daily lives. It is a film about the small daily transformations which women experience, allow, tend to, and which have been invisible in this male culture. In this film, two women touch. In all ways possible they show knowledge of. What they have lived through and what they will yet do, and *one sees in their movements how they have survived*. I am certain that one day this film will exist. (cited in Becker et al. 1981, emphasis mine)

Lesbian feminism: to remember a scene that has yet to happen, a scene of the ordinary; of the movements, little movements, which tell the story of our survival. It is a touching scene. Sometimes you have to battle for an ordinary. When you have to battle for an ordinary, when battling becomes ordinary, the ordinary can be what you lose.

Even if we lose it, we have a glimpse of it.

A loss can be a glimpse.

Moments can become movements.

Think of this: how for many women, life has been understood as a sphere of immanence, as dwelling in, not rising above; she is there; there she is; not transcending things by creating things. A masculinist model of creativity is premised on withdrawal. She is there; there she is: engaged in the endless repetitive cycle of housework. We can follow Adrienne Rich, who makes this starting point into an instruction: "Begin with the material," she says, with "matter, mma, madre, mutter, moeder, modder" (1986, 213). Lesbian feminism is materialist right from the beginning. If women are expected to be here, in matter, in materiality, in work, at work, this is where lesbian feminism begins. We begin in the lodge where we are lodged. We begin with the lodge when we are dislodged.

A poignant lesbian scene of ordinary life is provided by the first of the three films that make up *If These Walls Could Talk 2* (dir. Jane Anderson, 2000). We begin with that ordinary: we begin with its warmth. The quietness of intimacy: Edith and Abby, going to see a film together, coming home together. Yes maybe there are comments made by some kids on the street, but they are used to it: they have each other, a place to return to; home becomes shelter, a place to withdraw to.

Everything is shattered, when Abby slips and falls.

Everything shatters.

We are in the hospital waiting room. Edith is waiting to hear how Abby is. Another woman arrives, visibly upset, and says, "They just took my husband in. He had a heart attack." Edith comforts her. When this woman asks about Edith's husband, Edith replies, "I never had a husband." And the woman says, "That's lucky, because you won't have the heartbreak of losing one." The history of heterosexuality is presented as a history of broken hearts, or even just a history of hearts. To be recognized as having a heart is to be recognized as having the potential to be broken. With such recognition comes care, comfort, support. Without recognition, even one's grief cannot be supported or held by the kindness of another.

And so Edith waits. The temporality of this wait feels like a shudder, as each moment passes, as we wait with her, the mood of the film becoming unbearably sad, as it lingers over her loss by lingering. When she asks the hospital staff to see Abby they say, "Only family are allowed." She is excluded from the sphere of intimates. She is a nonrelative, or not-family. The nurse asks, "Is she any relation of yours, madam?" She replies, "I'm a friend, a very good friend." They respond only with another question, "Does she have any family?" The friend disappears in the weight of the address. The recognition of family ties as the only ties that are binding means Abby dies alone; it means Edith waits all night, alone. Their relationship is hidden as friendship, while friendship itself becomes produced as a lesser tie, less binding, another kind of fragile. The power of the distinction between friends and family is legislative, as if only family counts, as if other relationships are not real, or simply are not.

When lesbian grief is not recognized, because lesbian relationships are not recognized, then you become nonrelatives. You become unrelated; you become not. You are alone in your grief. You are left waiting.

We know this history. It is a history of what we know.

Support is how much you have to fall back on when you fall. In chapter 2, I suggested that heterosexuality can be understood as an elaborate support system. And in chapter 7, I considered how fragility is unevenly distributed. To leave a support system can mean to become more fragile, less protected from the bumps of ordinary life. Class of course can be understood in these terms. To be middle or upper class is to have more resources to fall back on when you fall. What is behind you can be what holds you up; what is behind you can stop you from going down.

To say that heterosexuality can do the work of holding you up when you fall shows how intersectionality is not only about stopping and starting, as I discussed in chapter 5, but also a matter of ups and downs. Maybe if the life you live severs a family tie or snaps a bond, one that would otherwise have held you up when things break up, then you have left not only heterosexuality but the stability of a class position as a way of accessing resources.[3] To leave heterosexuality can be to leave those institutional forms of protecting, cherishing, holding. When things break, your whole life can then unravel. So much feminist and queer invention comes from the necessity of creating our own support systems.

When family is not there to prop you up, when you disappear from family life, you have to find other ways of being supported. When you disappear from family life: does this happen to you? You go home, you go back home. And it feels like you are watching yourself disappear: watching your own life unravel, thread by thread. No one has willed or intended your disappearance. Just slowly, just slowly, as talk of family, of heterosexuality as the future, of lives that you do not live, just slowly, just slowly, you disappear. They welcome you; they are kind, but it is harder and harder to breathe. And then when you leave, you might go and find a lesbian bar or queer space; it can be such a relief. You feel like a toe liberated from a cramped shoe: how you wiggle about! And we need to think about that: how the restriction of life when heterosexuality remains a presumption can be countered by creating spaces that are looser, freer, not only because you are not surrounded by what you are not but because you are reminded there are many ways to be. Lesbian bars, queer space: wiggle room.

The loss of possibility can be experienced as a physical restriction. The remainder of this short film depicts the arrival of Abby's family for the funeral.

Before they arrive, Edith removes traces of their relationship from the house, including photographs from the wall, exposing the lighter spaces underneath. If relationships leave traces on the wall so too does the removal of those relationships. The house is figured as a zone of intimacy; their love literally occupies the walls, keeping them busy. The house is not represented as property, but as a space in which they have extended themselves; mementos, cards, photographs; their intimacy leaves an impression on the walls. A photo of them marching, traces of the lesbian and gay histories of activism that allow this zone to become theirs. The objects that Edith takes down are objects that embody their love, which create their own horizon. These objects betray their secret. The removal of signs of their intimacy empties the house, re-creating the house as a vacant space, as if the walls too must wait.

If the walls could talk, what would they say?

We need the walls to talk.

What a story.

When Abby's family arrive, the house is transformed from a zone of intimacy into property. The house was in Abby's name. There is no will. The objects, the house itself; it belongs to Abby's family.

The walls, too; they belong too.

They hold up the master's residence; the family home.

When Abby's family arrive, they occupy the house. Edith becomes their guest. Abby's nephew says, "I have no problem with you staying here. Maybe we can work out some sort of rental situation." Staying becomes a question of receiving his hospitality: he has the power to lend the house, which is the same power as the power to take it away. Indeed, the objects that embody their lesbian intimacy are taken away, by being transformed into property, as something that can be taken: they keep asking, "What was Aunt Abby's?" as a way of asking, "What is ours?" When a lesbian feminist past is reassembled as a heterosexual present, the future, her future, is lost.

It is a situation.

A sad, sad situation.

The sadness of the situation unfolds through things: they embody Edith's life; her life with Abby. But for Abby's relatives, these things were Abby's; they become objects that are inheritable. In particular, Abby's china porcelain birds, her most loved and precious objects, become the site of contestation over family values and the value of family. The daughter of her nephew—Alice, let's give her a name—says to Edith, "They are beautiful." When Alice picks up one of the birds, Edith says, "I gave her that one. It's a lovely gift." In the following exchange between Edith and Alice, we have a partial recognition of loss—which in underdescribing that loss works to annul the force of recognition. "It must be very sad for you to lose such a good friend." To which Edith replies, inadequately, "Yes it is." At this moment, Edith's face is blank, her eyes glimmering; she withholds. The affirmative response, "Yes it is," becomes a disavowal of the loss, a way of keeping the loss a secret, a way of keeping what was lost a secret.

It is at this moment that Edith is undone. For having said yes to this, Alice says, "I think you should have something of hers to remember her by. I would really like for you to pick one of these birds to have as a keepsake." These objects that signify her love for Abby, and Abby's love, are taken away in the very gesture of being returned: of being turned into a gift, a keepsake, as if she must be grateful for this return. The objects that Abby loved most, which were part of her, become kinship objects for Ted's family; they become family relatives, maybe even female relatives (if hers then ours), what can be inherited, objects to be passed down the family line, objects that give family its form. It is this loss, the loss of what her lover loved, that is too much.

Too much; it is too much.

Things shatter.

There are many ways to tell the story of recognition because there are many stories to tell. The desire for recognition is not necessarily about having access to a good life or being included in the institutions that have left you shattered. It is not even necessarily an aspiration for something: rather, it comes from the experience of what is unbearable, what cannot be endured. The desire for a bearable life is a desire for a life where suffering does not mean you lose your bearings when you become unhoused, when the walls come up, when they secure the rights of some to occupy space by the dispossession of others. The desire for a bearable life is a desire to have an ordinary life, an ordinary that is far more precious than property; indeed, an ordinary is what is negated when things become property, when things become alienable things, when things become family possessions.

I am not saying a desire for an ordinary does not take an institutional form, or that a zone of intimacy that covers the walls does not end up being an aspiration for a property, making things ours, so they cannot be taken away. There is more in an aspiration not to be unhoused than an aspiration for a house. To aspire is to breathe. With breath comes imagination. With breath comes possibility.

Perhaps a lesbian feminist struggle for recognition comes out of rage against the injustice of how some dwell by the dispossession of others. Perhaps the signs of this struggle are neutralized by being represented as a gift. As Sarah Schulman (1998, 102) has shown, when recognition is understood as a gift from the straight world, our collective labor and struggle are forgotten. It is like Edith being given the bird as a keepsake, as if that bird was theirs to give, rather than something that matters because it marks what was created by her and Abby being together; the effort to be together.

We have to keep trying. We want the walls to come down. Or, if they stay up, we want the walls to talk, to tell our story. A story too can shatter: a thousand tiny little pieces, strewn all over the place. Lesbian feminism: in making an ordinary out of the shattered pieces of a dwelling, we dwell.

We dwell, we tell.

How telling.

A WILLFULNESS ARCHIVE

I have noted how actions that are small can also become wall. Lesbian feminism might involve small actions. Maybe the chip, chip, chip of hammering can be transformed into a hammer: if he is a chip off the old block, we chip, chip, chip away at that block. Chip, chip, chip, who knows, eventually it might come right off. To persist in chipping at the blocks of heteropatriarchy, we have to become willful. I want to think of lesbian feminism as a willfulness archive, a living and a lively archive made up and made out of our own experiences of struggling against what we come up against, developing some of my arguments from chapter 3.

We could begin with the very figure of the lesbian feminist; how willful she is, how striking. She is without question a killjoy figure; so often coming up as being anti, antisex, antifun; antilife. The investment in her misery needs to be understood as just that: an investment. To live out a lesbian life is to become willingly estranged from the causes of happiness. No wonder she causes unhappiness.

It is important to note here that the investment in the misery of lesbians can also be detected even within queer studies. In some queer literatures, lesbian feminism itself appears as a miserable scene that we had to get through, or pass through, before we could embrace the happier possibility of becoming queer. For instance, Beatriz Preciado (2012), in a lecture on queer bulldogs, refers to lesbians as ugly with specific reference to lesbian styles, fashions, and haircuts. The lesbian appears as an abject figure we were all surely happy to have left behind, even if she continues to stalk queer talks as a reminder of a failed project. I suspect this reference to the ugliness of lesbians is intended as ironic, even playful. But of course contemporary sexism and homophobia is often ironic and playful. I don't find it particularly amusing.

And indeed what is also noticeable is how this investment in miserable lesbians leads to an erasure of the inventiveness in lesbian histories described in the previous section as a desire to be ordinary in a world in which your desires take you out of the ordinary. The bits and pieces from lesbian histories that are understood as more redeemable (for example, butch/femme as erotic styles or modes of being) become rewritten as a queer history, or a history of how queerness came to be. Of course there were moments in lesbian feminist history when butch and femme were critiqued as imitating the gender system, or when the butch lesbian was herself rendered a pale imitation of a man (moments that exposed the class as well as racial specificity of lesbian ideals); but that was not exhaustive either as a moment or as a critique. Lesbians are not a step on a path that leads in a queer direction.

A willful lesbian stone is not a stepping stone.

Try stepping on a stone butch and see what happens.

More is at stake in lesbian feminism as a politics of willfulness than how the figure of the lesbian feminist is menacing and miserable. Willfulness is also behind us. We can listen to who is behind us. Julia Penelope describes lesbianism as willfulness: "The lesbian *stands against* the world created by the male imagination. What *willfulness* we possess when we claim our lives!" (1992, 42, first emphasis mine). Marilyn Frye's radical feminism uses the adjective *willful*: "The willful creation of new meaning, new loci of meaning, and new ways of being, together, in the world, seems to me in these mortally dangerous times the best hope we have" (1992, 9). Together these statements are claims to willfulness as a lesbian and radical feminist politics, and I want us to think about the connections between them: willfulness as standing against; willfulness as creativity.

When a world does not give us standing, to stand is to stand against that world. And when a world does not give us standing, we have to create other ways of being in the world. You acquire the potential to make things, create things. Lesbian feminism: the actualization of a potential we have to make things. A movement is assembled by those who keep encountering in their everyday life what they stand against. Lesbian feminism is radical feminism (in the sense of feminist at its root) and thus lesbian feminism demands our full involvement; as Marilyn Frye describes, "Bodily energy, ardour, intelligence, vitality" all need "to be available and engaged in the creation of a world for women" (1991, 14).

To be engaged in the creation of a world for women is to transform what it means to be women. Let me explain what I mean by this by going back to the words. The history of the word *woman* teaches us how the categories that secure personhood are bound up with a history of ownership: *woman* is derived from a compound of *wif* (wife) and *man* (human being); woman as wife-man also suggesting woman as female servant. The history of woman is impossible to disentangle from the history of wife: the female human not only as in relation to man but as for man (woman as there for, and therefore, being for). We can make sense of Monique Wittig's (1992) audacious statement, "Lesbians are not women." She argues that lesbians are not women because "women" is being in relation to men: for Wittig, "women" is a heterosexual category, or a heterosexual injunction. To become a lesbian is to queer woman by wrestling her away from him. To create a world for women is to cease to be women for. To be a woman with a woman or a woman with women (we do not need to assume a couple form) is to become what Wittig calls an "escapee" or a stray. To be a lesbian is to stray away from the path you are supposed to follow if you are to reach the right destination. To stray is to deviate from the path of happiness. We deviate from the category "women" when we move toward women. Or if a lesbian is a woman, if we wrestle her away from this history, she is a willful woman.

Willful woman: how striking! Willful woman: how queer! By holding on to the figure of the lesbian as full of potential, we are not giving up on queer; rather, we are refusing to assume being queer means giving up on lesbian feminism.[4] In chapter 7, I drew on Eve Kosofsky Sedgwick's discussion of how the potential of queer resides in how it is cleaved to everyday childhood scenes of shame. Queer arrives as an affective inheritance of an insult.[5] That queer became an insult directed to sexual minorities refers us back to earlier meanings of queer as odd or strange. The lesbian as a figure might even overinherit queerness: in a heteropatriarchal world there might be nothing odder, or more striking, than women who have as their primary sexual and life partners other women. Lesbians: queer before queer.

Lesbian feminism: how revolting! We are revolting against the requirement to be in relation to men; we are revolting against the demand to be female relatives. Lesbian feminism: how we revolt; how we become revolting. The classic piece "Woman Identified Woman" by Radicalesbians thus begins with an explosive speech act: "A lesbian is the rage of all women condensed to the point of explosion" (1970, n.p.). This speech act renders the lesbian herself into a tipping point, a breaking point, what I called in the previous chapter feminist snap. She comes to embody the collective rage of women against the requirement to live their lives in relation to men, to become female relatives to the male universal. Such a rage, however, is only part of the story being told; becoming lesbian is an energetic becoming, a redirecting of women's energies away from the labor of maintaining relationships with men as our primary relationships.

A lesbian withdraws from a system that requires that she make herself available to men. Many antifeminist as well as antilesbian arguments explain and pathologize her withdrawal. One of the primary ways is through the explanation that lesbianism begins with disappointment; that some women become lesbians because they are not desirable to men; she is understood as a weak substitute, she yet again as not he. She can't get him so she settles for her.[6]

The rendering of the lesbian into an abject figure is an orientation device, a way of signaling the danger of not orientating your life as a woman around men. She acquires utility as a reminder of the unhappy consequence of getting things wrong. This statement by Radicalesbians shows exactly how abjection is used as a warning:

> As long as the label "dyke" can be used to frighten women into a less militant stand, keep her separate from her sisters, keep her from giving primacy to anything other than men and family—then to that extent she is controlled by the male culture. Until women see in each other the possibility of a primal commitment which includes sexual love, they will be denying themselves the love and value they readily accord to men, thus affirming their second-class status. As long as male acceptability is primary—both to individual women and to the movement as a whole—the term lesbian will be used effectively against women. Insofar as women want only more privileges within the system, they do not want to antagonize male power. They instead seek acceptability for women's liberation, and the most crucial aspect of the acceptability is to deny lesbianism—i.e., to deny any fundamental challenge to the basis of the female. But why is it that women have related to and through men? By virtue of having been brought up in a male society, we have internalized the male culture's definition of ourselves. That definition consigns us to sexual and family functions, and excludes us from defining and shaping the terms of our lives. (1970, n.p.)

The dyke is frightening. To become a dyke is not to be frightened off from militancy. To become a dyke is thus to become militant. She represents a cutoff point. For feminisms that are about becoming acceptable (code: more acceptable to men, or more acceptable to those who are being asked to give up some of their power), lesbians are still unacceptable; lesbianism stands for what is unacceptable; the woman who goes astray is the one who does make becoming acceptable to men her way. Or the work of being lesbian without losing face is the work of becoming as acceptable as one can be, the kind of diversity work I described in chapter 5 as institutional passing. Shiny happy lesbians: you can polish yourself by removing traces of dykes and other more frightening lesbian tendencies.

If in becoming woman we have already been directed a certain way, then to become woman in a different way requires a reorientation. To become woman can often mean, in this context, becoming unrelated. It requires work; the effort of redirection, turning away from men as turning the wrong way. At the end of the film *A Question of Silence*, discussed in chapter 8, we witness this work. When Janine exits the courtroom her husband signals to her to come to him. He beeps the horn of his car, aggressively. I hear that beep as the sound of patriarchy: attend to me; turn to me; listen to me; come back to me. But Janine does not turn to him, return to him; she turns instead toward the other women who have left the room. It is a subtle movement. It is a small step. But it is the beginning of a reorientation. When eventually Janine can turn away from the man who demands her attention, toward other women, it is only because something has already snapped, a bond not only to an individual man as a sexual and life partner, but to the world that makes that bond that which demands the fullness of her attention. Snap is what allows her turning, what allows her to see the women who are already there: right by her side. To identify as lesbian is to turn toward women, which, given the system we live in, requires an active and perpetual turning away from men.

In the statement "Woman Identified Woman," this turning toward women is described in terms of energy. They note, "On one level, which is both personal and political, women may withdraw emotional and sexual energies from men, and work out various alternatives for those energies in their own lives" (Radicalesbians 1970). I think woman identification has been read too quickly as being about gender expression. Woman identification here is about refusing as women to identify with male culture. To refuse to identify is to withdraw your own energy from relationships to men. You often have to become willful to withdraw that energy because you are expected to allocate it that way. Even to withdraw your energy from relationships to men will then be pathologized as hatred of men. This is why the lesbian appears so regularly as a man hater. And this is why woman identification makes woman such a willful subject;

she is willful when she is not willing to put her energies into her relationships with men; she is willful by how she redirects her attention. We could reclaim Adrienne Rich's (1993) somewhat maligned term "lesbian continuum" on similar grounds: not as taking the sex out of lesbianism (by putting friendships between women on the same continuum with sexual relationships) but as a call to redirect our attention.[7] To attend to women, we have to unlearn how we have learned to screen women out. We have to learn not to pass over her, just as we have been passed over.

It is something to aim for. When you aim not to reproduce a world that directs attention to men, you are threatening. When your being threatens life, you have to wrap life around being.

You have to wrap life around being. I would suggest that it is transfeminism today that most recalls the militant spirit of lesbian feminism in part because of the insistence that crafting a life is political work. Transfeminist manifestos carry the baton of radical lesbian manifestos such as "Woman Identified Woman": from Sandy Stone's (2006) "The Empire Strikes Back: A Posttranssexual Manifesto" to Julia Serano's (2007) "Trans Woman Manifesto" and Susan Stryker's (1994) "My Words to Victor Frankenstein." These texts assemble a politics from what they name: showing not only how the sex-gender system is coercive, how it restricts what and who can be, but how creativity comes from how we survive a system that we cannot dismantle by the force of our will alone (no matter how willful we are).

The monsters will lead the way. Susan Stryker describes how the transsexual appears as monster within some lesbian and gay writing. Rather than distancing herself from this figure, Stryker claims her, becomes her; a proximity initiated as a politics of transgender rage: "Through the operation of rage, the stigma itself becomes the source of transformative power" (1994, 261).

Remember, resonance.

Abject within feminism

Monstrosity

When lesbians insisted on speaking within feminist spaces, we were rendered monstrous: think back to Betty Friedan's description of a lesbian presence as a "lavender menace," a description that lesbian feminists such as Rita Mae Brown were willing to take up as their own. For Stryker, being willing to be the monster becomes a matter of how you live your life: "May your rage inform your actions and your actions transform you as you struggle to transform your world" (1994, 254). A political struggle can be the struggle to transform your world. It can take willfulness to bring politics back to life.

Willfulness might seem to be about an individual subject, as the one who has to become willful just to exist. She matters; to become a subject for some is to become a willful subject. But it is important not to reduce willfulness to individualism, as I have noted previously. We can think here of the character Molly Bolt from Rita Mae Brown's (1973) classic lesbian novel, *Rubyfruit Jungle*. It is interesting to note how this novel has been challenged by some critics for its individualism. Kim Emery in her reading of the novel strains hard (in the best way) to be sympathetic. But she notes, "I find it difficult to read *Rubyfruit Jungle* as being anything other than the simplistic, essentialist, and effectively anti-feminist aggrandizement of American individualism that critics like Bonnie Zimmerman hold it to be" (Emery 2002, 126). Emery in her reading also draws upon Rita Mae Brown's feisty lesbian feminist text *A Plain Brown Rapper*, in which Brown (1976, 126) describes woman identification as an ongoing activity, as a persistent practice of selfhood and solidarity. I think reading Molly Bolt through the lens of willfulness allows us to understand that actions that can be diagnosed as individualism provide the basis of lesbian feminist rebellion against social norms and conventions such as the family. When you fight against the family, you are often understood as fighting for yourself. Rebellion is dismissible as individualism. The word *willfulness* registers this dismissal.

I offered a reading of *Rubyfruit Jungle* in my book *The Promise of Happiness* (Ahmed 2010) as one instance of the genre of what I called female troublemaker fiction. Somewhat surprisingly (even to myself, looking back) Molly Bolt did not pop up in *Willful Subjects* (Ahmed 2014), though maybe she lent a hand to the many willful arms that haunted the pages. Molly is appealing. She captures something for us as lesbian readers precisely because of her willful energy: she is too much; she has to be too much, if she is not to be brought down by what she comes up against. It would be easy to dismiss this concern with character as individualism. For those who have to struggle to be, to become an individual is a profoundly communal achievement.

It is not surprising that girls who want girls are found to have wills that are wanting. A willful lesbian might be the one who makes bad object choices. A bad choice is when you willingly want the wrong things, the things you are supposed to give up, as well as willfully not wanting the right things, those that would or should secure your happiness. A willful lesbian archive is thus not only an unhappy archive, even though it includes unhappiness. As Elizabeth Freeman suggests, we might be able to glimpse in our archives "historically specific forms of pleasure" that have not been "subsumed into institutional forms" (2005, 66). Molly is not subsumed; her pleasures leak all over the place. She says in response to a question of how many women she has slept with: "Hundreds. I'm irresistible" (200). *Rubyfruit Jungle* offers us a story of a queer girl who refuses to give up her desires, even if they take her outside the horizon of happiness, even though they get her into trouble. When Molly is brought to the dean's office after rumors of lesbianism at film college, she is asked by the dean about her problem with girls, and replies:

> "Dean Marne, I don't have any problems relating to girls and I'm in love with my roommate. She makes me happy." Her scraggly red eyebrows with the brown pencil glaring through shot up. "Is this relationship with Faye Raider of an, uh—intimate nature?" "We fuck, if that's what you're after." I think her womb collapsed on that one. Sputtering, she pressed forward. "Don't you find that somewhat of an aberration? Doesn't this disturb you, my dear? After all, it's not normal." "I know it's not normal for people in this world to be happy, and I'm happy." (127)

Rather than being disturbed by being found disturbing, Molly performs the ultimate act of defiance, by claiming her happiness as abnormal. It is as if queers, by doing what they want, expose the unhappiness of having to sacrifice personal desires, in the perversity of their twists and turns, for the happiness of others.

The lesbian who persists is misdirected.

She is willing to be misdirected.

She is willing to miss.

Willfulness: not missing what you miss.

Despite all her charm, and her rather infectious enthusiasm for lesbian life worlds, it is not that Molly's experiences are happy ones, in the sense that she is able to make and get her way. Indeed, throughout, her experiences involve discrimination: violence and rejection from would-be lovers, who cannot bear the consequences of following queer desire out of the forms of recognition delivered by a straight world. She is just not defeated by these experiences. Of course, we need to take care to avoid turning characters such as Molly into good object lessons: as if we could create a moral imperative from the example of her fictional life. But we can still be infected by her enthusiasm that spills all over the pages, her refusal to be brought down. For me, as a lesbian feminist reader, characters like Molly Bolt with a spring in their step pick me up; feisty characters whose vitality is not at the expense of their lesbian desire, but how their desire roams across the pages.

If we think of lesbian feminism as a willfulness archive, we are not simply directing our attention to characters such as Molly Bolt, however appealing. A willfulness archive would derive as much from our struggle to write ourselves into existence as from who appears in what we write. This intimacy of standing against and creativity can take the form of a book.

A willful girl in a book

A willful girl as a book

I am rather taken by you

Gloria Anzaldúa describes her book *Borderlands/La Frontera: The New Mestiza* as follows: "The whole thing has had a mind of its own, escaping me and insisting on putting together the pieces of its own puzzle with minimal direction from my will. It is a rebellious, willful entity, a precocious girl-child forced to grow up too quickly" ([1987] 1999, 88). A book, a survival strategy, comes alive, acquires a life of its own, a will of its own, a willful will; history by the bone, own but not alone.

Lesbian feminism of color: the struggle to put ourselves back together because within lesbian shelters too our being was not always accommodated. I think of a brown history, a mixed history as a lesbian history, another way in which we can tell a history of women being in relation to women. I think of my own history, as a mixed lesbian, so many sides, all over the place. I think of all that lesbian potential as coming from somewhere. Brownness has a lesbian history, because there are brown lesbians in history; whether or not you could see us, whether or not you knew where to find us.

Intersectionality: let's make a point of how we come into existence. I am not a lesbian one moment and a person of color the next and a feminist at another. I am all of these at every moment. And lesbian feminism of color brings this all into existence, writing of all existence, with insistence, with persistence. There can be so much labor to bring ourselves about. When being is laboring, we are creating more than ourselves. Lesbian feminism of color is a lifeline made up out of willful books that had to insist on their own creation. Books are themselves material, paper, pen, ink, even blood. Words come out of us, like sweat, like blood; tears. Your texts are littered with love. Words can pulse with life; words as flesh, leaking; words as heart, beating.

A poem weeps

Audre Lorde spoke of herself as a writer when she was dying. For Lorde, writing was a survival strategy. She says, "I am going to write fire until it comes out of my ears, my eyes, my noseholes—everywhere. Until it's every breath I breathe. I'm going to go out like a fucking meteor!" (1988, 76–77).

And so she did

And so she did

She goes out; she makes something. She calls this capacity to make things through heat "the erotic." Lorde describes, "There is a difference between painting a black fence and writing a poem, but only one of quantity. And there is, for me, no difference between writing a good poem and moving into sunlight against the body of a woman I love" (1984a, 58). Words flicker with life, like the sunlight on her body.

A love poem

A lover as poem

I am warmed by the thought; of how we create things; of how we break open a container to make things. We watch the words spill. They spill all over you. I think too of Cherríe Moraga's poem "The Welder." Moraga speaks of heating being used to shape new elements, to create new shapes, "the intimacy of steel melting, the fire that makes sculpture of your lives, builds buildings" (1981, 219). We build our own buildings when the world does not accommodate our desires. When you are blocked, when your very existence is prohibited or viewed with general suspicion or even just raised eyebrows (yes they are pedagogy), you have to come up with your own systems for getting things through. You might even have to come up with your own system for getting yourself through.

How inventive

Quite something

Not from nothing

Something from something

A kitchen table becomes a publishing house

We assemble ourselves around our own tables, kitchen tables, doing the work of community as ordinary conversation. Lesbian feminist world making is nothing extraordinary; I have tried to show how lesbian feminist world making is quite ordinary. The ordinary can be what you are for. For: it comes from not. To stand against what is, we make room for what is not. Or even: we are for what is not. We might think of the work of making room as wiggling, a corporeal willfulness; like that toe that wiggles about in a shoe. A lesbian does not toe the line. Lesbians (as lesbians well know) have quite a wiggle; you have to wiggle to make room in a cramped space. We can be warmed by the work required to be together even if we sometimes wish it was less work. To recall the vitality of lesbian feminism as a resource of the present is to remember that effort required for our shelters to be built. When we have to shelter from the harshness of a world, we build a shelter.

Lesbian feminism gives us the tools to build a world in which we become each other's building blocks. We love our cobuilders; they are our lovers, which is not to say that we might not struggle at times to agree about what we are making. We have to find spaces that are for women: and for women means, for those who are assigned or assign themselves as women, for those who willfully accept being women as their assignment. And women's spaces are gradually being eroded, often through the assumption that they are no longer necessary. I have addressed this problem in relation to women's studies (chapter 7). The time for women's studies is not over until universities cease to be men's studies. We must be willful to will this cessation.

We are willful when we are not willing to cease. To recall the vitality of lesbian feminism as a resource of the present is to stay attuned to that effort required for those shelters to be built, brick by brick; she had a hand in it.

Helter-skelter

What a shelter

The roots; back to routes. *Skelter* from *skelt*: "to hasten, scatter hurriedly." Scattered; shattered; confusion. The helter?

Just there for the rhyme

Poetry in motion

To build from the ruin; our building might seem ruined; when we build, we ruin. It is a lesbian feminist hope: to become a ruin, to ruin by becoming. How easily though without foundations, without a stable ground, the walls come down. We keep them up; we keep each other up. We might then think of fragility not so much as the potential to lose something, fragility as loss, but as a quality of relations we acquire, or a quality of what we build. A fragile shelter has looser walls, made out of lighter materials; see how they move. A movement is what is built to survive what has been built. When we loosen the requirements to be in a world, we create room for others to be.

CONCLUSION: INTERSECTIONALITY IS ARMY

We could think of lesbian feminism as willful carpentry: she builds with her own hands; she is handy. Maybe I am thinking too of your arms, your strong butch arms and what they can do, whom they can hold; of how they can hold me. If a feminist history is army, as I described in the conclusion of chapter 3, that history is also a history of lesbian arms.

I think of being held by your arms

Yes, I do

I want to return one last time to the Grimm story. I keep coming back to the story because the arm keeps coming up. Is the willful child a lesbian? Is the arm a lesbian? The arm certainly seems queer: to come up is to be wayward.

We could tell a few lesbian stories about arms. When arms are not employed, they disobey; they wander away. Arms can be "matter out of place," to borrow an expression from the anthropologist Mary Douglas ([1966] 2002, 44), the sign of an improper residence. If you have the wrong arms, it means you are assumed to be in the wrong place. An example: A butch lesbian enters the female restroom. The attendant becomes flustered and says, "You are not supposed to be here." The butch lesbian is used to this: how many of her stories are restroom stories; to pass as male becomes a question mark of your right to pass into female space. "I am a woman," she says. We might have to assign ourselves with gender if we trouble the existing assignments. With a reassignment, she can go to the restroom. When she comes out, the attendant is embarrassed; the attendant points to her arm, saying, "So strong." The butch lesbian allows the moment to pass by joking, giving the attendant a show of her arms.

With arms we come out, with arm we come in. If the strong arms are called upon to answer a questioning of a right to be there, they are called upon to assert a right to be there. However, these moments do not always pass so easily. Many of these histories of passing or of not passing are traumatic.[8] Arms don't always help us get through. When arms are wayward, they can be beaten. If we told queer history as a history of arms, we would show the material consequences of being wayward. Arms after all can be gendering assignments. J. Halberstam in *Female Masculinity* notes with some surprise how Havelock Ellis uses the arm as a gender test in the case of Miss M.: "Miss M. he thinks, tries to cover over her masculinity but gives herself away to Ellis when he uses a rather idiosyncratic test of gender identification: 'with arms, palmed up, extended in front of her with inner sides touching, she cannot bring the inner sides of the forearms together as nearly every woman can, showing that the feminine angle of the arm is lost'" (Halberstam 1998, 80). If the arminess of the queer female arm is detected by a straightening rod, the arm is not straightened. The arm can be the fleshy site of a disagreement. The wayward arm is another call to arms.

You note the connection between the strong arms of the black woman (who has to insist on being woman) discussed in chapter 3 and the strong arms of the butch lesbian (who has to insist on being woman) discussed here. These arms can, of course, belong to the same body. Throughout feminist history many women had to insist on being women before they became part of the feminist conversation. Trans women have to insist on being women; trans women often have to keep insisting, again and again, often in the face of violent and repeated acts of misgendering; any feminists who do not stand up, who do not wave their arms to protest against this misgendering, have become the straightening rods. An antitrans stance is an antifeminist stance; it is against the feminist project of creating worlds to support those for whom gender fatalism (boys will be boys, girls will be girls) is fatal; a sentencing to death. We have to hear that fatalism as punishment and instruction: it is the story of the rod, of how those who have wayward wills or who will waywardly (boys who will not be boys, girls who will not be girls) are beaten. We need to drown these antitrans voices out, raising the sound of our own. Our voices need to become our arms: rise up; rise up.

We can make an army connection: if gender norms operate to create a narrow idea of how a female arm should appear, a white arm, a slight arm, an arm that has not labored, an arm that is delicately attuned to an assignment, then many who understand themselves as women, who sign up to being women, will be deemed not women because of their arms. It is the arms that lead us astray.

Arms not only have a history; they are shaped by history; arms make history flesh. No wonder arms keep coming up. It is the arms that can help us make the connection between histories that otherwise do not seem to meet. There are many arms; arms that are muscular, strong, laboring arms, arms that refuse to be employed, striking arms; arms that are lost in service to the industrial machine; broken arms.

Intersectionality is arm.
Intersectionality is army.

CONCLUSION 1 *A Killjoy Survival Kit*

Becoming a killjoy can feel, sometimes, like making your life harder than it needs to be. I have heard this sentiment expressed as kindness: as if to say, just stop noticing exclusions and your burden will be eased. It is implied that by not struggling against something you will be rewarded by an increasing proximity to that thing. You might be included if only you just stop talking about exclusions. Sometimes the judgment is expressed less kindly: disapproval can be expressed in sideways glances, the sighs, the eyes rolling; stop struggling, adjust, accept. And you can also feel this yourself: that by noticing certain things you are making it harder for yourself.

But the experiences we have are not just of being worn down; these experiences also give us resources. What we learn from these experiences might be how we survive these experiences. Toward the end of chapter 9 I raised the question of survival. Here survival is how I begin; it is the start of something. Survival here refers not only to living on, but to keeping going in the more profound sense of keeping going with one's commitments. As Alexis Pauline Gumbs suggests, we need a "robust and transformative redefinition of survival" (2010, 17). Survival can also be about keeping one's hopes alive; holding on to the projects that are projects insofar as they have yet to be realized. You might have to become willful to hold on when you are asked to let go; to let it go. Survival can thus be what we do for others, with others. We need each other to survive; we need to be part of each other's survival.

To be committed to a feminist life means we cannot not do this work; we cannot not fight for this cause, whatever it causes, so we have to find a way of sharing the costs of that work. Survival thus becomes a shared feminist project. So this tool kit contains my personal stuff, what I have accumulated over time; things I know I need to do and to have around me to keep on going on. We will accumulate different things, have our own stuff; we can peer into each other's kits and find in there someone else's feminist story. But I think the point of the kit is not just what we put in it; it is the kit itself, having somewhere to deposit those things that are necessary for your survival. Feminism is a killjoy survival kit.

We could think of this feminist survival kit as a form of feminist self-care. However, to think of a killjoy survival kit as self-care might seem to be a neoliberal agenda, a way of making feminism about the resilience of individuals.[1] I discussed the problem of resilience in chapter 7, the way in which we are asked to become resilient so we can take more (more oppression, more pressure, more work). But this is our problem: feminism needs feminists to survive. We might still need to be able to take it, the pressure we are put under when we refuse to take more, when we refuse to put up with a world.

Feminism needs feminists to survive: my killjoy survival kit is assembled around this sentence. It is a feminist sentence. And the reverse too is very true: feminists need feminism to survive. Feminism needs those of us who live lives as feminists to survive; our life becomes a feminist survival. But feminism needs to survive; our life becomes a feminist survival in this other sense. Feminism needs us; feminism needs us not only to survive but to dedicate our lives to the survival of feminism. This book has been my expression of my willingness to make this dedication. Feminists need feminism to survive.

Audre Lorde, in her extraordinary poem "A Litany of Survival," addresses those who were "never meant to survive," those for whom survival requires creativity and work; those for whom survival is politically ambitious. Let me share a few lines from this poem:

> For those of us who live at the shoreline
> standing upon the constant edges of decision
> crucial and alone
> for those of us who cannot indulge
> the passing dreams of choice
> who love in doorways coming and going
> in the hours between dawns (1978, 31)

Here through the art of light description Lorde evokes for us a "those of us," a those of us who live and love on the edges of social experiences, in doorways, shadows, those of us who fall like shadows fall, the fallen, those for whom coming into full view would be dangerous, those for whom survival might require not coming out in the full light of day.

Survival can be protest.

And then: how we care for ourselves becomes an expression of feminist care. Audre Lorde, as one might expect, helps us to differentiate survival from other styles of self-orientated politics. Lorde writes, "Caring for myself is not self-indulgence, it is self-preservation, and that is an act of political warfare" (1988, 131). This is a revolutionary, extraordinary sentence. It is a much-loved, much-cited sentence. It is an arrow, which acquires its sharpness from its own direction. It is from the epilogue to Lorde's *A Burst of Light*, a piece of writing so profound, so moving, that it never fails to teach me, often by leaving me undone, beside myself (that's why, as you will read, this book is in my survival kit). This writing is made up of fragments of notes put together as Audre Lorde learns that she has liver cancer, that her death can only be delayed, as she comes to feel that diagnosis in her bones. The expression "a burst of light" is used when she comes to feel the fragility of her body's situation: "that inescapable knowledge, in the bone, of my own physical limitation" (Lorde 1988, 121).

A Burst of Light is an account of how the struggle for survival is a life struggle and a political struggle. A death sentence is not only about what Jasbir Puar (2009) has called "prognosis time": it is not (or not only) about experiencing your death as imminent. When you are not supposed to live, as you are, where you are, with whom you are with, then survival is a radical action; a refusal not to exist until the very end; a refusal not to exist until you do not exist. We have to work out how to survive in a system that decides life for some requires the death or removal of others. Sometimes: to survive in a system is to survive a system. Some of us have to be inventive, Audre Lorde suggests, to survive.

Others: not so much.

When a whole world is organized to promote your survival, from health to education, to the walls designed to keep your residence safe, to the paths that ease your travel, you do not have become so inventive to survive. You do not have to be seen as the recipient of welfare because the world has promoted your welfare. The benefits you receive are given as entitlements, perhaps even as birthrights. This is why I describe privilege as a buffer zone; it is how much you have to fall back on when you lose something. Privilege does not mean we are invulnerable: things happen; shit happens. Privilege can however reduce the costs of vulnerability; you are more likely to be looked after.

Racial capitalism is a health system: a drastically unequal distribution of bodily vulnerabilities. Ruth Wilson Gilmore describes racism thus: "the state-sanctioned or extra-legal production and exploitation of group-differentiated vulnerability to premature death" (2007, 28). Being poor, being black, being of color puts your life at risk. Your health is compromised when you do not have the external resources to support a life in all of its contingencies. And then of course, you are deemed responsible for your own ill health, for your own failure to look after yourself better. When you refer to structures, to systems, to power relations, to walls, you are assumed to be making others responsible for the situation you have failed to get yourself out of. "You should have tried harder." Oh, the violence and the smugness of this sentence, this sentencing.

A health system is also a support system. The more precarious you are, the more support you need. The more precarious you are, the less support you have. When we say something is precarious, we usually mean it is in a precarious position: if the vase on the mantelpiece were pushed, just a little bit, a little bit, it would topple right over.[2] That position—of living on the edge—is what is generalized when we speak of precarious populations (see Butler 2015). Living on the edge: a life lived as a fragile thread that keeps unraveling; when life becomes an effort to hold on to what keeps unraveling.

When I think of this, I think of how fragility as an effort to hold on can become more revolting; how fragility can be militancy. Throughout *A Burst of Light* Audre Lorde compares her experience of battling with cancer (and she is willing to use this militaristic language; she is willing to describe this situation as war) to her experience of battling against antiblack racism. The comparison is effective, showing us how racism can be an attack on the cells of the body, her body, her black body, an attack on the body's immune system; the way in which your own body experiences what is outside itself as inside itself; death from the outside in. A world that is against you can be experienced as your body turning against you. This is why for Lorde caring for oneself is not self-indulgence but self-preservation. It is rebellious to fight for life when you have been given such a deadly assignment.

In this statement that caring for oneself is not self-indulgence we can thus hear a defense. Audre Lorde is defending self-care. What from? From whom? From, one might suspect, those who dismiss caring for oneself as an indulgence. Self-indulgence tends to mean being soft on one's self, but also can mean yielding to one's inclinations. Recently I have heard much feminist work being dismissed on these terms. Feminism: too soft, too safe, too focused on identity politics or individual suffering. Feminist student activism in particular has been dismissed like this: safe spaces, trigger warnings, self-care, all taken up as evidence of being coddled and weak. One thing I know from working in universities: student movements might be teaching us how attending to fragility, the histories that render some more fragile than others, can be a source of militancy.

And yet Audre Lorde could be read as a critic of self-care. After all, she gave us a strong critique of how structural inequalities are deflected by being made the responsibility of individuals (who in being given the capacity to overcome structures are assumed to fail when they do not overcome them). Her work explores how caring for oneself can become a technique of governance: the duty to care for one's self is often written as a duty to care for one's own happiness. In *The Cancer Journals* she shows how making our own happiness our first responsibility can be how we turn away from injustice. Lorde asks, "Was I really fighting the spread of radiation, racism, woman-slaughter, chemical invasion of our food, pollution of our environment, and the abuse and psychic destruction of our young, merely to avoid dealing with my first and greatest responsibility to be happy?" (1997, 76). Audre Lorde has given us the answer to her question.

We have something to work out here. Audre Lorde writes persuasively about how caring for oneself can lead you away from engaging in certain kinds of political struggle. And yet, in *A Burst of Light* (1988), she defends caring for oneself as not about self-indulgence but self-preservation. She is making for us a distinction. She is sharpening a tool. This kind of caring for oneself is not about caring for one's own happiness. It is about finding ways to exist in a world that makes it difficult to exist. This is why, this is how: those who do not have to struggle for their own survival can very easily and rather quickly dismiss those who attend to their own survival as being self-indulgent. They do not need to attend to themselves; the world does it for them.

For those who have to insist they matter to matter, self-care is warfare. We could think here of #blacklivesmatter, a movement with a hashtag; a hashtag can be snap; a movement begun by black feminist and queer activists Alicia Garza, Patrisse Cullors, and Opal Tometi to protest against how black lives do not matter, how black deaths are not mourned, how injustices against black people are not recognized. Mattering for some requires and involves collective agency: "Black Lives Matter affirms the lives of black queer and trans folks, disabled folks, black undocumented folks, folks with records, women and all black lives along the gender spectrum."[3] You have to affirm that some lives matter when a world is invested in saying they do not.

Protest can be a form of self-care as well as care for others: a refusal not to matter. Self-care can also be those ordinary ways we look out for each other because the costs of protesting are made so high, just as the costs that lead to protest remain so high. In directing our care toward ourselves, we are redirecting care away from its proper objects; we are not caring for those we are supposed to care for; we are not caring for the bodies deemed worth caring about. And that is why in queer, feminist, and antiracist work, self-care is about the creation of community, fragile communities as I explored in part III, assembled out of the experiences of being shattered. We reassemble ourselves through the ordinary, everyday, and often painstaking work of looking after ourselves; looking after each other.

We need a handle when we lose it. A killjoy survival kit is about finding a handle at the very moment one seems to lose it, when things seem to fly out of hand; a way of holding on when the possibility you were reaching for seems to be slipping away. Feminist killjoys: even when things fly out of hand, even when we fly out of hand, we need a handle on things.

ITEM 1: BOOKS

You need your favorite feminist books close to hand; your feminist books need to be handy. You need to take them with you; make them with you. Words can pick you up when you are down. And note: it is often books that name the problem that help us handle the problem. Kick-ass feminist books have a special agency, all of their own. I feel propelled by their kick.

Books in my tool kit include *Sister Outsider, A Burst of Light, Zami,* and *The Cancer Journals* by Audre Lorde; *Feminist Theory* and *Talking Back* by bell hooks; *The Politics of Reality* by Marilyn Frye; *Gender Trouble, Bodies That Matter,* and *Precarious Lives* by Judith Butler; *Mrs. Dalloway* by Virginia Woolf; *The Mill on the Floss* by George Eliot; *Rubyfruit Jungle* by Rita Mae Brown. Yes I know this list includes a lot of books by Audre Lorde and Judith Butler. Their words reach me. Their words teach me.

Wherever I go, they go.

ITEM 2: **THINGS**

A feminist life too is surrounding by things. Living a feminist life creates feminist things. We all have tendencies; we might be a feminist hoarder, keep every little poster, button, scrap of paper from a meeting; or we might not. But think of how a convention is a thing maker (the wedding photographs, the signs of a reproductive life that can gather like weights on walls). We need to have things too; things that gather around, reminders of a feminist life, happy objects even, reminders of connections, shared struggles, shared lives. We might have more or fewer things, but a feminist needs her things.

Surround yourself with feminism. In a conversation with Gloria Steinem, bell hooks describes how she surrounded herself with her precious objects, feminist objects, so that they are the first things she sees when she wakes up.[4] Think of that: you create a feminist horizon around you, the warmth of memories; feminism as memory making. Feminism too leaves things behind. Things can also be how you handle what you come up against: you are reminded why you are doing what you are doing. Things are reminders.

Our feminist politics makes things as well as breaks things.

ITEM 3: **TOOLS**

A survival kit is also a feminist toolbox. What are your feminist tools? Mine include a pen and a keyboard, a table; the things around me that allow me to keep writing, to send my words out. Maybe a survival kit is also a toolbox. We need to have things to do things with; a killjoy needs more tools, the more she is up against. Maybe she uses her computer to write a blog. A tool: a means to a killjoy end. The blog itself becomes a tool; it is how she can extend her reach; how she can find a community of killjoys. A feminist end is often a new means. We need more means available the harder it is to achieve our ends. We need to diversify our tools, expand our range; we need to become more and more inventive, because so often when we do one thing, we find ourselves blocked. She has to keep going when she is blocked; she can pick herself up again by picking something else up, maybe something she finds nearby. Of course, then, a feminist killjoy approaches things as potentially useful things, as means to her own ends. She has a use for things. She might not be using things the way she is supposed to. She might queer use or find a queer use for things. Her killjoy survival kit, to fulfill the purpose for which it is intended, will itself become another useful thing. But hand that survival kit to another, and it might not be quite so useful. In fact: a killjoy survival kit might even be deemed as compromising the health and safety of others. In fact: a killjoy survival kit might be deemed useless by others.

A feminist tool is sharp; we need to keep sharpening our tools. When we speak, we are often heard as sharp. Hear her: shrill, strident, the killjoy voice. A voice can be a tool. And yet somehow sharp can become blunt. One person once turned this bluntness into an insult, describing me "as not the sharpest tool in the house [of being]." I turn the insult into a willful aspiration: to make feminist points requires being willing to be blunt. My own citation policy in this book is a case in point.

In my previous chapter I described lesbian feminism as willful carpentry. So yes we need feminist carpenters, feminist builders; we need to make feminist buildings by not using the master's tools, as Audre Lorde notes, most willfully, by proclaiming unflinchingly that the master's tools will never dismantle the master's house. We might need feminist tools to make feminist tools. We can become tools; we can become bricks, feminist bricks.

Of course, sometimes a feminist has to go on strike. To strike is to put your tools down, to refuse to work by working with them. A feminist sometimes refuses to work, when the conditions of working are unjust. A tool can be what she puts down when she is striking.

ITEM 4: TIME

Did your heart quicken when you read that e-mail? Did your fingers quicken when you typed that response, as if driven by the force of your own rage? Do you have a sense that this is happening to you, and that you are caught by hap, and shudder because of what happens? Whatever you decide, whether to send something, or not, say something, or not, pause, breathe; take some time. Slow down. Frown. You might still send it, but you will be glad you have given yourself room to decide; you will be glad.

Time also means having time out. Even when you have willingly accepted the killjoy assignment, you are more than this assignment. Take breaks; do other things, with things. Time out might be required for time in.

Time out from being a killjoy is necessary for a killjoy if she is to persist in being a killjoy. Being a killjoy is not all that you are, and if you are too consumed by her, she can drain too much energy and will. Come back to her; she will come back to you: you will, she will.

ITEM 5: LIFE

There is so much in life, as we know, things that are ordinary or just there, beautiful things, to love; those things that come and go; things that are all the more valuable because they are fragile. Being a killjoy is too occupying, if it takes you away from the worlds you are in; the rise and fall of the sun, the way the trees are angled like that, the smile of a friend when you share a joke, the cold fresh water; the feel of the sea as immersion; the familiar smells of spices cooking.

Twice in my life an animal has come into my life and made life feel more possible, made life vibrate with possibility: when I was twelve, it was Mulka, a horse who was with me for almost thirty years (I mentioned him in chapter 2), always there even when we were living on separate continents. Mulka saved my life, of that I am sure, helped me to find another path when I was hurtling toward a miserable fate. He brought with him a world, a world of horsey people, in the Adelaide hills, a world apart from school and family. He brought with him Yvonne and Meredith Johnson, who in caring for him when I was away, cared for me. And then there was Poppy, our puppy, who came into my life while I was writing this book. It is the first time I have shared a life with a dog. She makes everything better. She brought with her so much, so intent on the task of being herself; a bounding presence who keeps me in the present. She wiggled her way into my affections. She also wiggled her way into this survival kit. She will wiggle right out again. Of that too, I am sure.

To survive as to be: to be with Mulka; to be with Poppy; to be in a present; to be out in the world; to be alive with a world.

Life matters; we are killjoys because life matters; and life can be what killjoys are fighting for; life requires we give time to living, to being alive, to being thrown into a world with others. We need to be thrown by how others are thrown. We need to be unsettled by what is unsettling. We need to let life in, in all of its contingencies. I think of this as being open to hap. And, as I suggested in chapter 8, to affirm hap is a kind of snap; we snap a bond that decides for us the kind of shape a life should have to count as a good life. But that does not mean breaking our bond to life. To snap a bond is for life. We believe in life all the more when we have to struggle for life, whether we have to snap, because we have to struggle to exist or struggle to transform an existence.

Being involved in a life project is affirmative. That is what those of us assigned killjoys know too well; yes we are assigned negative, but in being willing to receive that assignment we are affirming something. We might have different words, names, for this something.

ITEM 6: **PERMISSION NOTES**

There is only so much you can do. I have in my killjoy survival kit some permission notes to step back when it is too much. I noted in chapter 7 that you can learn to choose your battles wisely, but battles can also choose you. You don't always know when you can or will use your permission notes even when you have given them to yourself. But the mere fact of having them there, as a way you give yourself permission to exit a situation, can make the situation more bearable. You can leave; you can grieve.

I have already described how I left my academic post. I resigned because I gave myself permission to resign. That's not the only reason. But you need to be able to leave a situation, whether or not you do leave that situation. Being able to leave requires material resources, but it also requires an act of will, of not being willing to do something when it compromises your ability to be something.

I also have in my kit some sick notes. Do you anticipate that an event or meeting will be compromising? Do you feel you will be upset without being able to do anything? Well, put some sick notes in your kit. Use them sparingly, but given that we can be sick from the anticipation of being sick, the notes express a political as well as personal truth. Of course that is not to say that what we anticipate will happen will happen; of course not. But sometimes, just sometimes, we are not willing to take that risk. Be willful in your not willingness. Always.

ITEM 7: **OTHER KILLJOYS**

I think other killjoys are an essential part of my killjoy survival kit. I know it might sound odd to put other people in a place you have designated as your space (in a bag, I keep thinking of bags; how can we breathe in bags?). But I cannot think of being a killjoy without the company of other killjoys. This is not about identity; it is not about assuming a community of killjoys (I have discussed the problem with making this assumption). Rather, it is about the experience of having others who recognize the dynamics because they too have been there, in that place, that difficult place. This is not to say we cannot become killjoys to killjoys. We can and we do. And that is just one more reason that other killjoys need to be part of our survival kit. It helps us to recognize how we too can be the problem; we too can be involved in erasing the contributions or chances of others.

I learned this lesson recently when my own participation in a conversation on black British feminism was challenged by black women who saw me as participating in their erasure from public spaces and discussions. I responded too quickly and became defensive, hearing their voices as part of the same chorus of what I would call more questionable critiques that positioned brown women as gaining position by taking up places that did not belong to them, which used the familiar narrative that women of color use diversity as a career advancement. I heard as a killjoy. And that stopped me from hearing killjoys, those who were getting in the way of what I thought of as a lifeline: black British feminism as my intellectual community. Staying close to other killjoys is thus not about being on the same side. It is how we can ask more of ourselves; it is how we can be and stay vigilant.

Our crossness can and should be directed toward ourselves. We get things wrong. I did. And I do.

ITEM 8: **HUMOR**

A close kin of the figure of the feminist killjoy is the figure of the humorless feminist: the one who cannot or will not get the joke; the one who is miserable. Oh the proximity of kinship! Of course, we refuse to laugh at sexist jokes. We refuse to laugh when jokes are not funny. I consider this point to be so vital that it forms the fourth of the ten principles of my killjoy manifesto. But we do laugh; and feminist laughter can lighten our loads. In fact we laugh often in recognition of the shared absurdity of this world; or just in recognition of this world. Sometimes we make jokes out of the points left severed, the bleeding arteries of our institutional knowledge. Sometimes we laugh with each other because we recognize that we recognize the same power relations.

What I am implying here: lightening our loads becomes part of a killjoy survival strategy. When we are dealing with heavy histories, lightening becomes a shared activity. When we are dealing with norms that tighten the more we fail to inhabit them, making it difficult to breathe, loosening becomes a shared activity. Part of the work of lightening and loosening is sharing: because diversity work is costly, we have to share the costs of doing that work.

My interviews with diversity practitioners that I drew on in part II were thus full of laughter. Like the time a diversity practitioner talked about how she just had to open her mouth in meetings to witness eyes rolling as if to say, "Oh here she goes." How we laughed as killjoys recognizing that killjoy moment. Or like the time a diversity practitioner told me of how a friend asked, "Are they related?" about a photo of her (all white male) management team. How we laughed, at that moment, at that exposure of how institutions work as kinship structures. When we catch with words a logic that is often reproduced by not being put into words, it can be such a relief. We recognized that each other recognized the logic. Laughter, peals of it; our bodies catching that logic, too.

We don't always laugh, of course. Sometimes we have to let the full weight of a history bear down on us. Sometimes we need to let ourselves be down. But sometimes this sense of being down can convert into energy, because we can laugh at it; because what we come up against gives us the resources to bear witness, to expose things, to bring things to the surface, so they can be laughed at.

To laugh at something can be to make something more real, to magnify it, and to reduce something's power or hold over you, simultaneously.

ITEM 9: FEELINGS

Our emotions can be a resource; we draw on them. To be a killjoy is often to be assigned as being emotional, too emotional; letting your feelings get in the way of your judgment; letting your feelings get in the way. Your feelings can be the site of a rebellion. A feminist heart beats the wrong way; feminism is hearty.

One male professor where I work kept telling me, telling others, that he did not get the feminist killjoy; that she made no sense to him. He kept saying it repeatedly. Explain it to me. Really he was saying: explain yourself. And he kept saying things like, she doesn't make sense because we have women who are senior managers. In other words, he thought the right feminist feeling would be joy, gratitude even, for the good fortune of our arrival and progression. We have to be willing to be experienced as ungrateful, to use this refusal of joy as an exposure of what we have been commanded not to express. There was an implication in his refusal to get the feminist killjoy that my organizing of my own intellectual and political project through her was an institutional disloyalty; one that would potentially damage the institution.

I think of Adrienne Rich's (1979) killjoy invitation to be "disloyal to civilization." Our emotions are opened up when we refuse the commandment to be loyal and joyful. We don't always know how we feel even when we feel something intensely. Put all those feelings into your kit. See what they do. Watch the mess they stir up. A survival kit is all about stirring things up and living in the stew.

It is true, it is wearing. We can be worn down as well as becoming down. Bodies need to be looked after. Bodies need to be nourished and fed. Feminism too can be thought of as a diet; a feminist diet is how we are nourished by feminism. In my killjoy survival kit I would have a bag of fresh chilies; I tend to add chilies to most things. I am not saying chilies are little feminists. But you would have in your kit whatever you tend to add to things; however you adapt dishes to your own requirements. If we have a diversity of bodies, we have a diversity of requirements.

And this item is related to all the others. Bodies are the mediating relation. When we do not survive, we become body; a body is what is left. A body is behind. A body is vulnerable; we are vulnerable. A body tells us the time; bodies carry traces of where we have been. Perhaps we are these traces. A killjoy has a body before she can receive her assignment.

Bodies speak to us. Your body might tell you it is not coping with what you are asking; and you need to listen. You need to listen to your body. If it screams, stop. If it moans, slow down. Listen. Feminist ears: they too are in my survival kit.

So much energy is involved in the struggle not to be compromised by an existence. But as I have noted throughout this book, claiming the figure of the killjoy, saying in this situation or that "I am her" can be energizing; there is something about her, a sense of vitality, perhaps, a sense of rebelliousness and mischief, perhaps, naughtiness, even, which might be why and how killjoys keep circulating, keep proliferating; she seems to be popping up everywhere. As I said in an earlier chapter, if we pick her up, she picks up.

And that too is why bodies must be in our survival kit. Bodies that prance; bodies that dance; "bodies that matter," to borrow Judith Butler's (1993) terms; bodies that have to wiggle about to create space.

Wiggling is in my survival kit.

Dancing, too.

Bodies that dance: how often feminists have claimed dance as essential to their liberation. One might think of Emma Goldman's famous statement, "I won't join your revolution if I cannot dance." Or I think of the film about the survival of Audre Lorde, *The Berlin Years*, and its final sequences that show Audre dancing, sequences that seem to capture so well the generosity of her black feminist spirit. I think of the dancing at Lesbian Lives conferences that I have enjoyed over the years (the talking too, but the dancing is what I recall most quickly). A dancing feminist body, a dancing lesbian body, dancing black and brown bodies; the affirming of how we inhabit bodies through how we are with others. We are here, still. Anyone can dance with anyone to form a collective. I am not saying killjoys have a specific genre or style of dancing. I am not saying that that there is a killjoy dance. (Though maybe, just maybe, there is a killjoy dance.) Perhaps in her stance is a certain kind of prance; perhaps in the energy that saturates her figure, she becomes an assembly.

Look at her move: what a movement.

And, in putting dance in my killjoy survival kit, I am saying something affirmative. Is there a contradiction here? When I am joyful, have I ceased to be a killjoy? Dance can be how we embrace the fragility of being thrown. And joy too is part of killjoy survival, without any question. We need joy to survive killing joy; we can even take joy from killing joy. And so too is the erotic part of my kit, the kind of erotic that Audre Lorde spoke of with such eloquence; a feminist killjoy in being charged up is warmed up; she is an erotic figure. She might come to be as or in negation, but that negation trembles with desire; a desire for more to life, more desire; a desire for more. Feminist killjoys tend to spill all over the place. What a spillage.

Feminist killjoys: a leaky container.

And so:

Be careful, we leak.

We can recall again Shulamith Firestone's (1970, 90) call for a "smile embargo" in her revolutionary manifesto, *Dialectic of Sex*. She wants us to stop smiling as a force of habit; something that has become involuntary; to stop smiling until we have something to smile about. A smile boycott would be a collective action; it would only work if we all stopped smiling. Not smiling becomes a feminist strike. I will return to this striking feminism in my killjoy manifesto. But note too how Firestone's call is also a call to open up the erotic, to release the erotic from the habit of happiness that directs life down a "narrow, difficult-to-find alleyway of human experience" (1970, 155).

I explored in my chapter "Feminism Is Sensational" how feminism can be a coming alive to a world that had been closed off by the requirement to live your life in a certain way. Things come to life when they are not overlooked. So it is important to say this: we need to allow ourselves to be sad and angry; when joy and happiness become ideals, sadness becomes too quickly an obstacle, a failure to achieve or approximate the right feelings. Sadness can require a permission note (item 6). But at the same time, joy can be part of a killjoy survival kit. I personally don't need a permission note for joy; in my own experience, joy is culturally mandated even if it can be the site of rebellion (the collective joy of dissent); but if you do need to give yourself permission to be joyful, write yourself one. I think joy can only be part of a killjoy survival kit when we refuse to give joy the status of an aspiration. When joy becomes aspiration, then joy becomes what a killjoy has to kill. But even if survival for killjoys requires refusing to make joy (or its heavier friend happiness) into an aspiration, it does not mean we have an obligation to be sad or unhappy either. A killjoy is not joyless.

To return to Emma Goldman, to her book *Living My Life*, she affirms the freedom to dance when she is told not to dance; she dances and is told that it is not the right time to dance, because of the "death of a dear comrade" ([1931] 2008, 56). As she relays the story, she says a young boy with a solemn face whispered to her, "It did not behoove an agitator to dance." Goldman affirms at this moment dance as an affective rebellion against the requirement to be mournful; against the requirement not to live in her body through joyful abandon. This is what I call an affect alien moment. A killjoy survival kit is also about allowing your body to be the site of a rebellion, including a rebellion against the demand to give your body over to a cause or to make your body a cause. Maybe not dancing, too, can be what a body does; refusing to dance when dancing becomes a requirement, standing back, to one side, stopping.

AND FINALLY: A KILLJOY SURVIVAL KIT

Putting together a killjoy survival kit can also be a survival strategy. My killjoy survival kit is in my killjoy survival kit. Writing a feminist manifesto too might be a survival strategy. My manifesto, up next, is in my kit. In writing a feminist manifesto, you must first read other feminist manifestos. What a joy! Manifestos are "companion species," to borrow a description from one of Donna Haraway's (2003) manifestos. Reading manifestos is also in my killjoy survival kit. A kit can be a container for activities that are ongoing; projects that are projects insofar as they have yet to be realized.

A killjoy: a project that comes from a critique of what is.

Speaking of projects:

We are our own survival kits.

CONCLUSION 2 *A Killjoy Manifesto*

A manifesto: a statement of principle, a mission statement. Manifesto: a declaration of the intent of an individual or organization or group. How can one write a manifesto around a figure, the killjoy, or an activity, killing joy?

A manifesto: to make manifest. Moynan King in her discussion of Valerie Solanas's SCUM *Manifesto* addresses this sense of a manifesto as making manifest. She writes, "As a manifesto, SCUM's intention is to make manifest, to render perceptible, a new order of ideas" (King 2013, n.p.). To render a new order of ideas perceptible is simultaneously a disordering of ideas; manifestos often enact what they call for in surprising and shocking ways given how they expose the violence of an order. A feminist manifesto exposes the violence of a patriarchal order, the violence of what I called in chapter 2 "the machinery of gender."

A manifesto not only causes a disturbance, it aims to cause this disturbance. To make something manifest can be enough to cause a disturbance. This intimacy between manifestation and disturbance has implications for how we write a killjoy manifesto. A killjoy manifesto must be grounded in an account of what exists. Why is this important? It is about what we come up against. Some of the worst abuses of power I have encountered in the academy have been when individuals make use of an equality principle, as if to say, boundaries and rules are about hierarchy, so we are "free to do what we want," whereby "free to do what we want" really still means "you doing what I want you to do," given that the *we* is made up of an *I* who has power and a *you* that is subordinate by virtue of their positions within an organization. Note that "doing what we want" not only can be assumed to express an equality principle but can be articulated as a rebellion against institutional norms and authority (they would prevent us from having relationships because they assume boundaries and divisions that we have given up because we are free radicals). A killjoy manifesto cannot be about the freeing of radicals to pursue their own agendas.

A killjoy manifesto thus begins by recognizing inequalities as existing. This recognition is enacted by the figure of the killjoy herself: she kills joy because of what she claims exists. She has to keep making the same claim because she keeps countering the claim that what she says exists does not exist. The killjoy is often assumed to be inventive, to bring about what she claims; or, to use my terms from chapter 6, she is often assumed to be a wall maker. If a killjoy manifesto shows how the denial of inequality under the assumption of equality is a technique of power, then the principles articulated in that manifesto cannot be abstracted from statements about what exists. A killjoy manifesto is thus about making manifest what exists. In the labor of making manifest we make a manifesto.

To struggle for freedom is to struggle against oppression. Angela Davis in *Blues Legacies and Black Feminism* showed how the articulation of unfulfilled longings for freedom can also represent freedom "in more immediate and accessible terms" ([1989] 1998, 7). It is from oppression that freedom is given expression. A manifesto is required when a struggle is necessary to give expression to something. This is why the manifesto can be understood as a killjoy genre; we have to say it because of what is not being done. A manifesto makes an appeal by not being appealing: a manifesto is not an attractive piece of writing by existing norms or standards. It cannot be: it has to strain to be said. And yet a manifesto is appealing to those who read it; a manifesto appeals for something by appealing to someone. A killjoy manifesto appeals *to* killjoys.

Manifestos are often disagreeable because they show the violence necessary to sustain an agreement. It is not just that the feminist killjoy has a manifesto. The feminist killjoy is a manifesto. She is assembled around violence; how she comes to matter, to mean, is how she exposes violence. Just remember the *kill* in killjoy. This figure reminds us how feminism is often understood as a form of murder; calling for the end of the system that makes "men" is often understood as killing men. We could indeed compare the figure of the murderous feminist to that of the feminist killjoy. What Valerie Solanas ([1967] 2013) does in her manifesto, very controversially, is to literalize that fantasy of the murderous feminist through imagining a feminist collective, or a mind-set, that is SCUM (Society for Cutting Up Men). It should not surprise us, because one of her points was to be a cutoff point that the SCUM *Manifesto* was read literally; it was dismissed as literal or dismissed through literalism as intending the elimination of men. The manifesto works because it enacts the literalism that would enable its own dismissal. I have noticed this use of literalism as dismissal when working on my feminist killjoy blog. For example, when I tweeted a link to a blog post "white men," which was retweeted by a white man, another white man called it "genosuicide."[1] Genosuicide: the self-willed killing of a people. Or another time a student at Goldsmiths, Bahar Mustafa, allegedly used the hashtag #killallwhitemen.[2] Valerie Solanas is brought back to life on social media. Snap. But of course if this hashtag literalizes a fantasy, you literally encounter the fantasy. The hashtag is turned back into a command; heard as the planning of genocide.

The figure of the murderous feminist is useful: it allows the survival of men to be predicated on the elimination of feminism. Much feminist creativity has literalized a fantasy that does not originate with us, including the film *A Question of Silence*, discussed in chapters 8 and 9, where the man that is killed in an act of feminist revenge stands in for all men. And in a way of course you are being violent in exposing violence; if you are letting the violence come out of your own pen, to travel through you, you have to let the violence spill, all over the pages. And you are in a certain way calling for the end of white men because you are calling for the end of the institution that makes white men. "White men" is an institution, as I discussed in chapter 6. We do want to bring an end to him. But of course, at another level, it is harder to redeploy the figure of the murderous feminist than the figure of the feminist killjoy. Feminists are not calling for violence. We are calling for an end to the institutions that promote and naturalize violence. Much violence that is promoted by institutions is concealed by the very use of stranger danger, as I have discussed throughout this book: the assumption that violence only ever originates with outsiders. It is because we expose violence that we are heard as violent, as if the violence of which we speak originates with us.

To be a killjoy can also mean being understood as someone who kills life because there is such an intimacy between the life principle and the happiness principle. In being against happiness you are assumed to be against life. And as such there are life risks in being a killjoy. It is not that in being assigned a killjoy (and as I have argued, she always begins as an assignment because the feminist killjoy is announced from a position of exteriority; she already has a life of her own before we are assigned her) we are always willing or able to receive this assignment. In fact, as I explored in part I, the figure of the feminist killjoy often comes up in situations of intense pain and difficulty: when you are seated at the table, doing the work of family, that happy object, say, you threaten that object. And you threaten the object by pointing out what is already there, in the room; again, you are not being inventive. But what a feeling: when all the negative feeling that is not revealed when the family is working becomes deposited in the one who reveals the family is not working. I will never forget that feeling of wanting to eliminate myself from a situation that I had been assumed to cause.

It is a downer; we are downers.

A killjoy manifesto has company: books that bring things down, books that enact a collective frown. *The Dialectic of Sex* could be read as a killjoy manifesto, a book that has too quickly been dismissed as assuming technology would liberate women from biology, a book that showed that when the sexual division of labor structures everything, nothing will liberate anyone. Sarah Franklin describes how the "bulk of Firestone's manifesto was based on an analysis of what has held a certain gender stratification in place for millennia" (2010, 46). *The Dialectic of Sex* is optimistic because it accounts for how liberation is difficult to achieve. No wonder she has her killjoy moments. Firestone wants to explain why this system that is not working keeps on going, a system that she has no doubt eventually will kill us all. And for explanations, she turns to love, to romance, to the family. These institutions are promises of happiness. An institution can be organized around a promise. And they become ways of organizing living by assuming that proximity to a form will get you there. So, of course, Shulamith Firestone in turning in this direction turns to happiness. As I have already noted, she describes her "dream action" for the women's liberation movement as a smile boycott (Firestone 1970, 90). Perhaps we could call this action, following Lisa Millbank (2013), a smile strike, to emphasize its collective nature. Collectively we would strike by not smiling, a collectivity built out of individual action (not smiling is an action when smiling is a requirement for women and for those understood as serving others through paid or unpaid work) but which requires more than an individual. A smile strike is necessary to announce our disagreement, our unhappiness, with a system.

We must stay unhappy with this world.

The figure of the feminist killjoy makes sense if we place her in the context of feminist critiques of happiness, some of which I discussed in chapter 2 (see also Ahmed 2010). Happiness is used to justify social norms as social goods.

As Simone de Beauvoir described so astutely, "It is always easy to describe as happy a situation in which one wishes to place [others]" ([1949] 1997, 28). Not to agree to stay in the place of this wish might be to refuse the happiness that is wished for. To be involved in political activism is thus to be involved in a struggle against happiness. The struggle over happiness provides the horizon in which political claims are made. We inherit this horizon.

A killjoy becomes a manifesto when we are willing to take up this figure, to assemble a life not as her (I discussed the risks of assuming we are her in chapter 7) but around her, in her company. We are willing to killjoy because the world that assigns this or that person or group of people as the killjoys is not a world we want to be part of. To be willing to killjoy is to transform a judgment into a project. A manifesto: how a judgment becomes a project.

To think of killjoys as manifestos is to say that a politics of transformation, a politics that intends to cause the end of a system, is not a program of action that can be separated from how we are in the worlds we are in. Feminism is praxis. We enact the world we are aiming for; nothing less will do. Lesbian feminism, as I noted in chapter 9, is how we organize our lives in such a way that our relations to each other as women are not mediated through our relations to men. A life becomes an archive of rebellion. This is why a killjoy manifesto will be personal. Each of us killjoys will have our own. My manifesto does not suspend my personal story. It is how that story unfolds into action.

It is from difficult experiences, of being bruised by structures that are not even revealed to others, that we gain the energy to rebel. It is from what we come up against that we gain new angles on what we are against. Our bodies become our tools; our rage becomes sickness. We vomit; we vomit out what we have been asked to take in. Our guts become our feminist friends the more we are sickened. We begin to feel the weight of histories more and more; the more we expose the weight of history, the heavier it becomes.

We snap. We snap under the weight; things break. A manifesto is written out of feminist snap. A manifesto is feminist snap.

And: we witness as feminists the trouble feminism causes. I would hazard a guess: feminist trouble is an extension of gender trouble (Butler 1990). To be more specific: feminist trouble is the trouble with women. When we refuse to be women, in the heteropatriarchal sense as beings for men, we become trouble, we get into trouble. A killjoy is willing to get into trouble. And this I think is what is specific about a killjoy manifesto: that we bring into our statements of intent or purpose the experience of what we come up against. It is this experience that allows us to articulate a *for*, a *for* that carries with it an experience of what we come up against. A *for* can be how we turn something about. A manifesto is *about* what it aims to bring *about*.

There is no doubt in my mind that a feminist killjoy is for something; although as killjoys we are not necessarily for the same things. But you would only be willing to live with the consequences of being against what you come up against if you are for something. A life can be a manifesto. When I read some of the books in my survival kit, I hear them as manifestos, as calls to action; as calls to arms. They are books that tremble with life because they show how a life can be rewritten; how we can rewrite a life, letter by letter. A manifesto has a life, a life of its own; a manifesto is an outstretched hand. And if a manifesto is a political action, it depends on how it is received by others. And perhaps a hand can do more when it is not simply received by another hand, when a gesture exceeds the firmness of a handshake. Perhaps more than a hand needs to shake. If a killjoy manifesto is a handle, it flies out of hand. A manifesto thus repeats something that has already happened; as we know the killjoy has flown off. Perhaps a killjoy manifesto is unhandy; a feminist flight.

When we refuse to be the master's tool, we expose the violence of rods, the violences that built the master's dwelling, brick by brick. When we make violence manifest, a violence that is reproduced by not being made manifest, we will be assigned as killjoys. It is because of what she reveals that a killjoy becomes a killjoy in the first place. A manifesto is in some sense behind her. This is not to say that writing a killjoy manifesto is not also a commitment; that it is not also an idea of how to move forward. A killjoy has her principles. A killjoy manifesto shows how we create principles from an experience of what we come up against, from how we live a feminist life. When I say principles here, I do not mean rules of conduct that we must agree to in order to proceed in a common direction. I might say that a feminist life is principled but feminism often becomes an announcement at the very moment of the refusal to be bound by principle. When I think of feminist principles, I think of principles in the original sense: principle as a first step, as a commencement, a start of something.

A principle can also be what is elemental to a craft. Feminist killjoys and other willful subjects are crafty; we are becoming crafty. There are principles in what we craft. How we begin does not determine where we end up, but principles do give shape or direction. Feminist principles are articulated in unfeminist worlds. Living a life with feminist principles is thus not living smoothly; we bump into the world that does not live in accordance with the principles we try to live.

For some reason, the principles I articulate here ended up being expressed as statements of will: of what a killjoy is willing (to do or to be) or not willing (to do or to be). I think we can understand the some of this reason. A killjoy manifesto is a willful subject; she wills wrongly by what she is willing or is not willing to do. No wonder a willful subject has principles; she can be principled. She can share them if you can bear them.

PRINCIPLE 1: **I AM NOT WILLING TO MAKE HAPPINESS MY CAUSE.**

It is often made into a specific requirement: you are asked to do something in order to make others happy. You are more likely to be asked to do something to make others happy when they know you are not happy with what they are doing. Maybe you are asked to participate in a wedding ceremony by those who know you are against the institution of marriage celebrated by such ceremonies. They appeal to you by appealing to their own happiness. If you refuse that appeal you are judged as being selfish, as putting your own happiness before the happiness of others.

Mean: how could you?

A killjoy manifesto: meaning from the mean.

If you are willing to refuse these appeals, then happiness is not the principle you uphold. You have not found the appeal appealing. And you do not uphold this principle in general because you have come up against this principle before: you have been asked not to say things, to do things, because it would make others unhappy. It does not follow that a killjoy does not care for the happiness of others, or that she might not at times decide to do something because it contributes to the happiness of others. She is just not willing to make causing happiness her political cause.

From this everyday situation of living with the consequences of not making happiness your cause, you learn the unhappiness that happiness can cause. This first principle has been the basis of much feminist knowledge and activism: the identification of how institutions are built as promises of happiness; promises that often hide the violence of these institutions. We are willing to expose this violence: the violence of the elevation of the family, the couple form, reproductivity as the basis of a good life; the violence reproduced by organizations that identify speaking about violence as disloyalty. We will expose the happiness myths of neoliberalism and global capitalism: the fantasy that the system created for a privileged few is really about the happiness of many or the most.

To expose happiness myths is to be willing to be given a killjoy assignment.

PRINCIPLE 2: **I AM WILLING TO CAUSE UNHAPPINESS.**

Not making happiness your cause can cause unhappiness. A killjoy is willing to cause unhappiness.

A committed killjoy has a lifetime of experience of being the cause of unhappiness. And she knows this too: when you cause unhappiness, by virtue of the desires you have or the worlds you are not willing to take up as your own, unhappiness is assumed as your cause. It is not. Being willing to cause unhappiness does not make unhappiness your cause, although we live with the assumption that unhappiness is our cause. When our desires cause unhappiness, it is often assumed we desire to cause unhappiness. You might be judged as wanting the unhappiness you cause, which is another way you become an unhappiness cause.

A killjoy is willing to live with the consequences of what she is willing. She is thus willing to be the cause of someone else's unhappiness. It does not follow that she will not be made sad by other people being sad about her life (because they think her life is sad); it does not follow, even, that she would not feel sympathy in response to those made unhappy by her life. She will not let that unhappiness redirect her. She is willing to be misdirected.

Whose unhappiness are we willing to cause? Anybody's unhappiness: that can be the only answer to this question. But there is an "if" here. We are willing to cause institutional unhappiness if the institution is unhappy because we speak about sexual harassment. We are willing to cause feminist unhappiness if feminists are unhappy because we speak about racism. This means that: we are unhappy with this if. This means that: we are unhappy with what causes unhappiness. It can cause unhappiness to reveal the causes of unhappiness.

We are willing to cause unhappiness because of what we have learned about unhappiness from what we have been assumed to have caused. An "I" turns up here; she knows what is up from what turns up. When I spoke out publicly about sexual harassment at my college, I was identified by some as a killjoy without any sense of irony (there might have been a sense of irony given I had already professed to be her). What is important for us to note is that some feminists were part of this some. A feminist colleague said that in speaking out I was compromising "the happy and stimulating" environment that "long-standing feminists" had worked to create. I assumed I was not one of the long-standing feminists because of the stand I took. Yes, even speaking out about sexual harassment can cause feminist unhappiness. If so then: I am not willing to make feminist happiness my cause.

We have learned to hear what is at stake in such accusations. Feminism by implication is a bubble within the institution. But a feminist bubble can also operate as a mode of identification. To protect the feminist bubble you might want to protect it from exposure to the violence of the institution, a violence that is happening elsewhere (another center, another department). Protecting the feminist bubble ends up becoming a means of protecting the institution. You do not want the institutional violence exposed to others. You would prefer to resolve the violence "in house," even though the "in house" has failed to dismantle the master's house. Is this why there is such secrecy and silence about institutional violence even among some feminists?

If feminism is a bubble, we need the bubble to burst.

When we turn away from what compromises our happiness we are withdrawing our efforts from work that needs to be done to enable a more just and equal world. But this principle of being willing to cause unhappiness cannot be upheld by being assumed to refer only to the unhappiness of others. It is possible that we do not register some situations because to register those situations would make us unhappy. Maybe that is why the killjoy appears: because we are desperate not to register what she notices. Maybe this is why the killjoy appears to those who profess to be killjoys: our happiness too might depend on what we do not notice. Perhaps we keep our happiness through a willed oblivion. We must refuse this oblivion. If something would make us unhappy, when acknowledged, we need to acknowledge it. We are willing to cause our own unhappiness, which does not make our unhappiness our cause.

PRINCIPLE 3: I AM WILLING TO SUPPORT OTHERS WHO ARE WILLING TO CAUSE UNHAPPINESS.

A killjoy might first recognize herself in that feeling of loneliness: of being cut off from others, from how they assemble around happiness. She knows, because she has been there: to be unseated by the tables of happiness can be to find yourself in that shadowy place, to find yourself alone, on your own. It might be that many pass through the figure of the killjoy and quickly out again because they find her a hard place to be; not to be surrounded by the warmth of others, the quiet murmurs that accompany an agreement. The costs of killing joy are high; this figure is herself a cost (not to agree with someone as killing the joy of something).

How do you persist? As I suggested in my survival kit, we often persist by finding the company of other killjoys; we can take up this name when we recognize the dynamic she names; and we can recognize that dynamic when others articulate that dynamic for us. We recognize others too because they recognize that dynamic.

Those moments of recognition are precious; and they are precarious. With a moment comes a memory: we often persist by being supported by others. We might also experience the crisis of being unsupported; support matters all the more all the less we feel supported. To make a manifesto out of the killjoy means being willing to give to others the support you received or wish you received. Maybe you are in a conversation, at home or at work, and one person, one person out of many, is speaking out. Don't let her speak on her own. Back her up; speak with her. Stand by her; stand with her. From these public moments of solidarity so much is brought into existence. We are creating a support system around the killjoy; we are finding ways to allow her to do what she does, to be who she is. We do not have to assume her permanence, to turn her figure into personhood, to know that when she comes up, she might need others to hold her up.

Audre Lorde once wrote, "Your silence will not protect you" (1984a, 41). But your silence could protect them. And by them I mean: those who are violent, or those who benefit in some way from silence about violence. The killjoy is testimony. She comes to exist as a figure, a way of containing damage, because she speaks about damage. Over time, the time of being a feminist, we might call this feminist time, I have come to understand, to know and to feel, the costs of speaking out. I have thus come to understand, to know and to feel, why many do not speak out. There is a lot to lose, a lot, a life even. So much injustice is reproduced by silence not because people do not recognize injustice, but because they do recognize it. They also recognize the consequences of identifying injustice, which might not be consequences they can live with. It might be fear of losing your job and knowing you need that job to support those you care for; it might be concern about losing connections that matter; concern that what you say will be taken the wrong way; concern that by saying something you would make something worse. To suggest that the feminist killjoy is a manifesto is not to say that we have an obligation to speak out. We are not all in the same position; we cannot all afford to speak out. Killing joy thus requires a communication system: we have to find other ways for the violence to become manifest. We might need to use guerrilla tactics, and we have a feminist history to draw on here; you can write down names of harassers on books; put graffiti on walls; red ink in the water. There are so many ways to cause a feminist disturbance.

Even if speaking out is not possible, it is necessary. Silence about violence is violence. But feminist speech can take many forms. We become more inventive with forms the harder it is to get through. Speaking out and speaking with, sheltering those who speak; these acts of spreading the word, are world making. Killing joy is a world-making project. We make a world out of the shattered pieces even when we shatter the pieces or even when we are the shattered pieces.

PRINCIPLE 4: I AM NOT WILLING TO LAUGH AT JOKES DESIGNED TO CAUSE OFFENSE.

This principle might seem very specific: it might seem that it derives from my initial three principles and that it is not worthy of being one all on its own. But I think humor is such a crucial technique for reproducing inequality and injustice. I think the fantasy of the humorless feminist (as part of a more general fantasy of humorlessness of those who question a social as well as political arrangement) does such important work. The fantasy is what makes the figure of the killjoy do her work. It is assumed she says what she does (points out sexism, points out racism) because she is herself deprived of any joy, because she cannot bear the joy of others. Often once someone has been assigned a feminist killjoy, others then will make certain jokes, in order to cause her offense, in order to witness her ill humor. Do not be tempted to laugh. If the situation is humorless, we need not to add humor to it. If the situation is unfunny, we need not to make light of it; we need not to make it fun.

It is often through humor (say through irony or satire) that people can keep making sexist and racist utterances. Humor creates the appearance of distance; by laughing about what they repeat, they repeat what they laugh about. This *about* becomes the butt of the joke. It is no laughing matter. When it is no laughing matter, laughter matters.

But, of course, humor can challenge things by bringing things to the surface; I noticed this in my survival kit. But there are differences that matter in what laughter does. Feminist humor might involve the relief of being able to laugh when familiar patterns that are often obscured are revealed. We might laugh at how white men assemble themselves by reducing whatever we do as "not white men" to identity politics. We might laugh even about being poster children of diversity; and laughing does not mean we do not experience pain and frustration at being called upon by institutions to provide them with smiling colorful faces; to make our faces theirs. But this is not laughter that allows us to repeat what causes offense; it is a reorientation toward that cause. We do not repeat it; we withdraw.

The killjoy exists in close proximity to the figure of the oversensitive subject who is too easily offended. This figure is always evoked whenever social critique is successful: that something has been closed down or removed or lost (a loss that is mourned) because others are offended, where to be offended is to be too easily offended, to be weak, soft, impressionable. "Toughen up" has become a moral imperative, one that is (like most moral imperatives) articulated by those who think they have what they claim others need. Indeed this figure of the oversensitive subject might come up in advance of such a loss, or to avoid such a loss. The moral panic over trigger warnings often evokes this figure, specifically the figure of the oversensitive student who is not attuned to the difficulty and discomfort of learning, as if to say: if we let your sensitivities become law, we lose our freedom. I would argue that freedom has become reduced to the freedom to be offensive, which is also about how those with power protect their right to articulate their own views, no matter what, no matter whom.

If not wanting histories that are violent to be repeated with such violent insistence, or at least if asking questions about the terms that enable that repetition means being deemed oversensitive, we need to be oversensitive. When you are sensitive to what is not over, you are deemed oversensitive. We are sensitive to what is not over. We are sensitive because it is not over.

PRINCIPLE 5: I AM NOT WILLING TO GET OVER HISTORIES THAT ARE NOT OVER.

It is not over. We say that, with insistence, as we watch others declare things over. So many declarations, and they participate in the same thing. The former British prime minister, David Cameron, says that one thing that made Great Britain great was that we "took slavery off the high seas." Great Britain is remembered as the liberator of the slaves, not as perpetrator of slavery; not as a country that has benefited from the mass enslavement of others, from the colonization of others. When colonialism is referred to in the book upon which citizenship tests are based in the United Kingdom, it is described as the system that introduced democracy, law, bringing benefits to others. A violent history of conquest and theft imagined as the gift of modernity. And today, wars are still justified as gifts, as giving freedom, democracy, and equality.

When it is not over, it is not the time to get over it.

A killjoy is willing to bring this history up. A memory can be willful. And so we know what happens when we do this. You are accused as the one who is getting in the way of reconciliation. You are judged as the one who has yet to do what others have done: get over it; get over yourself; let it go. You become the open wound because you won't let things heal.

We are willing to be the ones who fail the project of reconciliation. We know the success of that project is the failure to address these histories of injustice that manifest not only in the unresolved trauma of those for whom this history is a bodily inheritance, a transgenerational haunting, but also in a grossly unequal distribution of wealth and resources.

How a world is shaped is memory.

And they say: but look what you have been given. Equality, diversity: they all become gifts for which we are supposed to be grateful; they become compensatory. We are not grateful when a system is extended to include us when that system is predicated on inequality and violence.

PRINCIPLE 6: **I AM NOT WILLING TO BE INCLUDED IF INCLUSION MEANS BEING INCLUDED IN A SYSTEM THAT IS UNJUST, VIOLENT, AND UNEQUAL.**

It is often an invitation: come in, be part, be grateful. Sometimes we have few options: we are workers; we work; we make do. We have to survive or even progress within an institution. But even for those of us who are included, even when we do receive benefits (we might have salaries; we might have pensions), we are not willing that inclusion: we are agreeing that inclusion requires being behind the institution, identifying with it. We are willing to speak out about the violence of the system, to strike, to demonstrate. We are willing to talk about the rods, to risk being identified as the wayward arm.

But there is a difficulty here. Because surely if you are employed by an organization, if you receive the benefit of employment, it could be said that to maintain a killjoy stance is a form of political dishonesty: you get to benefit from the institutions you critique. We need to start with our own complicity: this is why part II began with the compromised nature of diversity work. To be complicit should not become its own reproductive logic: that all we can do is to reproduce the logics of the institutions that employ us. In fact those who benefit from an unjust system need to work even harder to expose that injustice. For those killjoys who are in regular employment—let's call ourselves professional killjoys; some of us might even be professor killjoys—when we profess we kill joy; there is no way of overcoming this difficulty, so we must start from it. We need to use the benefits we receive to support those who do not receive these benefits, including those within our own institutions who do not have the same securities that give us the opportunity to expose the insecurities. Within higher education this means we need to enact our solidarity with students who are fighting for education as a right, for adjunct lecturers and faculty who do not have tenure or who are on short-term contracts, with those professional staff who do the work of maintaining the very buildings and facilities in which we do our work: cleaners, security staff, porters. I have tried to show how killing joy and willfulness also relate to the politics of labor: arms matter, which is to say some end up doing the work to reproduce the conditions that enable the existence of others. When our professional existence is enabled by the work of others, we need to use our existence to recognize that work. We need to expose the injustice of how institutions give support to some by not supporting others. And we need to support those who challenge the conditions in which they work unsupported. Willfulness is striking.

And: we must keep exposing the violence within the institutions that have included us, especially when our own inclusion occurs under the sign of diversity and equality, especially when our bodies and the products of our labor are used by institutions as evidence of inclusion. We become wall breakers. So we must talk about walls; we must show how history becomes concrete. We are not willing to allow our inclusion to support a happiness fantasy. We might need to leave, at a certain point, if our inclusion requires giving up too much, though we are not all in a position to leave.

A killjoy manifesto: requires an ongoing and willful refusal to identify our hopes with inclusion within organizations predicated on violence. I am not grateful to be included in an institution that is unequal. I am not grateful to be included in an institution in which talking about sexism and racism is heard as ungrateful. We have a history of ungrateful feminists to pick up from. Ungrateful feminists; grumpy; grump.

Together: grumps are a feminist lump. A lumpen proletariat: in feminist form with a feminist consciousness.

PRINCIPLE 7: I AM WILLING TO LIVE A LIFE THAT IS DEEMED BY OTHERS AS UNHAPPY AND I AM WILLING TO REJECT OR TO WIDEN THE SCRIPTS AVAILABLE FOR WHAT COUNTS AS A GOOD LIFE.

I have already noted how happiness involves the narrowing down of ways of living a life. We can be disloyal by refusing to be narrowed. We live lives deemed by others to be not happy, to be not reaching the right points of ceremony. Two women living together, refusing to have a civil partnership, refusing to get married; we are enacting our rejection of heteropatriarchy. To enact a rejection is an action performed with others.

We can come to embody an alternative family line, as I suggested in chapter 8, or an alternative to the family line. I quite like being a lesbian feminist auntie. I know that as a young woman I would have liked to have had lesbian feminist aunties, though I certainly had feminist aunties to whom I owe a great deal. We need to tell our stories to children, to those who are to come; generations need to tell each other our stories, assembled around other lives, those that are faint from under-inscription. We need to tell each other stories of different ways you can live, different ways you can be; predicated not on how close you get to the life you were assumed or expected to have, but on the queer wanderings of a life you live.

I would have liked to have known there were other ways of living, of being. I would have liked to have known that women do not have to be in relation to men. Of course, I struggled for this realization: I became a feminist; I found women's studies; I met women who taught me what I did not have to do; I found women who helped me deviate from an expectation.

Queer: the moment you realize what you did not have to be.

We can become part of a widening when we refused to be narrowed. And each time we reject or widen the happiness script, we become part of an opening. We have to create room if we are to live a feminist life. When we create room, we create room for others.

PRINCIPLE 8: I AM WILLING TO PUT THE HAP BACK INTO HAPPINESS.

I have noted how the word *happiness* derives from the Middle English word *hap*, suggesting chance. One history of happiness is the history of the removal of its hap, such that happiness is defined not in terms of what happens to you but of what you work for. In my book *The Promise of Happiness* I explored how happiness even ends up being redefined against hap, especially in the psychology of flows and positive psychology: as not something that happens (or just happens). The narrow scripts of happiness are precisely about the violence of the elimination of the hap. We need to recognize the elimination of hap before we can restore hap. We cannot simply use the lighter word as if it can get us out of here. We have to recognize the weight of the world, the heaviness of happiness, how we are brought down by the expectation that we are down. We stumble. When we stumble, when we are in line, we might feel ourselves as the obstacle to our own happiness; we might feel ourselves to be getting in the way of ourselves. Can we let ourselves be in the way? Can we be willing what we seem to be undoing? I stumble; maybe by stumbling I found you, maybe by stumbling I stumbled on happiness, a hap-full happiness; a happiness that is as fragile as the bodies we love and cherish. We value such happiness because it is fragile: it comes and goes, as we do. I am willing to let happiness go; to allow anger, rage, or disappointment be how I am affected by a world. But when happiness happens, I am happy.

A fragile happiness might be attuned to the fragility of things. We can care about the things that break off, the broken things. To care about such things is not to care for their happiness. Caring for happiness can so often translate into caring for others on the condition that they reflect back an idea you have of how a life should be lived. Perhaps we can think of care in relation to hap. We are often assumed to be careless when we break something, as I noted in chapter 7. What would it mean to care for something, whether or not it breaks? Maybe we can reorientate caring from caring for someone's happiness to caring what happens to someone or something: caring about what happens, caring whatever happens. We might call this a hap care rather than a happiness care. A hap care would not be about letting an object go, but holding on to an object by letting oneself go, giving oneself over to something that is not one's own. A hap care would not seek to eliminate anxiety from care; it could even be described as care for the hap. Caring is anxious—to be full of care, to be careful, is to take care of things by becoming anxious about their future, where the future is embodied in the fragility of an object whose persistence matters. Our care would pick up the pieces of a shattered pot. Our care would not turn the thing into a memorial, but value each piece; shattering as the beginning of another story.

But we would not end up with a liberal notion: everything is equally fragile; we must care for everything equally. It is not; I do not. Some things become more fragile than others in time. In time, we attend. To attend to something that has become more easily breakable is to attend to its history, with love, and with care.

PRINCIPLE 9: **I AM WILLING TO SNAP ANY BONDS, HOWEVER PRECIOUS, WHEN THOSE BONDS ARE DAMAGING TO MYSELF OR TO OTHERS.**

So many times, when a bond has been snapped, I have been told it is sad, as I noted in chapter 8. But bonds can be violent. A bond can be diminishing.

Sometimes we are not ready to recognize that we have been diminished. We are not ready. It can take psychic as well as political work to be ready to snap that bond. When you do, when you snap, it can feel like an unexpected moment that breaks a line that had been unfolding over time, a deviation, a departure. But a moment can be an achievement; it can be what you have been working for.

You might be willing to snap the bond. You might need to be willful to be willing. And you might need to recognize that others too need to work to reach a point when they can let go. Share that work. We have to share the costs of what we give up. But when we give up, we do not just lose something even when we do lose something. We find things. We find out things we did not know before—about ourselves, about worlds. A feminist life is a journey, a reaching for something that might not have been possible without snap, without the snappy encouragement of others. But a feminist life is also a going back, retrieving parts of ourselves we did not even realize we had, that we did not even realize we had put on hold.

We can hold each other by not putting ourselves on hold.

PRINCIPLE 10: I AM WILLING TO PARTICIPATE IN A KILLJOY MOVEMENT.

Whether or not you are being difficult, you are heard as making things difficult for yourself as well as others. So much difficulty, you would think feminist killjoys would give up. And yet, when I first began presenting and talking about the feminist killjoy, when I first began working with her as well as on her, picking her up, I noticed how energetic the room would be. Sometimes speaking of her, letting her into the room to do her thing, felt like an electric shock. And she finds herself quickly in a company of killjoys: transfeminist killjoys (Cowan 2014), ethnic killjoys (Khorana 2013), crip killjoys (Mullow 2013), indigenous feminist killjoys (Barker 2015). There will be more of that I am sure.

Why? Because the figure of the killjoy comes up whenever there are difficult histories to bring up. The killjoy is appealing not despite what she brings up but because of what she brings up. She acquires vitality or energy from a scene of difficulty. To be willing to be a killjoy, to be willing to get in the way of happiness, grasps hold of a judgment and takes it on.

We even transform the judgment into a rebellious command.

Killjoy?

Just watch me.

Bring it on.

It can be quite a pickup when we pick her up. There can be joy in finding killjoys; there can be joy in killing joy. Our eyes meet when we tell each other about rolling eyes.

You too; you too.

A fragile movement.

Snappy.

So many moments are abbreviated in our equation "rolling eyes = feminist pedagogy." We are willing those moments. Moments can become movement. Moments can build a movement, a movement assembled from lighter materials. This is not a secure dwelling. We are shattered, too often; but see how the walls move.

We are willing to participate in a killjoy movement.

We are that movement.

Watch us roll.

NOTES

Introduction

1. Literally, I mean: one time when I was a PhD student, a feminist member of the staff pulled my off-the-shoulder top over my shoulders, saying something like, "You are supposed to be a feminist."

2. For further discussion of hope in relation to the past tense, see my book *The Cultural Politics of Emotion* (Ahmed 2004).

3. Flavia Dzodan, "My Feminism Will Be Intersectional or It Will Be Bullshit!," Tigerbeatdown, October 10, 2011, http://tigerbeatdown.com/2011/10/10/my-feminism-will-be-intersectional-or-it-will-be-bullshit/.

4. There is so much racism at stake in which sexism comes up: sexism is often seen as a problem with cultures (or a cultural problem) "over there" rather than "here." Also note: the elsewhere is often understood as behind in time.

5. I have called this melancholic universalism: you identify with the universal that has repudiated you. For some preliminary observations, see my blog post "Melancholic Universalism," feministkilljoys, December 15, 2015, http://feministkilljoys.com/2015/12/15/melancholic-universalism/.

6. I will be developing the arguments about practical phenomenology from the conclusion to *On Being Included* (Ahmed 2012), though I use different terms in this book, ones that do not point so quickly back to this philosophical tradition. See especially part II, "Diversity Work," for discussion of how we know things because of our effort to transform things.

7. I have made the decision not to cite any of the work of (self-described) radical feminists who are writing against the phenomena they describe as "transgenderism" (often called trans exclusionary radical feminism, or TERFS), because I find this work so violent and reductive that I have not wished to bring it into the body of my own text. I have noticed in reading discussions on social media how the mechanisms for excluding trans women from feminism are mobile (rather like the walls I discuss in part II). In some cases, I have heard people refer to "biology 101," or a scientific basis of female and male sex differences, to claim trans women are not biologically women as the grounds for justifying the exclusion of trans women. I want to rebuke: "Biology 101? Well, patriarchy wrote that textbook," and pass them a copy of Andrea Dworkin's *Woman Hating*,

a radical feminist text that supports transsexuals having access to surgery and hormones and challenges what she calls "the traditional biology of sexual difference" based on "two discrete biological sexes" (1972, 181, 186). At other times in trans-exclusionary work, it is not biology but socialization that is used: trans women cannot be women because they were socialized as men and benefited from male privilege. Here it is the social rather than the biological that becomes what is immutable: as if socialization goes one way, relates only to one category (gender), and is not contested and disputed in everyday life depending on how one might embody or not embody that category. Feminism itself depends on the failure of socialization to bring about willing gendered subjects. Another typical argument is that transgenderism as a set of medical practices depends on essentialist notions of gender because it corrects gender-nonconforming behaviors and is shaped by a heterosexist imperative. Of course there have been decades of scholarship by transgender theorists that is critical of how gender and heteronorms become an apparatus of truth within medical institutions; that has shown how in order to gain access to surgery and hormones, trans subjects have to tell a narrative that is legible to authorities because it maintains gender scripts: from Sandy Stone's "The Empire Strikes Back: A Posttranssexual Manifesto" (2006) to more recent work by Dean Spade (2006) and Riki Wilchins (2014). This work shows how not being accommodated by a gender system (which requires you to stay with an assignment made by authorities at birth) can involve becoming more vigilant and reflexive about that system (although it is very important not to expect those who are not accommodated by a system to become pioneers or transgressors of norms, either). I think what is going on in anti-trans feminist work is the desire to exclude and police the boundaries of women on whatever basis can be found (hence the target is a moving target). The policing of the category of women is how a specific group of women have secured their right to determine who belongs within feminism (whiteness has been another key mechanism for policing feminism). The policing of the boundaries of women has never not been disastrous for feminism. For a useful collection on transfeminist perspectives, see Enke (2012). One last point—feminism begins with a premise that is a promise: we do not have to live by other people's assignments.

8. This is a very blunt citational policy (and I might need to add cis, straight, and able-bodied to the general body I am evoking). Perhaps you need to form a blunt policy in order to break a long-standing habit. This policy is blunt rather than precise because I understand white men as a cumulative effect rather than a way of grouping together persons who share a common attribute (for discussion, see chapter 6). I am quite aware that in specific instances we could have a debate as to whether such-and-such individual is or should be regarded as part of the institutional apparatus of white men. Note also, by using some primary materials (for example, the Grimm story in chapter 3), I am in effect citing white men. This policy relates to the intellectual horizon of the book rather than the cultural materials upon which I draw.

9. I first used this idea of desire lines in *Queer Phenomenology* (Ahmed 2006). The term is from landscape architecture for the paths on the ground created when enough people do not take the official route.

1. Feminism Is Sensational

1. I am using *you* here as an address to myself, not to another. These experiences happened to me. Others will have different experiences of gender-based violence. But in writing these experiences down, I needed to address myself as *you*, at times, and at other times as *I*. These switching points might be necessary to bring something into words: how violence can estrange you from yourself.

2. Though one funny detail: I spelled *patriarchy* wrong throughout! *Patriarchy* became *patriachy*. Maybe that was a willful desire not to get patriarchy right.

3. See the website Everyday Sexism Project (http://everydaysexism.com/). Laura Bates, who founded the project and site, has since published *Everyday Sexism* (2014).

4. For a longer discussion of the significance of being mixed race with particular reference to my relationship to whiteness, see chapter 5 of this book and chapter 3 of *Queer Phenomenology* (Ahmed 2006). See also Gail Lewis's (2009) wonderful piece reflecting on her relation to her white mother as a mixed-race subject, which combines autobiography with a reading of psychoanalytic and sociological texts.

5. When I completed a research project in diversity that I discuss in part II, we encountered this way of hearing directly. We wrote a report on how racism was being obscured by the feel-good mantra of diversity and by the emphasis on good practice as a positive technique. The response was: surely you are exaggerating. You encounter the disbelief that there could be so much racism. You are heard as exaggerating and that exaggeration is heard as a form of malice or ill will. They never published our report. Hearing accounts of racism as sensationalist is a way of not hearing accounts of racism. See Swan (2010b) for a good discussion of the audit process. And with my thanks to Elaine Swan for sharing this work and for willful solidarities.

6. I am telling my own story of becoming a feminist as a story of the family table. It is important to acknowledge that not all families gather around a table. Tables too might have their own biographies; their own stories to tell. See my book *Queer Phenomenology* (Ahmed 2006) for a more sustained discussion of tables as kinship objects.

7. This is why, as I explore more in chapter 7, we can be alarmed ourselves when the feminist killjoy turns up, because we know the consequences of fulfilling the expectation that we will become her.

8. In chapter 3 I discuss how feminists are often judged as suffering from a weakness of will.

2. On Being Directed

1. I return to how norms are dwellings in chapter 5, developing the arguments from my chapter "Queer Feelings" in *The Cultural Politics of Emotion* (Ahmed 2004) about how norms can be inhabited differently.

2. Of course we learn that grammar is also gendered: for her, to reach a point is a cessation, becoming Mrs. Dalloway, marriage as the acquisition of a new name. We know why feminism requires new words, Ms., but the addition of Ms. does not stop the choice offered so often: is that Miss or Mrs.? Mr. stays Mr.

3. Not just children. When I got a new puppy, someone said to me that when she was older she and the person's male dog could be "boyfriend and girlfriend."

4. I made this argument in my chapter "Melancholic Migrants" from my book *The Promise of Happiness* (Ahmed 2010) with reference to a reading of the film *Bend It like Beckham*. In this film, Jess comes to embody a happiness hope because her desires take her away from (what are narrated as) the traditional expectations of her Sikh family. For important discussions of melancholia and migration, see Cheng (2001) and Eng and Han (2003).

5. One might consider such experiences of being misattuned from a gender system as providing another basis for the affinity between feminism and transpolitics: getting gender wrong and experiencing oneself as the wrong gender. Within transgender and queer studies, this narrative of being in the wrong body—and the model of gender dysphoria—has been a subject of rigorous critique (see Stone 1996, 228; Halberstam 1998, 145). However, we might think of experiences of wrongness as bodily experiences of not being at home in a body, which is to say, not being at home in how one has been assigned: wrong as not feeling right; wrong as what, for some, transsexuality "feels like" (Prosser 1998, 8). Feeling wrong, or getting gender wrong, does not assume that there is a right way of doing gender; they are consequences of the assumption that there is a right way.

6. Of course, that it is the bride who must be happy, who must bear the burden of the happiness of the day, teaches us something about gender and its uneven distributions of what we might call happiness hopes. It teaches us to notice what might seem obvious. If we search for the happiness of the bride to confirm the happiness of the day, then happiness hopes for women remain tied to marriage, even if the scripts of gender have become more flexible.

3. Willfulness and Feminist Subjectivity

1. This version of the story can be downloaded here: "The Wilful Child," *Grimm's Fairy Tales*, Universal Library, posted by John Mark Ockerbloom, accessed February 16, 2015, http://www.cs.cmu.edu/~spok/grimmtmp/090.txt. See also Grimm and Grimm (1884, 125).

2. Of course, this strategy would not work for everyone. Sometimes a scream is what is intended.

3. I should note here that there is a tradition in feminist literary criticism that treats madness primarily as a metaphor for female rebellion. Elizabeth J. Donaldson (2011, 94) has argued very convincingly that such a metaphor can be problematic not only for how it romanticizes mental illness but in its erasure of mental illness as a lived experience. Lisa Merri Johnson has also explored the "rush to metaphor" within queer theory (the use of metaphors of cutting, for example), calling for "queer theorists to acknowledge able-bodied/able-minded privilege as a potentially distorting factor in their interpretations of texts marked by illness and disability" (2014, n.p.). I have learned from this important work, and I recognize that my brief reading of Charlotte Perkins Gilman's "The Yellow Wallpaper" risks this rush to metaphor. I also think the text points us to a history of feminist mental illness (not just feminism as mental

illness) that is being explored in the body of work called feminist disability studies, from which I am learning so much. See also Lamp and Cleigh for discussion of ableism in Gilman's writings, but also on how she gradually began to "understand the source of her disability as socially constructed" (2011, 184).

4. I want to stress the significance of being "not black" as a British Asian/person of color. I have commented in previous work on how *black* was used differently in the United Kingdom to signify all people of color (see Ahmed 2010, 2012). Some have called this use of blackness "political blackness." There were reasons that this usage developed in the European context: *black* was used not only as an expression of solidarity but also in response to shared conditions of arrival, of arriving in the imperial center from the former colonies ("We are here because you were there") after so-called decolonization. This solidarity was particularly important for antiracist activists from the subcontinent and the Caribbean. However, this use of blackness has become more and more untenable in the European context (although it is still used by earlier generations of activists and by current activist groups such as Southall Black Sisters). I think this shift is partly about the increasing recognition of antiblack racism within communities of color, including Asian communities. It is also a reflection of the changing landscapes of race in Europe: the experience of colonization by European countries does not provide a common ground in the same way it once did. So the expression *person of color* is increasingly being adopted within Europe (it was formerly understood as a U.S. term), as well as the word *brown*, which is increasingly used as an indicator of a racialized position.

5. I return to this idea of the police as the rods in chapter 8, on feminist snap.

6. We might also describe the domination of children as a primary technique for the domination of people. As Eli Clare puts it, "What better way to maintain a power structure—white supremacy, patriarchy, capitalism, a binary and rigid gender system—than to drill the lessons of who is dominant and who is subordinate into the bodies of children" ([1999] 2015, 150).

7. I gave a talk drawn from this material at the University of Alberta at Edmonton in 2014. I mentioned that the Grimm story could be thought of as a form of colonial rule, that the willful child evoked by the story could be understood to denote the colonized. Maria Campbell, a Métis author and activist, stood up after my lecture. She shared with us that the nuns in her residential school had told the story of the girl and her willful arm but that she had not known its origin. The story is there. There she is.

8. For a longer discussion of the use of this figure of the willful child in responses to the so-called riots, see the third chapter, "The General Will," of my book *Willful Subjects* (Ahmed 2014).

9. The slave is both person and property; a property of will that has will. Saidiya V. Hartman observes this paradox with reference to the captive female: she must be both "will less and always willing" (1997, 81). Hartman describes the "negation of the captor's will" as "*willful* submission to the master" (81, emphasis in original). A willful submission is one in which the slaves are willing to extend the will of the master: "The purportedly binding passions of master-slave relations were predicated on the inability of the slave to exercise her will, in any ways other than serving her master" (84). See

also Spillers for an important discussion of how the body of the slave is severed from "its motive will" (1987, 67).

10. Maria Zackodnick (2011, 99), for instance, notes that other accounts of this event did not include references to Truth baring her arm.

11. I will return to the significance of arms as a form of fleshy intersectionality in the conclusion of my final chapter.

Part II. Diversity Work

1. For a longer discussion of how I ended up doing the project, see the introduction to *On Being Included: Racism and Diversity in Institutional Life* (Ahmed 2012).

2. These two senses of diversity work were introduced briefly in the conclusion of *On Being Included*. I am developing the arguments from that book by taking up these two senses and considering how they meet.

4. Trying to Transform

1. Words such as *equity*, even when they are tired, can still be sticky. See for example Malinda Smith's (2010) discussion of how *equity* is used by white feminists only with reference to gender equity. With thanks to Malinda Smith for her important critical work.

2. This definition is from the Chartered Institute of Public Relations, "What Is PR," CIPR, http://www.cipr.co.uk/content/careers-advice/what-pr (last accessed May 23, 2016).

3. Goldsmiths' "Statement on Sexual Harassment," June 2016, is online at http://www.gold.ac.uk/governance/official-responses/statement-on-sexual-harassment/. Anna Bull, Tiffany Page, and Leila Whitley's response, "Statement on Sexual Harassment in Higher Education (SHHE) at Goldsmiths," is available to read on the conference website: https://shhegoldsmiths.wordpress.com/statement/ (last accessed July 3, 2016).

4. This would of course be an overoptimistic expectation, especially in the United Kingdom (although the overoptimism of the expectation can still teach us something). In the United Kingdom, all single honors undergraduate women's studies programs have closed (although we have quite a few postgraduate gender studies programs). No critical race or critical ethnic programs or black studies degrees were introduced during this period (although a few centers and postgraduate programs were introduced). The calls to decolonize the curriculum in the United Kingdom are very recent: one example would be the initiative Why Is My Curriculum White?, begun at University College London in 2014. See their video: UCLTV, "Why Is My Curriculum White?," YouTube, November 11, 2014, https://www.youtube.com/watch?v=Dscx4h2l-Pk.

5. As I explained in the introduction to *On Being Included*, I have had two academic appointments in my career, both to teach courses on race (one in women's studies, one in media and communications). It is very easy to become the race person when you take up these appointments. We need to tell our stories of arrival. In both instances, the experience of being appointed felt like being appointed by whiteness: people of color being interviewed for jobs on race by white panels, speaking to white audiences

about our work. In fact, in both cases the experience was one of solidarity with those who have to face this situation. Whiteness can be a situation we have or are in; and when we can name that situation (and even make jokes about it), we recognize each other as strangers to the institution, and find in that estrangement a bond. Of course, at the same time, I should stress here that we do want there to be posts on race and ethnicity. We also want there to be more than one; we want not to be the one. In the last few years, a number of black and minority ethnic (BME) appointments have been made in my department—BME colleagues who are also working in different ways on race. Although we cannot reduce diversity to a body count, bodies do count. It has been a relief not to be so singular.

6. I would like to thank my colleagues who are participating in this effort to radicalize our curriculum, in particular Lisa Blackman and Richard Smith. The canon is like a wall: we have to chip, chip, chip away at it.

7. I am indebted to this blog post: PhDisabled, "Event Organizers: Give Access Information up Front. Please?," October 30, 2014, https://phdisabled.wordpress.com/2014/10/30/event-organizers-give-access-information-up-front-please/. With thanks to the PhD students involved in this blog and this project.

5. Being in Question

1. Intersectionality is a key black feminist concept: the term was first introduced by Kimberlé Williams Crenshaw (1989), although intersectionality existed as a method and politics before the arrival of the term itself. A number of critiques of intersectionality have associated it with identity and stabilization (for example, Puar 2007). I think these critiques would be best understood as critiques of how intersectionality has been institutionalized (see Bilge 2013). The word and concept are not exhausted by these critiques: intersectionality can bring us back to life because it is full of life. For a useful elaboration of how intersectionality works to challenge "additive models," see Brewer (1993). For an excellent "cartographic" approach to intersectionality, see Brah (1996).

2. And note that I have witnessed this injustice: I once heard a question from an audience member that talked of the "complicity" of black staff with organizational values, as if by virtue of being black they should risk not being complicit.

6. Brick Walls

1. In the United Kingdom, universities are increasingly being asked to become border police by reporting on the attendance of international students (see Topping 2014).

2. For a further discussion of this problem with reference to specific examples of how feminists have identified critiques of sexism as a knee-jerk response or a bad feminist habit, see Ahmed (2015).

3. This sentence is written in solidarity with the Rhodes Must Fall protest movement that began in Cape Town, South Africa, and moved to other universities including Oxford University and Edinburgh University in the United Kingdom. Bringing down statues of Rhodes from university campuses is an act that calls for a full decolonizing of education—in all of its structures and spaces. As Grace Almond writes: "By

removing the statue, the campaign does not seek to remove Rhodes from the public historical memory. On the contrary, the act would address our colonial past in an effort to decolonise our collective conscience" (2015, n.p.).

4. This definition of *vandal* comes from the Online Etymology Dictionary, http://www.etymonline.com/ (last accessed May 24, 2016).

7. Fragile Connections

1. We could think here more generally about how privilege works through the use of fragility, even though fragility is often understood as weakness. Masculinity, for example, can work through fragility: he might be spared so much because his fragile ego has to be protected from potential damage. Here I think temporality is crucial: in these contexts fragility points to the future. It works as an anticipatory causality, as a way of avoiding certain situations because of what they might cause.

2. My mother's condition that was kept a secret was multiple sclerosis, which is a degenerative disease. So when I learned of her condition in my late teens, I learned she had multiple sclerosis. Not long after I found out about it, after new tests, the diagnosis was changed to transverse myelitis, which is not a degenerative disease. My mother had lived with multiple sclerosis as her diagnosis for over twenty years. One can understand then: how a diagnosis becomes experienced as one kind of sentencing, and what a shock it can be when that diagnosis is deemed a misdiagnosis. That shock can be the realization that a life you could have lived—without a diagnosis of degeneration—was taken from you.

3. I have been using *wiggle* in this book. These two words, *wiggle* and *wriggle*, both imply sudden movements, but they have a different affective quality, at least for me. *Wiggle* is often defined as quick irregular *sideways* movements. *Wriggle* can mean to turn and twist in quick writhing movements. *Wriggle* also has a more sinister sense: when you wriggle out of something, you get out of something by devious means. In deviation there is an implication of deviance.

8. Feminist Snap

1. Again: it would be very easy to interpret this action as being because my father was Muslim (racism is an easy script, trying to resolve complex situations from old and stale tales). It was not. I do not need to add this, but let me add this: my wider Muslim family, especially my Muslim aunties, have been unflinchingly warm and accepting. Being accepting does not have to take the form of a response to coming out because it is not about having an identity that has to be revealed (that is one model of sexuality). Rather, this is the acceptance that goes: this is you; this is who you are with; this is what you do; this is you. We love you, we love this.

2. Thanks to Elena Loizidou for teaching me to hear the significance of this laughter.

3. This character was played by feminist and civil rights activist Florynce "Flo" Kennedy. This is extremely effective: the life of an activist becomes part of the life of a film about activism. See Randolph (2015) for an important account of Kennedy as a black feminist radical.

4. As Kimberlé Williams Crenshaw and Andrea Ritchie describe, "say her name sheds light on black women's experience of police violence in order to produce a gender inclusive approach to racial justice" (2015, n.p.).

5. Finger snapping could be considered a black queer genealogy. Marlon Riggs, for example, describes finger snapping for African American gay men as "emotionally and politically charged as a clenched fist" (1999, 308). Riggs documents how this gesture is appropriated by mainstream culture. For a good discussion of the many layers of snapping as a complex and contested signifier for African American women and African American gay men, see Johnson (2009).

6. One of the stories in *Born in Flames* is in fact the cutbacks to domestic violence services, another reason this film is frighteningly familiar. It described then a future where we are now.

7. See Sisters Uncut, "Safer Spaces Policy," 2016, http://sistersuncut.org/saferspaces/ (last accessed May 23, 2016). Thanks to all those, including Sisters Uncut, who participated in the Centre for Feminist Research's panel on Violence against Women on November 24, 2015.

8. See Sisters Uncut, "Safer Spaces Policy," 2016, http://sistersuncut.org/saferspaces/.

9. Lesbian Feminism

1. I acknowledge here the feminist digital media site Everyday Feminism, launched in 2012, with its mission to "help people heal from and stand up to everyday violence, discrimination, and marginalization through applied intersectional feminism" (http://everydayfeminism.com/, last accessed September 18, 2015).

2. When writing this sentence about how women have to get their whole body behind an action, I was reminded of Iris Marion Young's description of "throwing like a girl," which I referred to in chapter 1. A girl throws by not putting the whole of her body behind the action. Young gives us a phenomenological account of how the girl comes to experience her body as restriction. But one aspect of her account we could reflect upon is the extent to which it accepts that a girl, when throwing like a girl, throws in a way that is less good than a boy (in other words, the extent to which it accepts the association of femininity and failure). It might seem obvious that her way of throwing is deficient: that the boy throws faster and farther than the girl. But if we think of how the girl has to put so much energy into accomplishing things, because of the obstacles that she encounters, things that are in her way, could we not see her way of throwing as wisdom: she is saving her energy for more important things? See also Dahl (2015) for an important queer femme critique of how feminists associate femininity with failure.

3. This would be true of course only for those who have lost connection to middle-class or resource-rich families. My argument here suggests that we need to rethink the distinction between a politics of recognition and a politics of redistribution (see Butler's [1997] critique of Nancy Fraser's use of this distinction). Sexuality, race, and gender as a series of norms are very much about access to resources that cannot be separated from the class system (indeed, which mess with that system at certain

points). We can witness this messiness when we return to life, which is to say, to ups and downs, to the distribution of vulnerability across a life course as well as a social system (see also Butler 2004).

4. I was very struck, when I gave a lecture in February 2015 on living a lesbian life, based on material from this chapter, how my argument was translated as calling for a return to lesbian feminism by giving up on queer.

5. We could show how Sedgwick's argument can be applied to queer studies: that the potential for queer studies resides in how queer cleaves to those scenes of shame. In other words, queer is all the more queer because of what queer refers to. I add this because I have detected some anxiety within queer studies about the status of queer as a literal referent. We can queer the referent. We might even become rather literal about this; go back to the letter. We preserve histories by the words we use, which does not mean that the act of preservation should not be contested (which histories, which words, who, when, where?). Let's think about the word *reference*. It is itself a rather queer word. To refer is to relate or to carry back. Heather Love (2007) describes "feeling backward" as a way of doing queer history. Perhaps we can do feminist and queer theory by using backward terms, terms that point us back. To use terms that go back is not to make these terms into a ground: going back is another invitation to go back again; referral as deferral. We can refuse the injunction to move forward by assuming that going back is what would stop us from moving at all. Words can keep histories alive, or words remind us of how histories are alive. To use queer as if it can simply be freed from this history would be to lose something; it would detach queer from the very histories that render queer affective or charged. When we lose that charge, queer can end up being reorganized around the same old bodies, doing the same old things. We need to retain that charge in how we use the word: pointedly. And, as I discuss in this chapter, we can then use queer to question how queer can be taken up as if it replaces other words (such as lesbian) that are assumed to be more containing, because they are assumed to be always and only about identity. This book also aims to show how some words become pointers of identity (identity words), attached to bodies who are deemed too attached to themselves, by how other words are freed or detached from bodies, becoming lighter, even universal. We need the heavier words to point us back, to teach us how lighter words that are assumed to be detached still point to some bodies more than others.

6. For a much longer discussion of the figure of the "contingent lesbian" (derived from a reading of psychoanalysis and inversion), see chapter 2 in my book *Queer Phenomenology* (Ahmed 2006).

7. We might return as well to Alice Walker's powerful womanist prose. As I noted in chapter 3, in her *In Search of Our Mothers' Gardens*, Walker defines a womanist as a "black feminist or feminist of color" and as "usually referring to outrageous, audacious, courageous or *willful* behavior" (2005, xi). Walker also describes a womanist as a "woman who loves women, sexually and nonsexually" (xi). A womanist is a queer as well as a willful black woman or woman of color.

8. For discussions of bathrooms as places of gender policing, see Cavanagh (2010) and Halberstam (1998, 20–29).

Conclusion 1

1. For discussion of how critiques of neoliberalism can be used in conservative ways (and even in ways that justify a withdrawal from commitments to equality), see my blog posts "Selfcare as Warfare," feministkilljoys, August 25, 2014, http://feministkilljoys.com/2014/08/25/selfcare-as-warfare/; and "Against Students," feministkilljoys, June 25, 2015, http://feministkilljoys.com/2015/06/25/against-students/.

2. We cannot make our distinctions too clear here (clear distinctions do not get us closer to messy worlds), but it is worth thinking of the relation between *fragility* as the word I have been using and *precarity*, which is the more used word in academic conversations. Fragility seems to be used to indicate a quality of something that is material or physical while precarity is more likely to indicate a position: so a vase would be fragile because it is made from porcelain but precarious because it is close to the edge. I think the reason I have chosen to work with the term *fragility* rather than *precarity* is because I tend to work with words that have a certain kind of resonance in everyday life because they tend to be used to indicate a quality: of a feeling (feeling fragile) or of an object or person (being fragile).

3. See Black Lives Matter, "About #BlackLivesMatter," http://www.blacklivesmatter .com (last accessed September 22, 2015).

4. The conversation is available here: New School, "bell hooks and Gloria Steinem at Eugene Lang College," YouTube, October 8, 2014, https://www.youtube.com /watch?v=tkzOFvfWRn4.

Conclusion 2

1. Sara Ahmed, "White Men," feministkilljoys, November 4, 2014, http://feministkilljoys.com/2014/11/04/white-men/.

2. With my thanks to Bahar Mustafa for her important political work. For a longer discussion of the issues surrounding Bahar's harassment on mainstream and social media, see Sara Ahmed, "A Campaign of Harassment," feministkilljoys, May 26, 2015, http://feministkilljoys.com/2015/05/26/a-campaign-of-harassment/.

REFERENCES

Ahmed, Sara. 2015. "Introduction: Sexism—a Problem with a Name." *New Formations,* no. 86: 5–13.

———. 2014. *Willful Subjects.* Durham, NC: Duke University Press.

———. 2012. *On Being Included: Racism and Diversity in Institutional Life.* Durham, NC: Duke University Press.

———. 2010. *The Promise of Happiness.* Durham, NC: Duke University Press.

———. 2006. *Queer Phenomenology: Orientations, Objects, Others.* Durham, NC: Duke University Press.

———. 2004. *The Cultural Politics of Emotion.* Edinburgh: Edinburgh University Press.

———. 2000. *Strange Encounters: Embodied Others in Post-coloniality.* London: Routledge.

———. 1998. *Differences That Matter: Feminist Theory and Postmodernism.* Cambridge: Cambridge University Press.

Alexander, M. Jacqui. 2006. *Pedagogies of Crossing: Meditations on Feminism, Sexual Politics, Memory, and the Sacred.* Durham, NC: Duke University Press.

Almond, Grace. 2015. "Rhodes Must Fall: Why British Universities Need to Decolonize not Diversify." *Consented,* December 29. http://www.consented.co.uk/read/rhodes-must-fall-why-british-universities-need-to-decolonize-not-diversify/.

Ang, Ien. 2001. *On Not Speaking Chinese: Living between Asia and the West.* London: Routledge.

Anzaldúa, Gloria. (1987) 1999. *Borderlands/La Frontera: The New Mestiza.* San Francisco: Aunt Lute.

———. 1983. "La Prieta." In *This Bridge Called My Back: Writings by Radical Women of Colour,* edited by Cherríe Moraga and Gloria Anzaldúa, 198–209. Watertown, MA: Persephone.

Barker, Joanne. 2015. "The Indigenous Feminist Killjoy." *Tequila Sovereign,* July 24. https://tequilasovereign.wordpress.com/2015/07/24/the-indigenous-feminist-killjoy/.

Bates, Laura. 2014. *Everyday Sexism.* London: Simon and Schuster.

Beauvoir, Simone de. (1949) 1997. *The Second Sex.* Translated by H. M. Parshley. London: Vintage.

Becker, Edith, Michelle Citron, Julia Lesage, and B. Ruby Rich. 1981. "Lesbians and Film." *Jumpcut*, nos. 24–25: 17–21.

Berlant, Lauren. 2011. *Cruel Optimism*. Durham, NC: Duke University Press.

———. 2008. "Thinking about Feeling Historical." *Emotion, Space and Society* 1 (1): 4–9.

———. 2007. "Slow Death: Sovereignty, Obesity, Lateral Agency." *Critical Inquiry* 33 (4): 754–80.

Bilge, Sirma. 2013. "Saving Intersectionality from Feminist Intersectionality Studies." *Du Bois Review: Social Science Research on Race* 10 (2): 405–24.

Brah, Avtar. 1996. *Cartographies of Diaspora: Contesting Identities*. London: Routledge.

Braidotti, Rosi. 2006. *Transpositions: On Nomadic Ethics*. Cambridge: Polity.

Brewer, Rose M. 1993. "Theorizing Race, Class and Gender: The New Scholarship of Black Feminist Intellectuals and Black Female Labor." In *Theorizing Black Feminisms: The Visionary Pragmatism of Black Women*, edited by Stanlie Myrise James and Abena P. A. Busia, 13–30. London: Routledge.

Brontë, Charlotte. (1847) 1999. *Jane Eyre*. London: Wordsworth.

Brown, Kimberly Juanita. 2015. *The Repeating Body: Slavery's Visual Resonance in the Contemporary*. Durham, NC: Duke University Press.

Brown, Rita Mae. 1976. *A Plain Brown Rapper*. Oakland: Diana.

———. 1973. *Rubyfruit Jungle*. New York: Bantam.

Brown, Wendy. 2010. *Walled States, Waning Sovereignty*. Cambridge, MA: MIT Press.

———. 1995. *States of Injury: Power and Freedom in Late Modernity*. Princeton, NJ: Princeton University Press.

Butler, Judith. 2015. *Notes toward a Performative Theory of Assembly*. Cambridge, MA: Harvard University Press.

———. 2004. *Precarious Life: The Powers of Mourning and Violence*. London: Verso.

———. 1997. "Merely Cultural." *Social Text*, nos. 52–53: 265–77.

———. 1993. *Bodies That Matter: On the Discursive Limits of "Sex."* London: Routledge.

———. 1990. *Gender Trouble: Feminism and the Subversion of Identity*. New York: Routledge.

Cavanagh, Sheila L. 2010. *Queering Bathrooms: Gender, Sexuality and the Hygienic Imagination*. Toronto: University of Toronto Press.

Cheng, Anne-Anlin. 2001. *The Melancholia of Race: Psychoanalysis, Assimilation and Hidden Grief*. Oxford: Oxford University Press.

Clare, Eli. (1999) 2015. *Exile and Pride: Disability, Queerness, and Liberation*. Durham, NC: Duke University Press.

Collins, Patricia Hill. 2000. *Black Feminist Thought: Knowledge, Consciousness and the Politics of Empowerment*, 2nd ed. New York: Routledge.

Cowan, T. L. 2014. "Trans/Feminist Killjoys: Rage, Love and Reparative Performance." *Transgender Studies Quarterly* 1 (4): 501–16.

Crenshaw, Kimberlé Williams. 1989. "Demarginalizing the Intersection of Race and Sex: A Black Feminist Critique of Antidiscrimination Doctrine, Feminist Theory and Antiracist Politics." *University of Chicago Legal Forum*, 139–67.

Crenshaw, Kimberlé Williams, and Andrea Ritchie. 2015. "Say Her Name: Resisting Police Brutality against Black Women." African American Policy Forum. Update, July 16, 2015. http://www.aapf.org/sayhernamereport/.

Dahl, Ulrika. 2015. "Sexism: A Femme-inist Perspective." *New Formations*, no. 86: 54–73.

Davis, Angela. (1989) 1998. *Blues Legacies and Black Feminism: Gertrude "Ma" Rainey, Bessie Smith and Billie Holiday*. New York: Vintage.

———. 1983. *Women, Race and Class*. New York: Vintage.

DiAngelo, Robin. 2011. "White Fragility." *International Journal of Critical Pedagogy* 3 (3). http://libjournal.uncg.edu/ijcp/article/view/249.

Donaldson, Elizabeth L. 2011. "Revisiting the Corpus of the Madwoman: Further Notes toward a Feminist Disability Studies Theory of Mental Illness." In *Feminist Disability Studies*, edited by Kim Q. Hall, 91–114. Bloomington: Indiana University Press.

Douglas, Mary. (1996) 2002. *Purity and Danger: An Analysis of the Concepts of Pollution and Taboo*. London: Routledge Classics.

Duggan, Lisa. 2003. *The Twilight of Equality: Neoliberalism, Cultural Politics, and the Attack on Democracy*. Boston: Beacon.

Dworkin, Andrea. 1972. *Woman Hating*. New York: E. P. Dutton.

Echols, Alice. 1989. *Daring to Be Bad: Radical Feminism in America, 1967–1985*. Minneapolis: University of Minnesota Press.

Eliot, George. (1861) 1994. *Silas Marner*. Hertfordshire: Wordsworth Classics.

———. (1860) 1965. *The Mill on the Floss*. New York: New American Library.

———. (1895) 1961. *Adam Bede*. New York: Signet Classics.

Emery, Kim. 2002. *The Lesbian Index: Pragmatism and Lesbian Subjectivity in the Twentieth Century*. Albany: State University of New York Press.

Eng, David L., and Shinhee Han. 2003. "A Dialogue on Racial Melancholia." In *Loss: The Politics of Mourning*, edited by David L. Eng and David Kazanjian, 343–71. Berkeley: University of California Press.

Enke, Anne, ed. 2012. *Transfeminist Perspectives: In and beyond Transgender and Gender Studies*. Philadelphia: Temple University Press.

Fanon, Frantz. (1967) 2008. *Black Skin, White Masks*. Translated by Charles Lam Markmann. London: Pluto.

Firestone, Shulamith. 1970. *The Dialectic of Sex: The Case for Feminist Revolution*. New York: Bantam.

Frankenberg, Ruth, and Lata Mani. 1993. "Crosscurrents, Crosstalk: Race, 'Postcoloniality' and the Politics of Location." *Cultural Studies* 7 (2): 292–310.

Franklin, Sarah. 2015. "Sexism as a Means of Reproduction." *New Formations* 86: 14–33.

———. 2010. "Revisiting Reprotech: Firestone and the Question of Technology." In *Further Adventures of the Dialectic of Sex: Critical Essays on Shulamith Firestone*, edited by Mandy Merck and Stella Stanford, 29–59. London: Palgrave Macmillan.

Freeman, Elizabeth. 2005. "Time Binds, or, Erotohistoriography." *Social Text* 23 (3–4): 57–68.

Friedan, Betty. 1965. *The Feminine Mystique.* Harmondsworth: Penguin.

Frye, Marilyn. 1992. *Willful Virgin: Essays in Feminism, 1976–1972.* Freedom, CA: Crossing Press.

———. 1991. "Introduction." In Marilyn Murphy, *Are Your Girls Traveling Alone? Adventures in Lesbianic Logic,* 11–16. Los Angeles: Clothes Spin Fever.

———. 1983. *The Politics of Reality: Essays in Feminist Theory.* Trumansburg, NY: Crossing Press.

Garland-Thomson, Rosemarie. 2014. "The Story of My Work: How I Became Disabled." *Disability Studies Quarterly* 34 (2): n.p.

———. 2011. "Misfits: A Feminist Materialist Disability Concept." *Hypatia: A Journal of Feminist Philosophy* 26 (3): 591–609.

Gatens, Moira. 1983. "The Critique of the Sex/Gender Distinction." In *Beyond Marxism: Interventions after Marx,* edited by Judith Allen and Paul Patton, 143–60. Sydney: Interventions.

Gill, Rosalind. 2007. "Postfeminist Media Culture: Elements of a New Sensibility." *European Journal of Cultural Studies* 10 (2): 147–66.

Gilman, Charlotte Perkins. (1904) 2002. *The Home: Its Work and Influence.* Lanham, MD: Rowman and Littlefield.

———. (1892) 1997. *The Yellow Wallpaper and Other Stories.* New York: Dover.

Gilmore, Ruth Wilson. 2007. *Golden Gulag: Prisons, Surplus, Crisis, and Opposition in Globalizing California.* Berkeley: University of California Press.

Goldman, Emma. (1931) 2008. *Living My Life,* vol. 1. New York: Cosimo.

Gordon, Lewis R. 1999. "Fanon, Philosophy, Racism." In *Racism and Philosophy,* edited by Susan E. Babbitt and Sue Campbell, 32–49. Ithaca, NY: Cornell University Press.

Grimm, Jacob, and Wilhelm Grimm. 1884. *Household Tales,* vol. 2. Translated by Margaret Hunt. London: George Bell.

Gumbs, Alexis Pauline. 2010. "We Can Learn to Mother Ourselves: The Queer Survival of Black Feminism, 1968–1996." PhD dissertation, Duke University.

Gunaratnam, Yasmin. 2014. "Morbid Mixtures: Hybridity, Pain and Transnational Dying." *Subjectivity* 7 (1): 74–91.

Gupta, Camel. 2014. Presentation to Black British Feminism panel, Centre for Feminist Research, Goldsmiths, December 11.

Gutiérrez y Muhs, Gabriella, Yolanda Flores Niemann, Camren G. González, and Angela P. Harris, eds. 2006. *Presumed Incompetent: The Intersections of Race and Class for Women in Academia.* Boulder: University Press of Colorado.

Halberstam, J. 2011. *The Queer Art of Failure.* Durham, NC: Duke University Press.

———. 2005. *In a Queer Time and Space.* Durham, NC: Duke University Press.

———. 1998. *Female Masculinity.* Durham, NC: Duke University Press.

Hall, Radclyffe. (1928) 1982. *The Well of Loneliness.* London: Virago.

Haraway, Donna. 2003. *A Companion Species Manifesto: Dogs, People and Significant Otherness.* Chicago: Prickly Paradigm.

Hartman, Saidiya V. 1997. *Scenes of Subjection: Terror, Slavery and Self-Making in Nineteenth-Century America.* New York: Oxford University Press.

Hemmings, Clare. 2011. *Why Stories Matter: The Political Grammar of Feminist Theory.* Durham, NC: Duke University Press.

Hesford, Victoria. 2013. *Feeling Women's Liberation.* Durham, NC: Duke University Press.

Hochschild, Arlie Russell. (1983) 2003. *The Managed Heart: Commercialization of Human Feeling.* Berkeley: University of California Press.

hooks, bell. 2000. *Feminist Theory: From Margin to Centre.* London: Pluto.

———. 1996. "Inspired Eccentricity: Sarah and Gus Oldham." In *Family: American Writers Remember Their Own*, edited by Sharon Sloan Fiffer and Steve Fiffer. New York: Vintage.

———. 1988. *Talking Back: Thinking Feminism, Thinking Black.* Boston: South End.

———. 1981. *Ain't I a Woman: Black Women and Feminism.* Boston: South End.

Jacques, Juliet. 2015. *TRANS: A Memoir.* London: Verso.

———. 2010. "'Confidence Is the Key to Passing—or at Least to Silencing the Hecklers.'" *Guardian*, July 28. http://www.theguardian.com/lifeandstyle/2010/jul/28/passing-as-a-woman.

Jaggar, Alison M. 1996. "Love and Knowledge: Emotion in Feminist Epistemology." In *Women, Knowledge, and Reality: Explorations in Feminist Philosophy*, edited by Ann Garry and Marilyn Pearsall, 166–90. New York: Routledge.

James, Robin. 2015. *Resilience and Melancholy: Pop Music, Feminism, Neoliberalism.* London: Zero.

Johnson, E. Patrick. 2009. "Snap! Culture: A Different Kind of 'Reading.'" *Text and Performance Quarterly* 15 (2): 122–42.

Johnson, Lisa Merri. 2014. "Bad Romance: A Crip Feminist Critique of Queer Failure." *Hypatia: A Journal of Feminist Philosophy* 30 (1): 251–67.

Kafai, Shayda. 2013. "The Mad Border Body: A Typical In-Betweeness." *Disability Studies Quarterly* 33 (1): n.p.

Kafer, Alison. 2013. *Feminist, Queer, Crip.* Bloomington: Indiana University Press.

Kelley, Robin D. G. 2014. "Why We Won't Wait." *Counterpunch*, November 25. http://www.counterpunch.org/2014/11/25/why-we-wont-wait/.

Khorana, Sukhmani. 2013. "On Being an Ethnic Killjoy in the Asian Century." *The Conversation*, November 19. http://theconversation.com/on-being-an-ethnic-killjoy-in-the-asian-century-19833.

King, Moynan. 2013. "Revenge as a Radical Feminist Tactic in the SCUM Manifesto." *Nomorepotlucks*, July/August. http://nomorepotlucks.org/site/revenge-as-radical-feminist-tactic-in-the-scum-manifesto-moynan-king/.

Kuhn, Annette. (1995) 2002. *Family Secrets: Acts of Memory and Imagination.* London: Verso.

Lamp, Sharon, and W. Carol Cleigh. 2011. "A History of Ableist Rhetoric in American Feminism from the Eugenics Period." In *Feminist Disability Studies*, edited by Kim Q. Hall, 175–90. Bloomington: Indiana University Press.

Lewis, Gail. 2009. "Birthing Racial Difference: Conversations with My Mother and Others." *Studies in the Maternal* 1 (1): 1–21.

Lorde, Audre. 1997. *The Cancer Journals.* San Francisco: Aunt Lute.

———. 1988. *A Burst of Light: Essays.* Ithaca, NY: Firebrand.

————. 1984a. *Sister Outsider: Essays and Speeches*. Trumansburg, NY: Crossing Press.

————. 1984b. *Zami: A New Spelling of My Name*. London: Sheba Feminist.

————. 1978. *Black Unicorn*. New York: Norton.

Love, Heather. 2007. *Feeling Backward: Loss and the Politics of Queer History*. Cambridge, MA: Harvard University Press.

McKittrick, Katherine. 2015. "Yours in the Intellectual Struggle: Sylvia Wynter and the Realization of the Living." In *Sylvia Wynter: On Being Human as Praxis*, edited by Katherine McKittrick, 1–8. Durham, NC: Duke University Press.

McRobbie, Angela. 2009. *The Aftermath of Feminism*. London: Sage.

Millbank, Lisa. 2013. "The Scope of Action, Smiling, Smile 'Strikes' and Individual Action." Radtransfem. http://radtransfem.tumblr.com/post/40249024485/the-scope-of-action-smiling-smile-strikes-and.

Miller, Alice. 1987. *For Your Own Good: The Roots of Violence in Child-Rearing*. London: Virago.

Mingus, Mia. 2013. "Video Interview w/Mia Mingus on Disability Justice." Icarus Project, December 11. http://www.theicarusproject.net/disability/video-interview-wmia-mingus-on-disability-justice.

Mirza, Heidi. 2015. "Decolonizing Higher Education: Black Feminism and the Intersectionality of Race and Gender." *Journal of Feminist Scholarship*, nos. 7–8: 1–12.

Mohanty, Chandra Talpade. 2003. *Feminism without Borders: Decolonizing Theory, Practicing Solidarity*. Durham, NC: Duke University Press.

Moraga, Cherríe. 1981. "The Welder." In *This Bridge Called My Back: Writings by Radical Women of Color*, edited by Cherríe Moraga and Gloria Anzaldúa, 219. Watertown, MA: Persephone.

Moreton-Robinson, Aileen. 2003. "'Tiddas Talkin' Up to the White Woman': When Huggins et al. Took on Bell." In *Black Lines: Contemporary Critical Writing by Indigenous Australians*, edited by Michele Grossman, 66–78. Melbourne: Melbourne University Press.

Morrison, Toni. 1979. *The Bluest Eye*. London: Picador.

Mullow, Anna. 2013. "Bellyaching." *Social Text*, October 24. http://socialtextjournal.org/periscope_article/bellyaching/.

Ngai, Sianne. 2007. *Ugly Feelings*. Cambridge, MA: Harvard University Press.

Oakley, Ann. 2007. *Fractured: Adventures of a Broken Body*. Bristol, U.K.: Policy.

————. 1980. *Women Confined: Towards a Sociology of Childbirth*. New York: Schocken.

Orelus, Pierre. 2011. *Courageous Voices of Immigrants and Transnationals of Color: Counter Narratives against Discrimination in Schools and Beyond*. New York: Peter Lang.

Penelope, Julia. 1992. *Call Me Lesbian: Lesbian Lives, Lesbian Theory*. New York: Crossing Press.

Peters, Julie Anne. 2003. *Keeping You a Secret*. Boston: Little, Brown.

Preciado, Beatriz. 2012. "Queer Bulldogs: Histories of Human-Canin [*sic*] Co-breeding and Biopolitical Resistance" [video]. Presented at conference, Documenta 13, September 10. http://d13.documenta.de/#/research/research/view/on-seeds

-and-multispecies-intra-action-disowning-life-beatriz-preciado-queer-bulldogs
-histories-of-human-canin-co-breeding-and-biopolitical-resistance.

Probyn, Elspeth. 1996. *Outside Belongings*. London: Routledge.

Prosser, Jay. 1998. *Second Skins: The Body Narratives of Transsexuality*. New York: Columbia University Press.

Puar, Jasbir. 2009. "Prognosis Time: Towards a Geo-politics of Affect, Debility and Capacity." *Women and Performance: A Journal of Feminist Theory* 19 (2): 161–72.

———. 2007. *Terrorist Assemblages: Homonationalism in Queer Times*. Durham, NC: Duke University Press.

Puwar, Nirmal. 2004. *Space Invaders: Race, Gender and Bodies out of Place*. Oxford: Berg.

Radicalesbians. 1970. "The Woman Identified Woman." Duke University Libraries, Digital Collections. http://library.duke.edu/digitalcollections/wlmpc_wlmms01011/.

Randolph, Sherie M. 2015. *Florynce "Flo" Kennedy: The Life of a Black Feminist Radical*. Chapel Hill: University of North Carolina Press.

Rankine, Claudia. 2014. "Poet Claudia Rankine: 'Racism Works Purely on Perception' in America." *Guardian*, December 27. http://www.theguardian.com/books/2014/dec/27/claudia-rankine-poetry-racism-america-perception.

Rich, Adrienne. 1993. "Compulsory Heterosexuality and Lesbian Existence." In *The Lesbian and Gay Studies Reader*, edited by Henry Abelove, Michèle Aina Barale, and David M. Halperin, 227–54. New York: Routledge.

———. 1986. "Notes toward a Politics of Location." In *Blood, Bread, and Poetry: Selected Prose, 1979–1985*. New York: Norton.

———. 1979. "Disloyal to Civilization." In *On Lies, Secrets and Silence: Selected Prose, 1966–1978*. New York: Norton.

Riggs, Marlon T. 1999. "Black Macho Revisited: Reflections of a Snap! Queen." In *Black Men on Race, Gender and Sexuality: A Critical Reader*, edited by Devon W. Carbado, 306–11. New York: New York University Press.

Sandahl, Carrie. 2002. "Considering Disability: Disability Phenomenology's Role in Revolutionizing Theatrical Space." *Journal of Dramatic Theory and Criticism* 16 (2): 17–32.

———. 1993. "Queering the Crip or Cripping the Queer: Intersection of Queer and Crip Identities in Solo Autobiographical Performance." GLQ 9 (1–2): 25–56.

Saunders, James Robert. 1988. "Womanism as the Key to Understanding Zora Neale Hurston's *Their Eyes Were Watching God* and Alice Walker's *The Color Purple*." *Hollins Critic* 25 (4): 1–11.

Schulman, Sarah. 1998. *Stage Struck: Theatre, AIDS, and the Marketing of Gay America*. Durham, NC: Duke University Press.

Schwarz, Judith. 1986. *Radical Feminists of Heterodoxy*. Hereford, AZ: New Victoria.

Sedgwick, Eve Kosofsky. 1993. "Queer Performativity: Henry James's *The Art of the Novel*." GLQ 1 (1): 1–14.

———. 1985. *Between Men: English Literature and Male Homosocial Desire*. New York: Columbia University Press.

Serano, Julia. 2007. *Whipping Girl: A Transsexual Woman in Sexism and the Scapegoating of Femininity*. Berkeley, CA: Seal.

Sharpe, Christina. 2010. *Monstrous Intimacies: Making Post-slavery Subjects*. Durham, NC: Duke University Press.

Smith, Malinda. 2010. "Gender, Whiteness, and 'Other Others' in the Academy." In *States of Race: Critical Race Feminism for the 21st Century*, edited by Sherene Razack, Malinda Smith, and Sunera Thobani, 23–35. Toronto: Between the Lines.

Solanas, Valerie. (1967) 2013. *SCUM Manifesto*. Chico, CA: AK Press.

Spade, Dean. 2006. "Gender Mutilation." In *The Transgender Studies Reader*, edited by Susan Stryker and Stephen Whittle, 315–32. London: Routledge.

Spelman, Elizabeth V. 1989. "Anger and Insubordination." In *Women, Knowledge and Reality: Explorations in Feminist Philosophy*, edited by Ann Garry and Marilyn Pearsall, 263–74. New York: Routledge.

Spillers, Hortense. 1987. "Mama's Baby, Papa's Maybe: An American Grammar Book." *Diacritics* 17 (2): 64–81.

Spivak, Gayatri Chakravorty. 1988. "Can the Subaltern Speak?" In *Marxism and the Interpretation of Culture*, edited by Cary Nelson and Lawrence Grossberg, 271–313. Basingstoke, U.K.: Macmillan Education.

Stone, Sandy. 2006. "The Empire Strikes Back: A Posttransexual Manifesto." In *The Transgender Studies Reader*, edited by Susan Stryker and Stephen Whittle, 244–56. London: Routledge.

Stryker, Susan. 1994. "My Words to Victor Frankenstein above the Village of Chamounix: Performing Transgender Rage." *GLQ* 1 (3): 237–54.

Swan, Elaine. 2010a. "Commodity Diversity: Smiling Faces as a Strategy of Containment." *Organization* 17 (1): 77–100.

———. 2010b. "States of White Ignorance, and Audit Masculinity in English Higher Education." *Social Politics* 17 (4): 477–506.

Thobani, Sunera. 2003. "War and the Politics of Truth-Making in Canada." *International Journal of Qualitative Studies in Education* 16 (3): 399–414.

Titchkosky, Tanya. 2011. *The Question of Access: Disability, Space, Meaning*. Toronto: University of Toronto Press.

Topping, Alexandra. 2014. "Universities Being Used as Proxy Border Police, Say Academics." *Guardian*, March 2. http://www.theguardian.com/education/2014/mar/02/universities-border-police-academics.

Trowbridge, Katherine M. 1855. "Jane Munson: Or the Girl Who Wished to Have Her Own Way." In *Student and Family Miscellany*, edited by Norman Allison Calkins, 16–20. New York: N. A. Calkins.

Tyler, Imogen. 2013. *Revolting Subjects: Social Abjection and Resistance in Neo-liberal Britain*. London: Zed.

———. 2007. "The Selfish Feminist: Public Images of Women's Liberation." *Australian Feminist Studies* 22 (53): 173–90.

Valentine, Gill. 1996. "(Re)Negotiating the 'Heterosexual Street': Lesbian Productions of Space." In *BodySpace: Destabilizing Geographies of Gender and Sexuality*, edited by Nancy Duncan, 146–55. London: Routledge.

Walker, Alice. 2005. *In Search of Our Mothers' Gardens*. Phoenix, AZ: New Edition.

Wekker, Gloria. 2016. *White Innocence: Paradoxes of Colonialism and Race*. Durham, NC: Duke University Press.

Whitley, Leila. 2014. "More Than a Line: The Border as Embodied Site." PhD dissertation, Goldsmiths, University of London.

Whitley, Leila, and Tiffany Page. 2015. "Sexism at the Centre: Locating the Problem of Sexual Harassment." *New Formations*, no. 86: 34–53.

Wilchins, Riki. 2014. *Queer Theory, Gender Theory*. New York: Riverdale Avenue.

Wittig, Monique. 1992. *The Straight Mind and Other Essays*. Boston: Beacon.

Woolf, Virginia. (1925) 1996. *Mrs. Dalloway*. London: Wordsworth.

———. 1920. *A Room of One's Own*. London: Hogarth.

Wynter, Sylvia. 2006. "On How We Mistook the Map for the Territory and Reimprisoned Ourselves in Our Unbearable Wrongness of Being, of *Désêtre*: Black Studies toward the Human Project." In *Not Only the Master's Tools: African American Studies in Theory and Practice*, edited by Lewis R. Gordon and Jane Anna Gordon, 107–72. Boulder, CO: Paradigm.

Yancy, George. 2013. "Walking while Black." *New York Times*, September 1.

Young, Iris Marion. 1990. *Throwing like a Girl and Other Essays*. Bloomington: Indiana University Press.

Zackodnik, Teresa. 2011. *Press, Platform, Pulpit: Black Feminist Publics in the Era of Reform*. Knoxville: University of Tennessee Press.

INDEX

Abby (character), 218–21
able-bodied privilege, 181–82
academy, the. *See* university settings
accessibility, 109–10, 113–14, 124–25,
  180–84, 276n3 (ch. 7)
Adam Bede (Eliot), 166–68. *See also* Mrs.
  Poyser
Adelaide Norris (character), 207–10
affect aliens, 53–57, 194, 254
Alexander, M. Jacqui, 90–91
alienation, 39–42, 53–57, 194
alignment, 55
Almond, Grace, 275n3
Amendment to the Race Relations Act of
  2000, 94–95, 103
Ang, Ien, 117
anger, 172, 177–78, 184, 201
Antigone, 74
antitransism, 14–15, 174–75, 234, 269n7
Anzaldúa, Gloria, 9, 183, 191, 230
archive of shared experience, 185, 222–32.
  See also lesbian feminism
arms and armies: broken bones of, 183–84;
  feminine angle of, 233; lesbian feminist
  intersectionality and, 232–34; of "The
  Willful Child," 66–68, 75–80, 84–85, 158–
  59, 174, 233, 273n7; of willful feminists,
  84–88, 158–60, 273–74nn9–11, 275n3
attunement, 41–42

background racism, 168–69
Bano, Gulzar, 4–5, 192
Bates, Laura, 271n3
Beauvoir, Simone de, 255

becoming feminist, 18, 19–20; alienation
  in, 39–42, 57; becoming audible in, 73,
  272n2; becoming the problem in, 36–39,
  271nn5–7; directionality of power and,
  20, 43–64; gender fatalism and, 25–26;
  memory work in, 22–24; naming of
  difficulties in, 31–36, 271n4; nervous
  conditions and madness in, 76–77, 272n3;
  as sad inheritance, 62–64; sensation in,
  20–42; willful subjectivity and, 65–88.
  See also feminist killjoys
being feminist. *See* becoming feminist;
  diversity work; living consequences
being outside the norm. *See* embodied
  diversity
Bend It like Beckham, 272n4 (ch. 2)
Berlant, Lauren, 13, 194–95, 198
Berlin Years, The (Lorde), 247
#blacklivesmatter movement, 239–40
Blackman, Lisa, 275n6
Blues Legacies and Black Feminism (Davis),
  252
Bluest Eye, The (Morrison), 17, 40–41
bodies. *See* embodied diversity
Bodies That Matter (Butler), 240
books. *See* companion texts
Borderlands / La Frontera: The New Mestiza
  (Anzaldúa), 191, 230
Born in Flames (dir. Borden), 188, 206–11,
  276n3 (ch. 8), 277n6
boying, 51
breakage: of bodies, 180–84, 276nn2–3
  (ch. 7); carefulness and, 14, 169–71; of
  fragile feminist spaces, 175–79, 259, 276n1

breakage (*continued*)
(ch. 7); of fragile objects, 164–68; of
fragile relationships, 168–75
breaking points. *See* feminist snap
brick walls, 91, 96–97, 135–60; in academic
citation practices, 148–58; bodies as,
145–48; feminist killjoys as makers of,
142; heterogender as, 215–17; material and
tangible resistance of, 136–42, 147–48;
sexual harassment complaints and,
139–42; stranger danger and, 142–45;
willful feminists and, 158–60, 275n3
Brown, Rita Mae, 16–17, 227–30, 240
Brown, Wendy, 145
building a feminist world. *See* feminist
movement
Bull, Anna, 111
Burst of Light, A (Lorde), 237–40
butch lesbians, 223
Butler, Judith, 25–26, 240, 247, 255

Cameron, David, 262
Campbell, Maria, 273n7
Cancer Journals, The (Lorde), 184, 239, 240
carefulness, 14, 169
cis women, 14–15, 120
citation policies, 15–17; feminist theory on,
15–16, 269–70nn7–9; racism and sexism
in, 148–58
Clare, Eli, 182–83, 273n6
Clarissa Dalloway (character). *See Mrs.
Dalloway*
class, 148, 219, 237–38, 277n3, 279n2 (cncl. 1)
Claudia (character, *The Bluest Eye*), 40–41
clenched fist, the, 85, 86
collective snap, 188, 200–212, 254, 276n3
(ch. 8), 277n4, 277nn6–7
Collins, Patricia Hill, 87–88
coming out, 51–53
communication strategies, 95–96
companion texts, 16–17, 237, 240, 254, 256
compulsory heterosexuality, 46, 48–49
consciousness of injustice, 27–31, 47, 61–62
consequences of being feminist. *See* living
consequences
contingent lesbians, 278n6
costs of living as a feminist. *See* living consequences

Crenshaw, Kimberlé Williams, 275n1 (ch. 5),
277n4
crip (as term), 184–85
criticality, 155
critical theory, 9–11
cruel optimism, 194–96
Cullors, Patrisse, 239–40
cultural feminism, 1–2, 213. *See also* feminism
Cultural Politics of Emotion, The (Ahmed),
181, 271n1 (ch. 2)
cultural studies, 132

Dahl, Ulrika, 55
dancing, 247–48
Daring to Be Bad (Echols), 213
Davis, Angela, 87, 252
de-girling, 54–55
Delmar, Rosalind, 213
desire lines, 15, 270n9
Dialectic of Sex, The (Firestone), 248, 254
DiAngelo, Robin, 179
Differences That Matter (Ahmed), 8
directionality of power, 20, 43–64, 272n4
(ch. 2); alignment and habituation with,
55–57; changing direction and, 47–48;
feminist killjoys as affect aliens and,
53–57, 194; following the flow of, 44–48;
the happiness path and, 48–52, 272nn3–4
(ch. 2); normativity of, 43, 271n1 (ch. 2).
See also happiness (and unhappiness);
Mrs. Dalloway
disability, 148; accessibility challenges in,
109–10, 113–14, 180–84, 276n3 (ch. 7);
questioning wrongness in, 124
disciplinary fatalism, 150–51
disorientation, 133–34
diversity work, 6, 18, 89–91, 214; brick walls
in, 91, 96–97, 135–60; communication
strategies in, 95–96; embodied diversity
in, 91, 111, 115–35, 274n5; on institutional
reproduction, 154; intersectionality in,
119–20, 147–48, 275n1 (ch. 5); overing
and, 155–58; public relations role of, 103,
105; pushing for outcomes in, 107–13;
sweaty concepts of, 94; transformative efforts of, 91, 93–114; in university settings,
90–91, 94–97, 148–58; as willful work,
113–14; words used for, 98–102

dogs, 243
domestic violence services, 277n6
Donaldson, Elizabeth J., 272n3
Douglas, Mary, 233
Duggan, Mark, 81
Dworkin, Andrea, 269n7
Dzodan, Flavia, 5

Echols, Alice, 213
Edith (character), 218–21
Eliot, George, 16–17, 68, 164–68, 240; Maggie
    Tulliver of, 68–69, 74, 165; Mrs. Poyser of,
    166–68, 171, 175, 179, 208; as philosopher
    of will, 165; Silas Marner of, 165–66, 199
Ellis, Havelock, 233
embodied diversity, 91, 111, 115–35, 274n5;
    bodies as borders in, 145–47; discomfort
    and disorientation in, 123, 133–34; insti-
    tutional passing in, 126–31, 275n2 (ch. 5);
    intersectionality in, 119–20, 147–48, 275n1
    (ch. 5); questioning gender and sexuality
    in, 120–25; questioning race in, 116–20;
    stranger danger and, 142–45. See also
    racism
"Embodying Strangers" (Ahmed), 177
Emery, Kim, 227
emotional labor, 58–62, 246
"Empire Strikes Back: A Posttransexual
    Manifesto, The" (Stone), 227, 269–70n7
Equality Act of 2010, 103
Equality Challenge Unit, 103–4
equity fatigue, 98–99, 274n1 (ch. 4)
Eve, 74
Everyday Feminism, 277n1
Everyday Sexism project (Bates), 30, 271n3
*Exile and Pride: Disability, Queerness, and
    Liberation* (Clare), 182–83
eye rolls. See rolling eyes

false consciousness, 61–62
family background, 187–88. See also class;
    privilege
Fanon, Frantz, 133–34
feelings, 58–62, 246
Female Masculinity (Halberstam), 233
female relatives, 216
feminism, 9; breaking through the happi-
    ness seal in, 58–62, 210, 255; critiques of

lesbian feminism in, 213–14; definitions
    of, 5; dismissiveness toward, 2, 38, 40,
    154–56, 239, 269n1, 271n8, 275n2 (ch. 6);
    instrumentalization of, 15–16; snappy
    tongues of, 191–92. See also becom-
    ing feminist; diversity work; living
    consequences
"Feminism Is Sensational" (Ahmed),
    248–49
feminist classics, 17, 47
feminist consciousness, 62
feminist diet, 247
feminist disability studies, 272n3
feminist killjoys, 11, 20; alienation and,
    39–42, 53–57, 194; becoming the problem
    as, 36–39, 271nn5–7; eye rolls and, 38,
    99, 142, 207, 268; failure to habituate
    by, 55–57; feminists of color as, 176–79;
    fragile shelters of, 175–79; in institutional
    settings, 99–101, 113, 131; killing joy by,
    53–57, 168, 255; lesbian feminists as, 222–
    23, 255; manifesto of, 74–75, 249, 251–68;
    principles of, 255–68; self-breakage by,
    171–75; snappiness of, 189–91; snapping
    bonds by, 195–96, 266–67; survival kit
    of, 16–17, 54, 235–49; as wall makers, 142;
    as wenches in the works, 158; as willful
    feminists, 74–75, 83. See also diversity
    work; living consequences
feministkilljoys.com blog, 11
feminist mementos, 241
feminist movement, 2–7; being moved
    in, 5–6; as building project, 14–15;
    classic texts of, 16–17, 237, 240, 254, 256;
    intersectionality in, 5, 119–20, 147–48,
    212, 219, 230–34, 275n1 (ch. 5); as a killjoy
    movement, 267–68; persistence needed
    for, 6, 96–98; recognition of what hasn't
    ended in, 5–6, 269n4; shelters and spaces
    of, 175–79, 259; survival kit for, 235–49.
    See also becoming feminist; diversity
    work; living consequences
feminist principles, 255–68. See also killjoy
    manifesto
feminist snap, 3, 162, 187–212, 255; beginning
    points in, 192, 210–12; breaking bonds
    and, 193–200, 266–67, 276n1 (ch. 8);
    breaking points in, 187–88; collective acts

feminist snap (*continued*)
  of, 188, 200–212, 276n3 (ch. 8), 277n4,
  277nn6–7; description of, 188–92; laughter and, 204–5; of snappy killjoys, 189–91
feminist subjectivity. *See* willful feminists
feminist theory, 7–10; animation by everyday life of, 10–12, 19–20; in becoming a
  feminist, 20; citation policies in, 15–16,
  148–58, 269–70nn7–9; companion texts
  in, 16–17, 237, 240, 254, 256; as digested
  and past, 112–13; as lived theory, 214–15;
  practicing feminism and, 14–15; sweaty
  concepts of, 12–14, 269n6; universal focus
  of, 29
Feminist Theory (hooks), 240
femme lesbians, 223
finger snapping, 210, 277n5
Firestone, Shulamith, 215, 248, 254
flying off the handle, 171
For Your Own Good (Miller), 67–68
fragility, 163–86; of bodies, 180–85,
  276nn2–3 (ch. 7); of broken objects,
  164–68; of broken relationships, 168–75,
  185–86; depletion of energy and, 163–64;
  of feminist killjoys, 171–75; of feminist
  spaces, 175–79, 259, 276n1 (ch. 7); gender
  norms of, 169–70; judgment of meanness
  and, 179; of oneself, 169–71; of precarious
  populations, 238, 279n2 (cncl. 1); white
  forms of, 179, 276n1 (ch. 7)
Franklin, Sarah, 158, 254
Freeman, Elizabeth, 228–29
Friedan, Betty, 86, 102, 227
Frye, Marilyn, 240; on feminist theory as
  lived theory, 214; on oppression, 49–50,
  54, 189; on willful radical feminism, 223

Gage, Frances Dana Barker, 87
Garland-Thomson, Rosemarie, 124–25
Garza, Alicia, 239–40
gender dysphoria, 148, 272n5
gender fatalism, 25–26, 48–49, 150, 234
gender systems, 55–57, 233, 272n5
Gender Trouble (Butler), 240, 255
genosuicide, 253
gentrification, 145–46
Gilman, Charlotte Perkins, 76–77, 272n3
Gilmore, Ruth Wilson, 238

girling, 25–26, 54–55
Goldman, Emma, 247, 249
Gordon, Lewis, 133–34
Griffin, Sue, 217
Grimm story. *See* "Willful Child, The"
Gumbs, Alexis Pauline, 235
Gunaratnam, Yasmin, 181
Gupta, Camel, 52–53

Halberstam, J., 233
Hall, Stuart, 112
hap care, 266
happiness (and unhappiness), 20, 62–64,
  168; affirming the hap of, 196–97, 265–66;
  breaking through the seal of, 58–62, 210,
  255; emotional labor of, 58; expected
  paths to, 48–52, 187, 197, 272nn3–4
  (ch. 2); feminist killjoys as affect aliens
  and, 53–57, 194; of lesbian feminists, 222–
  23, 228–30; Lorde's critique of, 60–61; as
  pressure and oppression, 49–54, 187–88,
  253–55, 272n6; smile strikes in response
  to, 254; sympathy for another's grief and,
  58–62. *See also* directionality of power
Haraway, Donna, 16
Hartman, Saidiya V., 273n9
health systems, 238
Heterodoxy Club, 78
heterogender, 215–17
Hochschild, Arlie Russell, 56, 58, 85, 101
homework: feminist theory as, 7–10; gender
  fatalism as, 26; replication of disruptions
  in, 9–10, 269n5; willfulness as, 83–84
homonormativity, 46
homosociality, 152
hooks, bell, 9, 177–78, 240; definition of
  feminism of, 5; on talking back, 191–92;
  on unhappy housewives, 86
horses, 54, 243
Hours, The (dir. Daldry), 62–63
"How to Tame a Wild Tongue" (Anzaldúa),
  191
humor: causing offense with, 261–62; laughter and, 201, 204–5, 245–46

identity politics, 154–58
If These Walls Could Talk 2 (dir. Anderson),
  218–21

impatience, 179, 208, 211
individualism, 83
inherited intentionality, 25
In Search of Our Mothers' Gardens (Walker), 278n7
institutional passing, 127–31, 275n2 (ch. 5); building rapport and, 130–31; minimizing signs of difference in, 129–30
institutional sexism, 35–36. *See also* university settings
intellectual work of feminism. *See* feminist theory
intersectionality, 5, 212, 219, 230–34; embodied diversity and, 119–20, 147–48, 275n1 (ch. 5); of lesbian feminists of color, 230–31

Jacques, Juliet, 120
Jaggar, Alison, 27
James, Robin, 189
Jane Eyre (Brontë), 191
"Jane Munson: Or the Girl Who Wished to Have Her Own Way" (Trowbridge), 69–71
Janine van den Bos (character), 200–205, 226
Johnson, Lisa Merri, 272n3
Johnson, Meredith, 243
Johnson, Yvonne, 243

Kafai, Shayda, 76
Kafer, Alison, 185
Keeping You a Secret (Peters), 51–52
Kennedy, Florynce "Flo," 276n3 (ch. 8)
killjoy manifesto, 249, 251–68; in companion texts, 254, 256; critique of happiness in, 254–55; fantasies of violence in, 252–54; feminist principles in, 255–68; on humor that causes offense, 261–62; on a killjoy movement, 267–68; on not getting over histories that are not over, 262–63; on not making happiness of others our cause, 74–75, 253–55, 257; on putting the hap back into happiness, 265–66; recognition of inequality in, 252–53; on supporting those who cause unhappiness, 259–61; on unwillingness to be complicit in an unjust institution, 263–64; on widening the

scripts for a good life, 264–65; on willingness to cause unhappiness, 258–59; on willingness to snap bonds, 266–67
killjoy survival kit, 235–49; bodily nourishment in, 247; classic feminist texts in, 16–17, 237, 240, 256; feelings and emotions in, 246; feminist objects and mementos in, 241; feminist tools in, 241–42; humor in, 245–46; killjoy manifesto in, 249, 251–68; other killjoys in, 244–45; other living creatures in, 54, 243; permission notes in, 244; time and time out in, 242; wriggling and dancing in, 247–49
King, Moynan, 251
knee-jerk responses, 155, 275n2 (ch. 6)
Kramer vs. Kramer, 39
Kuhn, Annette, 126

laughter, 201, 204–5, 245–46
lesbian continuum, 227
lesbian feminism, 162, 213–34, 255; charged connection between terms in, 214; color and, 230–31; diversity work and, 214; feminist critiques of, 213, 227; as feminist killjoys, 222–23; happiness and unhappiness of, 222–23, 228–30; on how one lives, 213–14; intersectional army of, 232–34; safe spaces of, 232; struggle for ordinary recognition in, 217–22, 277n3; tools to interpret data in, 215–17, 277n2; transfeminism and, 227; willfulness archive of, 185, 228–32; willful turn away from men in, 222–28
Lesbian Lives conferences, 247–48
Lewis, Gail, 271n4
"Litany of Survival, A" (Lorde), 236–37
living consequences, 18, 161–62; feminist snap in, 3, 162, 187–212; fragility in, 163–86; handling hostility in, 162; killjoy manifesto for, 249, 251–68; killjoy survival kit for, 235–49; reviving lesbian feminism for, 162, 213–34; snapping bonds and, 193–200, 266–67, 276n1 (ch. 8)
Living My Life (Goldman), 249
living on the edge, 238
Lorde, Audre, 9, 12, 240; dancing of, 247; on the erotic, 230–31, 248; on happiness, 60–61; on her cancer and mastectomy,

privilege, 125–26, 276n1 (ch. 7); of the able-bodied, 181–82; as a buffer zone, 148, 219, 237–38, 277n3, 279n2 (cncl. 1)
Probyn, Elspeth, 54
professional killjoys, 263–64
Promise of Happiness, The (Ahmed), 10; on affirming the hap, 196–97, 265–66; on female troublemaker fiction, 228; on the path of happiness, 48, 272n4 (ch. 2); on social hopes of migrant families, 52–53
pronoun labor, 122
Puar, Jasbir, 237
Puwar, Nirmal, 9, 125

queer (as term), 184–85, 224, 278nn4–5. *See also* lesbian feminism
Queer Phenomenology (Ahmed), 270n9, 271n4; on questionable identities, 121–22; on well-trodden paths, 45–46
queer studies, 278n5
Question of Silence, A (dir. Gorris), 187, 200–205, 226, 253

Race Relations Act of 2000 amendment, 94–95, 103
racial capitalism, 238
racism: in academic citation practices, 148–58; background forms of, 168–69; critical reproduction of, 155; feminists of color as killjoys when they speak about, 176–79; feminist vigils against, 209–10, 277n4; Gilmore's definition of, 238; in humor, 261–62; Lorde on feminism and, 83, 177–78; Lorde on self-preservation and, 238–39; materiality of, 147–48; overing of, 155–58; polite forms of, 118–19; racialization of the stranger in, 33–34, 117–18, 130–31, 143–45; racialization of violence in, 72, 144–45; reproduction of, 9, 154–58; "Walking While Black" and, 143–44; of whiteness as universal, 133–34, 146–47
racism (as term), 31–36; brick wall against usage of, 140; learning and using as grown-up word, 32–36, 271n4
Radicalesbians, 224–26
radical feminism, 223; critiques of lesbian feminism in, 213, 227; trans exclusion in, 14–15, 174–75, 234, 269n7

raised eyebrows, 216–17
Rankine, Claudia, 144
resilience, 189, 236, 279n1 (cncl. 1)
Rhodes Must Fall movement, 275n3
Rich, Adrienne, 46, 218, 227, 246
Riggs, Marlon, 277n5
Ritchie, Andrea, 277n4
rolling eyes, 38, 99, 142, 207, 268
Rubyfruit Jungle (Brown), 16–17, 227–30, 240

Sandahl, Carrie, 184–85
Saunders, James, 78
Schulman, Sarah, 222
SCUM (Society for Cutting Up Men), 253
SCUM Manifesto (Solanas), 251–53
second-wave feminism, 3–4, 30
Sedgwick, Eve Kosofsky, 152, 185, 224, 278n5
self-girling, 54–55
sensation, 20–42; alienation and attunement in, 39–42, 57; arousal by injustice in, 22–26, 271n1 (ch. 1); awareness of injustice in, 27–31, 47, 61–62; cataloging of injustice and, 30; exposing and becoming the problem (killjoy) and, 36–39, 271nn5–7; gender fatalism in, 25–26; making things sensational and, 21, 37, 271n5; memory work of the body and, 22–24; naming of racism and sexism and, 31–36, 271n4
sensational (as term), 22
Serano, Julia, 120, 227
sexism, 14, 30–36; in academic citation practices, 148–58; brick wall against usage (as term) of, 140; collective feminist snap against, 200–205, 210–12; critical reproduction of, 155; as grown-up word, 32–36, 271n4; in humor, 261–62; lesbian feminism's tools to interpret data of, 215–17; overing of, 155–58; reproduction of, 9, 154–58
sexual harassment complaints: brick walls in, 139–42; snapping bonds and, 198–99, 203
Sharpe, Christina, 79
shatter/shattering, 12, 17, 22, 164, 168–69, 175, 179, 182–83, 185–86, 266
Silas Marner (Eliot), 165–66, 199
Single Equality Scheme, 103–4

willful feminists, 6, 11, 20, 65–88, 158–60, 216; arms and armies of, 84–88, 158–60, 174, 273–74nn9–11, 275n3; becoming feminists as, 71–77; as being for oneself, 74–77; as female behavior, 68–71, 79, 273n6; as feminist killjoys, 74–75, 83, 171–75; of feminist snappy tongues, 191–92; fragility and, 164–68, 173–75; judgment and discipline of, 67–71; justification of violence toward, 72–74, 80–81; lesbian feminists as, 165, 222–32, 255; political activism of, 82–84; racial valence of, 80–81, 272n4; reclaiming of willfulness by, 77–84; of slavery, 87–88, 273–74nn9–10; womanists as, 78–82, 193, 234, 278n7
willfulness (as term), 65–66, 68
willfulness charge, 65, 74–75, 174–75
Willful Subjects (Ahmed), 10–11, 66, 228; on Eliot's characters, 68, 165; on *A Question of Silence*, 200
Wittig, Monique, 224
woman (as term), 224
"Woman" (Ahmed), 8

Woman Hating (Dworkin), 269n7
"Woman Identified Woman" (Radicalesbians), 224–26
womanism, 78–82, 193, 234, 278n7
Women, Race and Class (Davis), 87
women's studies, 112–13, 161–62, 274n4; decline of, 232; as fragile dwelling space, 175–76
Woolf, Virginia, 16–17, 44, 74, 240. See also *Mrs. Dalloway*
work of a feminist. *See* diversity work
Wynter, Sylvia, 111

Yancy, George, 143–44
"Yellow Wallpaper, The" (Gilman), 76–77, 272n3
Young, Iris Marion, 25, 277n2

Zackodnick, Maria, 274n10
Zami (Lorde), 185–86, 240
Zella Wylie (character), 207, 276n3 (ch. 8)
Zimmerman, Bonnie, 227
Zimmerman, George, 143–44

CPSIA information can be obtained
at www.ICGtesting.com
Printed in the USA
LVHW082111040422
715272LV00003B/151

9 780822 363040